Tea
6th Sept
Bre

C000001348

Started   9th Sept.
Finished

LONDON'S
LORD MAYORS
800
YEARS OF SHAPING
THE CITY

LONDON'S LORD MAYORS

800

YEARS OF SHAPING THE CITY

EMMA HATFIELD

AMBERLEY

First published 2015

Amberley Publishing
The Hill, Stroud
Gloucestershire, GL5 4EP

www.amberley-books.com

Copyright © Emma Hatfield, 2015

The right of Emma Hatfield to be identified as
the Author of this work has been asserted in
accordance with the Copyrights, Designs and
Patents Act 1988.

ISBN 978 1 4456 5029 6 (hardback)
ISBN 978 1 4456 5030 2 (ebook)

British Library Cataloguing in Publication Data.
A catalogue record for this book is available
from the British Library.

Typesetting and Origination by Amberley
Publishing
Printed in the UK.

CONTENTS

Introduction

A CORPORATION IS BORN

When Richard I gave Henry Fitz-Ailwin the title of Mayor of London in 1189, he could hardly have anticipated the longevity of the post. Widely considered to be the oldest civic position in existence, it is also one of the most successful; certainly London's Lord Mayors have played a crucial role in securing the City's fortunes. Through insurrection, disease, fire and war, London's sworn guardians have steered their citizens through turmoil and disaster, and it is now, through their eyes, that we gain a unique perspective on the City's seminal events.

It is in the panicked words of Thomas Bludworth that we truly understand the scale of alarm that spread through the City almost as quickly as the flames on that fateful September day in 1666. And we can still read, to this day, the hastily prepared orders of London's Lord Mayor Sir John Lawrence as he solemnly promised to remain in the plague-ridden City when most others in authority had fled. Though the country splintered in the throes of civil war, we can still see the remains of London's defences, so hastily ordered by an anxious Penington as he sought to repel the invading king, and it is in the persuasiveness of Lord Mayor Humphrey Weld that we see the pivotal role which London played in securing the destiny of England's colonies overseas.

From the earliest days of London's fledging government to the well-established structures of the present day, London's Lord Mayors have variously acted as guardians, educators, reformers and liberators – and many of the City's landmarks pay testament to their acts today. Step into the stately Fishmonger's Hall at the foot of London Bridge and you will encounter the commanding figure of Sir William Walworth, who so swiftly put an end to the Peasant's Revolt. Walk up the polished stone steps of the medieval Guildhall and you will see the Corporation's own copy of the Magna Carta, to which the only commoner involved, Lord Mayor William Hardel, unhesitatingly added his own personal seal. Flick through the financial accounts of the Mercers, one of the City's oldest and most successful guilds, and you can even calculate the expenses incurred as London's Lord Mayor and the City's guilds accompanied the irrepressible Anne Boleyn from Greenwich to Westminster on the joyous event of her coronation.

No portrait of London's Lord Mayors would be complete without an understanding of the livery companies to which the Lord Mayors belong. Today, more than one hundred livery, as they are collectively known, play a pivotal role in City life, and whether associated with trade or craft are notable not only for attending the mayor but also for their work in supporting the community. It was ever thus. In medieval times the City of London guilds (the term livery is a modern supposition and originates from the distinctive uniforms worn to distinguish membership to the separate trades), wielding enormous power and influence, were at the very heart of City life. Responsible for nominating each year's Lord Mayor (through their liverymen), the guilds also held considerable financial sway and in times of war or general deficit were called upon countless times to help fund a cash-strapped monarch. As the power of the City increased across the centuries, the guilds also loaned money to nobility, contributing substantial sums to City projects as well as helping finance the American colonies.

Until early in the sixteenth century the order of the guilds was a much-disputed matter, and in a highly competitive marketplace many an argument got out of hand in an attempt to establish a hierarchy. Basing their decision on the economic and political clout of the guilds at that time, the City fathers finally settled upon the following:

1. The Worshipful Company of Mercers
2. The Worshipful Company of Grocers
3. The Worshipful Company of Drapers
4. The Worshipful Company of Fishmongers
5. The Worshipful Company of Goldsmiths
6. The Worshipful Company of Merchant Taylors (alternates yearly with the Skinners)
7. The Worshipful Company of Skinners (alternates yearly with the Merchant Taylors)
8. The Worshipful Company of Haberdashers
9. The Worshipful Company of Salters
10. The Worshipful Company of Ironmongers
11. The Worshipful Company of Vintners
12. The Worshipful Company of Clothworkers

The Merchant Taylors and the Skinners, you will note, enjoy

alternate years at the position of number six – such was the highly spirited nature of the trades. Lord Mayor Robert Willimot, who served in 1742, was the first of London's Mayors not to have been chosen from the great twelve listed above. He was, in fact, of the Worshipful Company of Coopers.

While wielding a great deal of influence within the business and political spheres of the City, the guilds have also long added their unique flavour to the Corporation's elaborate ceremonial life. In chapter 6, we discover the distinctly flamboyant nature of the medieval Lord Mayors' Shows along with the ancient customs and celebrations of which the livery are a core part, while in chapter 9 we will see the Lord Mayors dispense justice – often to the apprentices and masters of these pivotal trades.

As we progress through this text it will become obvious that the Lord Mayor of London sits at the head of unique form of government. Elected each year on 29 September, the chosen candidate not only becomes the chief magistrate of the City but also holds a number of other responsibilities, including coroner, chief justice and escheator for London, the liberties and Southwark. Admiral of the Port of London, President of the City of London Reserve Forces and Cadets Association, Trustee of St Paul's Cathedral and Chancellor of the City University are all other responsibilities tied to this uniquely elected post.

Originally referred to by the Saxon name of 'wardmote', the administrative and judicial segregations of the City of London are each represented in the Court of Common Council by an alderman and a number of Common Councilmen who are elected by the registered voters within each ward. It is worthwhile, here, examining the wards of the City – the twenty-five distinct divisions which mark out both the judicial and military areas of the City from which the aldermen and Common Councilmen are selected. Each of these ancient units has a distinct history and tradition of its own.

Aldersgate After the City gate of the same name which originally stood southwards of St Botolph's church. A large ward, it is divided into Aldersgate Without and Aldersgate Within. One of the ward's main streets, Aldersgate Street was once home to London House, one-time home to the Bishop of London.

Aldgate Also from the City gate of the same name, formerly known as Ealdgate. The ward is home to the church of St Catherine Coleman, which in 1489 was substantially repaired and had a fourth aisle added by Sir William White, Lord Mayor of London in 1482.

Bassishaw One of the smallest wards in the City, this ward is home to Basinghall Street, the name of which is derived from a large hall belonging to the Basing family.

Billingsgate In the western boundary of this ward lies Pudding Lane, and the site of the bakery where the Fire of London began.

Bishopsgate A large part of this ward escaped the destruction of the Great Fire of London and therefore many of its buildings are among the oldest in the City. It is home to Crosby Square, named after London alderman Sir John Crosby.

Bread Street A medieval bread market took place here from at least 1302. It was also home to Gerard's Hall Inn, the residence of John Gysor, Mayor of London in 1245.

Bridge Ward Within A ward named after its proximity to the once highly populated London Bridge. Fishmongers' Hall stands within this ward, home to the stately statue of City hero William Walworth.

Broad Street Once the widest street in the City and home to both Carpenters' and Drapers' Hall.

Candlewick The centre for the medieval City's candlemakers, this ward is home to St Michael's Crooked Lane, a church enlarged by John Lewkyn (four times London Lord Mayor, 1348, 1358, 1365 and 1366).

Castle Baynard The castle constructed by William Baynard who, with William the Conqueror, invaded England. It is the liberty attached to the castle which constitutes the current ward. Castle Baynard was also home to Robert FitzWalter who, with Lord Mayor William Hardel, led the rebellion against King John which resulted in the great charter of liberties Magna Carta.

Cheap From the Saxon word for market, 'chepe'. The City's affairs are run here from Guildhall and it is also home to the Lord Mayor's church, St Lawrence Jewry.

Coleman Street This ward bears the foundation stone of Bethlem Hospital, laid in 1675, which once stood in Bishopsgate Ward but on becoming ruinous moved after the Lord Mayor, aldermen and Common Council relinquished land.

Cordwainer Named after the leatherworkers who traded here. This ward is home to St Mary Aldermary, which has benefitted from many donations from London citizens including Lord Mayor Henry Keble (1510).

Cornhill Ward Once home to the City's corn sellers, this ward is home to the church of St Peter-upon-Cornhill, the patronage of which passed through the hands of Richard Whittington to the Corporation of London, which still retains it to this day.

Cripplegate From the City gate of the same name where charity was once given to beggars. It is divided into Cripplegate Within and Cripplegate Without (the walls). Sir Ambrose Nicholas, Lord Mayor in 1575, founded a set of almshouses on the east side of Monkwell Street in 1575 and this ward was also the home of a now-disappeared church, St Alphage, which housed a monument to Sir Rowland Hayward, Lord Mayor of London in 1570.

Dowgate Thought to take its name from 'dwyr-gate', meaning water gate. In this ward are the Watermans' Hall and the Skinners' Hall.

Farringdon Within and Without Originally one ward named after City citizen and goldsmith William Farrendon, this was divided into two in 1395. The sessions house was once in this ward.

Langbourn Once a stream that ran from the Thames to Fenchurch Street. Fenchurch Street is one of the ward's main streets, as is Lombard Street, which took its name from the Italian merchants of Lombard who settled there. Pewterers' Hall is also here.

Lime Street Thought to be named after the area in which lime was sold. Although it runs through several parishes, it doesn't have a church. It is home to Leadenhall market.

Portsoken Takes its name from the word 'portsoken', meaning liberty at the gate, since it was once entirely outside the City walls.

Queenhithe From the harbour of the same name, once under the jurisdiction of Queen Eleanor. It obtained the 'queen' in the reign of Henry III because the customs collected were enjoyed by the queens of England.

Tower Ward Due to its proximity to the Tower of London. This ward includes the City of London's Trinity House and the Bakers' Hall.

Vintry Once a place on the Thames where Bordeaux wines were sold. Vintners' Hall stands on the spot of a house once occupied by Sir John Stody, Lord Mayor of London in 1357.

Walbrook Named after a brook which once crossed the City wall at Dowgate. The Lord Mayor's mansion house sits within this ward, which is also home to the famous London Stone. St Mary

Bothaw was a church in this ward thought by some to be where first London Lord Mayor Henry Fitz-Ailwin is buried.

Not only is the area of the City of London still divided into the segments of its ancient wards, but it still retains many of its earliest positions of authority. The post of alderman, or 'elder man', for example, can be found in records dating back to Saxon times. Today the Court of Aldermen does not wield as much influence as it formerly did as many of its functions have been taken on by the Court of Common Council. Consisting of twenty-five aldermen and a hundred Common Councilmen, it is this court, as opposed to the Court of Aldermen, which ultimately runs the City of London.

While the position of Lord Mayor reflects the long, unbroken threads of City governance, there is another office that actually predates the mayoralty and also still exists today, and that is the office of sheriff, which once formally represented the king under the title of 'shire reeve'. Responsible for collecting royal revenues and for enforcing royal justice, in 1385 it was deemed necessary that London's Lord Mayors should have gained the invaluable experience of having previously served as sheriff – an effective way of testing capability for the job. During one of the many ceremonial occasions associated with the Lord Mayor and the City of London, you may well come across another, less well-known figure who appears to be acting on behalf of an alderman, and that is the beadle. Also an elected officer, the beadle's responsibilities were also to ensure the City's citizens were invited to and attended the thrice-yearly Chief Folk-Moots, and to fine those who were not present. Beadles were also elected at these assemblies and were expected to maintain order and to open and close the meetings.

Each ward elects their own beadle, though some of the larger wards may have two or three.

Of all the aspects of the governance of the City of London, much has been written about the Freedom of the City, which freemen of the various City companies cannot join the livery without, but it is worth taking a moment to clarify the exact terms of reference. By today's standards, the key advantages of Freedom of the City may seem insignificant since they are now almost unanimously enjoyed across the nation; however, in medieval times the Freedom was a highly sought-after prize. Incorporating the essential right to trade, the freedom also included the right to vote, and exemption from market and fair tolls.

In addition to individual liberties, the City itself also enjoys a number of rights which have been variously granted by the Crown, and as custodians and chief protectors it is exactly these rights that London's Lord Mayors have been forced to defend. As we look through the great charters of the thirteenth century we see London's early Lord Mayors Serlo le Mercer and William Hardel defend the trading rights of the citizens of London, and in the process we learn exactly why the City played such a significant role in securing the terms of the Magna Carta. As we look towards the downfall of Charles I, we see why London's Lord Mayors, along with other leading citizens of the day, felt it necessary to risk their own lives by putting a reigning monarch on trial.

Today, the physical manifestations of the City's governance are a very tangible reminder of the way in which London's Lord Mayors have shaped the City's history. The palatial structure of the Guildhall, for example, one of only a handful of medieval structures to have survived the City's fires, speaks to us of the continued supremacy of a medieval authority that is still relevant to this day. Within its magisterial walls lie a vast collection of City records, and it was to these stately rooms that volunteers flocked in 1914 in response to the Lord Mayor's call to arms.

Crisp Gascoyne (1752) was the first of London's Lord Mayors to benefit from the newly built residence Mansion House, where London's Lord Mayors still reside. It is, as Lady Knill describes in her remarkably detailed text *Mansion House*, an unusually multi-functional building:

> Londoners give it a friendly glance as they hurry past, it stands for the dignity of their citizenship, strangers hardly regard it as a wonder, in a City so rich in historical buildings and yet, with the exception of the Palace of the Doges at Venice, it is perhaps the only edifice in existence which serves the purposes of court of justice, prison and residence; no favoured stranger having permission to visit the sumptuous apartments designed for entertaining with the magnificent Egyptian Banqueting Hall would dream that by opening a door he could pass into a London Police Court with dock handy, and that in cells below some poor wretch might be listening to the heavy tread of a warders' feet.

Certainly, to the uninitiated observer, the existence and impact of the City's Lord Mayors could easily be missed – though nonetheless they remain. From the halls of the great livery companies to the spot on which Wilkes raucously called for liberty, you have simply to know where to look.

I

LONDON'S LIBERTIES
1200–1315

High on the Holborn Viaduct, on the boundary of the City, stands the distinguished stone statue of Henry Fitz-Ailwin, London's very first Lord Mayor. Warden of the City's very first stone bridge (London Bridge), Fitz-Ailwin is also recorded as being one of the collectors – along with the Archbishop of Canterbury, the Bishop of London and the Earl of Arundel – of the not insubstantial ransom of 150,000 marks paid to release Richard I when he was imprisoned by Duke Leopold of Austria on his return from the Third Crusade. Owner of a small portion of land within the City of London, the earliest known reference to London's first chief magistrate is contained in the Pipe Rolls of Henry II, which refer to a payment made by Fitz-Ailwin to take on the lands of his recently deceased father. Fitz-Ailwin is also listed as an alderman (elder man with municipal authority) in the City's records of 1177, but while he was clearly a figure of some consequence and responsibility in early medieval London, it is the newly created post he occupied – an important marker in the City's move towards civic independence – with which we are first concerned.

The strands of London's emergence as a seat of governance date back at least to 833, when the City was selected to be the site of assembly by Egbert, king of the West Saxons, who wished to consult his advisors on the urgent matter of repelling the ferocious attacks of the Danes. Although the City subsequently fell to Scandinavian invaders in 851, King Alfred recovered possession in 883, creating the backbone of the City's constitution along with the office of sheriff (shire reeve or portreeve). However, it wasn't until the peace-seeking Edward the Confessor made London his home that the City made significant gains in terms of wealth and population. By the time the Norman Duke William managed finally to gain a foothold across the Channel, London was an extremely powerful city with its own very attractive store of gold – a fact not overlooked by the Conqueror, who went to some lengths to preserve its status. In his first charter to his new subjects he promised the citizens of London they would retain the rights and privileges they had known since the time of Edward the Confessor – rights which were crucial to their continuing trading success.

> William the king friendly salutes the bishop and Godfrey the portreeve, and all the burgesses within London, both French and English. And I declare, that I grant you to be all law-worthy, as you were in the days of King Edward; and I grant that every child shall be his father's heir, after his father's days; and I will not suffer any person to do you wrong. God keep you.

It is recorded, says Reginald R. Sharpe in *London and the Kingdom: Volume 1*, that William granted another charter to the citizens of London, vesting in them the City and Sheriffwick of London, which has since been lost, however the terms of the charter between London and the Conqueror were faithfully kept. Having ascended the English throne by the aid of the citizens of London, William, unlike many of his successors, was careful not to infringe the terms of their charter, whilst the citizens on the other hand continued loyal to their accepted king, and lent him assistance to put down insurgents in other parts of the kingdom.

William might have been quick to affirm the existing rights of his new citizens but it wasn't until his fourth son, Henry I, was on the throne (1100–35) that the citizens of London were granted significant new privileges. In a bid to win the crucial support of the City of London, Henry granted a pivotal set of civil freedoms, including release from various duties payable to the Crown and exemption from trial by battle. No citizen had now to plead any cause without the walls of the City, while the jurisdiction for civil matters in the county of Middlesex was given to the City for the sum of £300 a year. Furthermore, Henry's generous charter promised that London citizens would be free from 'scot, lot, Danegeld and the murdrum' (scot and lot were taxes, while Danegeld was levied to raise money to keep the Danes out and murdrum was a fine issued for unsolved murders). Most important of all was the statement that the citizens of London could henceforth elect their own representative as sheriff:

Know that I have granted to my citizens of London for themselves and their heirs that they may hold the shrievalty of London and Middlesex of me and my heirs for a farm of £300 by tale. The citizens may appoint as sheriff whomever they want from among themselves and as judge whomever they want from among themselves to take charge pleas of the crown and supervise their conduct; no-one else shall be judge over the men of London ... All London men and their goods are to be exempt from and free of toll, passage, lastage, and all other customs, throughout all England and the seaports ... A Londoner may not be penalized by an amercement greater than his were, that is, 100s; I refer to pleas which [have a penalty that] is pecuniary. Furthermore, miskenning is not to be [applicable] in the husting or the folkmoot, nor in any other pleas within the city. A husting may be held once a week, that is, on Monday. I will ensure my citizens have [justice regarding] their lands, pledges and debts, inside the city and outside. Concerning lands for which they bring a complaint before me, I shall uphold their rights according to the law of the city. If anyone exacts toll or customs from citizens of London, the citizens may in the city recover, from [members of] the borough or town where the toll or customs were taken, the same amount given by a Londoner for toll, and applicable damages. All debtors who owe debts to citizens must repay them, or in [the court of] London offer defence that they are not indebted. If they are unwilling to repay the debt or to come and defend themselves, then the citizens to whom the debts are owed may make distraint within the city, from [any member of] the borough or town or county in which the debtor resides. The citizens may have their hunting rights in the fullest and best form they were had by their ancestors, that is, in the Chilterns, Middlesex and Surrey.

Charter granted by Henry 1 to London.

Corporation of London Records Office, Liber Horn, f.362v. Transcription in C. Brooke, G. Keir and S. Reynolds, 'Henry I's charter for the City of London', *Journal of the Society of Archivists*, 4 (1973), pp. 575–6

Issued at Westminster, then described as a low-lying and swamp-infested island, no original copy of the charter is known to survive. What has endured, however, is the concession the citizens of London were given to choose their own sheriff – a pivotal judicial and administrative post which still survives to this day. Whether he fully realised it or not, in granting Londoners this charter, in which he also abolished various abuses and developed the Exchequer, Henry was taking the first tentative steps towards creating a state that functioned away from the personal rule of the monarchy, and the City followed suit. In gaining the right to elect its own sheriffs, London had begun to assert an authority all of its own, particularly since sheriffs were originally only appointed by royal command. Known to have existed as far back as the seventh century, and often referred to in towns as portreeves, these leaders of each county exercised their right to administer justice on a local level as well as collecting the bewildering and often highly unpredictable array of taxes inflicted on the local populace.

For a time, says Sharpe, the appointment of sheriffs was lost to the citizens. Throughout the reigns of Henry II and his successor they were appointed by the Crown. Richard's charter to the citizens makes no mention of the sheriffwick, nor is it mentioned in the first charter by John. But although the right to elect a sheriff had been lost, the move towards the City's autonomous status was ultimately too strong to be reversed. It would take a number of years, however, before the City would enjoy the benefits of a locally elected candidate, and until that time it would simply have to put up with the ceaseless attacks on its purse by the money-hungry monarchy.

In following his personal desire to participate in the Crusades to the Holy Land, Richard I left his administration with part of the problem of collecting enough funds to finance his risky adventures. Granting charters in return for fixed sums therefore became a favoured method of raising revenue, to the point where contemporary chronicler Richard of Devizes was quoted as saying that the monarch would sell London itself if only he could find a bidder.

It wasn't until 1191 that the news of Richard being taken hostage reached London, and in a bid to gain the City's support, prominent citizen Richard FitzReiner negotiated with the prisoner's younger brother John to support his claim against Lord Chancellor Longchamp for the supremacy of England. In return, John, along with his justices, granted the City of London its commune, from which its chief magistrate, Mayor Henry Fitz-Ailwin, would shortly emerge. This, says Sharpe, is the first record of the citizens of London as a corporate body, but,

> so far from granting to them something new, the very words their commune (*communam suam*) imply a commune of which they were already in enjoyment. How long the commune may have been in existence, unauthorised by the Crown, cannot be determined but that the term *communio*, in connection with the city's organisation was known half a century before we have already seen … whenever that happened to take place, there took place also a change in the chief governor of the city. The head of the city was no longer a Saxon 'portreeve' but a French 'Mayor', the former officer continuing in all probability to perform the duties of a portreeve or sheriff of a town in a modified form. From the time when this 'civic revolution' occurred down to the present day, the sheriff's position has always been one of secondary importance, being himself subordinate to the mayor.

John had successfully set the scene for his accession, and it was with the full support of the citizens of London that he secured his throne when his elder brother Richard received a fatal wound while besieging a castle in northern France. Having won the City's initial support, John went further to ensure that the Crown and the City remained on friendly terms, and shortly after his coronation on 27 May he granted the City three charters. Gillian Keir, in *London 800–1216: The Shaping of a City*, says:

> The first merely repeated the terms of his father's charter and thus confirmed privileges long enjoyed. The second, abolishing weirs on the River Thames and the River Medway, was couched in the same terms as a royal charter issued two years previously. The third, however, marked the king's personal acceptance of recent and possibly controversial customs. John formally allowed the citizens to appoint their own sheriffs at the modest farm of £300. Men who held such office, it was emphasised, were answerable to the Exchequer judges, but they retained the rights of London citizens. If they committed crimes punishable by the loss of life or limb, they were to be tried according to City law. On the other hand, they might be liable for fines as high as £20, a sum apparently four times greater than that usually accorded to citizens.

While John might have seemed somewhat free with the privileges he granted to London, in reality these liberties always came at a price. The 3,000 marks John expected Londoners to pay for the right to choose their own sheriffs took the City four long years to repay. This, on top of highly unpopular taxes and the 'gifts' the monarch so often expected, left contemporary chronicler Matthew

Paris recording that John's exhortations had left the citizens of London in a position no better than slaves.

Little wonder that by 1215 the City's officials were taking active measures for defence. Says Keir: 'The aldermen were ordered to survey the arms borne by those living in their wards and check that they were able to defend the City. Every alderman was to possess a banner behind which parish contingents might assemble.'

Most important, says Keir, were the demands that

> all evil taxes should be abolished and that no tallage should be taken without the agreement of both kingdom and City; the mint was to belong to the City as in former years; foreign merchants should come and go freely and responsibility for the River Thames should rest entirely with London ... The most startling exception was an article which called for a mayor to be elected annually in the folkmoot. Clearly it was time that the head of the commune, who had been addressed and therefore acknowledged in royal documents should receive full official recognition; but the provisions for his election point to a radical strain within city politics. Not only do they imply resistance to Fitz-Ailwin's long term as mayor, but the ignore the smaller, more efficient City courts like the Husting Court in favour of the old-fashioned and rather cumbersome popular assembly.

John, meanwhile, bent on recovering the Crown's lost lands in France, continued to drain the City of its hard-won wealth. By the beginning of the thirteenth century the relationship between the City and the Crown had once more broken down as the relationships between the king and his barons crumbled.

On 15 June 1215, London's fourth Lord Mayor, William Hardel, solemnly put his seal on what would become one of the most important charters in English history. Surrounded by some of the richest and most powerful barons of the day, Hardel, a mercer by trade, was the only member of the Magna Carta group to be listed in his official capacity and, notably, the only commoner involved. So how had London's newly elected Lord Mayor come to be caught up in the rebel barons' grievances, and why did he feel it necessary to be involved in what was, after all, a potentially dangerous act of rebellion against a reigning king?

In the thirteenth century, the City of London was independent, thriving and heavily reliant on trade. Viewed as a separate entity to Westminster – the seat of royal, administrative and religious life – the City was both the economic and residential heart of London, and as such a guaranteed source of loans for monarchs. From the barons' point of view, Hardel's support was a powerful bargaining chip and crucial in obtaining the charter conditions from John. But as the elected representative of the economic powerhouse of the country, Hardel was also there to protect the freedoms and liberties the Crown had, over centuries, conceded to the City – freedoms that were crucial to London's continuing expansion.

By the end of that now-infamous day in Runnymede, the twenty-five-strong rebel group, led by the dangerously persuasive Robert Fitzwalter, was successful in securing terms which limited royal authority and established the highly radical principle that the king was subject to, and not above, the law. Hardel, however, had additional reason to feel reassured. Although the bulk of Magna Carta focused on the interests of the barons, the Great Charter of Freedom also included what was, to Hardel's mind, a vitally important clause: 'That the City of London shall enjoy its ancient liberties and free customs, both by land and water.' While this did not afford Londoners any new rights or freedoms, it did protect the terms of all previous charters the City had received from the Crown. For London, a city of which it was said that merchants delivered commodities to from every nation in the world, it was the promise to uphold King Richard I's charter of conservancy which was of pressing issue.

While the river had served as a major thoroughfare for centuries, the charter of 1197 gave both its conservancy and its jurisdiction to the City of London – from its junction in the sea eastwards to as far west as it was known as the Thames. The reference to free customs by water was particularly important in the early thirteenth century since, to the acute detriment of the City's income, a practice had begun, in the main carried out by wealthy landowners, of creating weirs and dams fitted with nets to catch fish. Not only did this hinder navigation of the river, but it also encroached upon the City's reserves by hampering the efforts of the City's fishermen. It was a relief to all in the City to know that the privileges upon which so much trade depended were certain to be upheld – after all, not all monarchs had exploited the City as much as John. Many, in fact, had sought to protect and enhance the Capital's potential, including William the Conqueror, who ensured that London enjoyed an exceptional status under his full protection and was answerable only to him. This was a key determining factor in the City's growth, since under this new-found and previously rarely enjoyed stability livelihoods once again became secure.

When Hardel returned to the City, which remained, for the time being at least, under baronial control, it was with the knowledge that not only were London's freedoms secure but that the king would no longer be as free to interfere in the City's financial affairs. For too long John had abused the City's purse, though he was very far from being the only guilty party. Henry II had extracted free gifts from the City in 1158, 1159, 1170 and 1173, while Richard I had persuaded London's sheriff Henry de Cornhill to supply vast quantities of military accoutrements along with stores and provisions for his ill-fated Crusade.

What happened after King John put his seal on the unnamed charter is enshrined in the nation's history books. While the terms of the Magna Carta stipulated that the twenty-five barons would be enforcing its provision, John, furious at having been forced to acquiesce, wrote to Rome. Just two months after Magna Carta had been granted, a papal bull, issued on 24 August 1215 by Pope Innocent III, annulled the groundbreaking document with the explanation that John had been forced into accepting terms which were not only harmful to royal rights but were shameful to the English people.

With no choice but to accept the Pope's decree, the barons discarded all thought of reissuing the document and instead decided to focus on another way to achieve their goals: they invited Prince Louis (the eldest son of the King of France) to take the throne. Charles H. Browning, in his text *The Magna Charta Barons*, explains:

> The Dauphin himself disembarked at Sandwich where he proceeded to London and was met by a committee of the rebel barons and conducted to St Paul's Church 2 June 1216. Here he received the formal homage of the barons and knights and himself made an oath to govern the kingdom of England in the manner they desired. He then sent warnings to the King of the Scots, and to the Welsh princes and all who had not done homage to him at St Paul's to make their fealty at once, or to retire with all speed from his kingdom.

Had John not suddenly passed away in the October of 1216, the charter may have been consigned to oblivion. However, with Louis now governing some of the country, the advisors to John's nine-year-old-son Henry now took a bold step – they decided to reissue the Magna Carta in order to tempt the barons back to Henry's cause. Louis surrendered in a battle at Lincoln in 1217, peace was declared, and that year the second charter was issued. In 1225, yet a further reissue was commanded by Henry III and given his official seal. To further give the charter weight, the Church made known its approval, saying it would excommunicate anyone who broke its terms.

The history of the City of London's involvement with the Magna Carta is not confined to either one person (William Hardel) or to this single event. The barons, in fact, had sought the ear of another London Lord Mayor, Serlo le Mercer, earlier on in 1215. He had indicated that the City would be willing to support the barons' cause. To this end, he and four other prominent citizens of the City's authority offered their own finances to the sum of around 1,000 marks for Prince Louis. However, as history records, it was leading citizen and lord of Baynard's Castle Robert Fitzwalter (who styled himself 'Marshall of the army of God') who had directed the City's involvement in the fight against the king after being appointed, in the presence of London's Lord Mayor, as leader of the rebels. Says Sharpe:

> But it was in time of war that Fitz-Walter achieved for himself the greatest power and dignity. It then became the duty of the castellain to proceed to the great gate of St. Paul's attended by nineteen other knights, mounted and caparisoned, and having his banner, emblazoned with his arms, displayed before him. Immediately

upon his arrival, the mayor, aldermen, and sheriffs, who awaited him, issued solemnly forth from the church, all arrayed in arms, the mayor bearing in his hand the city banner, the ground of which was bright vermilion or gules, with a figure of St. Paul, in gold, thereon, the head, feet, and hands of the saint being silver or argent, and in his right hand a sword. The castellain, advancing to meet the mayor, informed him that he had come to do the service which the city had a right to demand at his hands, and thereupon the mayor placed the city's banner in his hands, and then, attending him back to the gate, presented him with a charger of the value of £20, its saddle emblazoned with the arms of Fitz-Walter, and its housing of cendal or silk, similarly enriched. A sum of £20 was at the same time handed to Fitz-Walter's chamberlain to defray the day's expenses. Having mounted his charger, he bids the Mayor to choose a Marshal of the host of the City of London; and this being done, the communal or 'mote-bell' is set ringing, and the whole party proceed to the Priory of Holy Trinity at Aldgate. There they dismount, and entering the Priory, concert measures together for the defence of the city.

While the Magna Carta will forever be remembered as a groundbreaking document, it did in fact strongly echo the terms of a previous charter – the Coronation Charter of King Henry I (1100), which was granted more than a hundred years earlier. Copies of this earlier document were sent to all the shires.

HENRY, king of the English, to Bishop Samson [bishop of Worcester and former royal chaplain] and Urso de Abetot [Sheriff of Worcester] and to all his barons and faithful subjects, both French and English, of Worcestershire,

1. Know that by the mercy of God and the common counsel of the barons of the whole kingdom of England I have been crowned king of this said kingdom; and because the kingdom has been oppressed by unjust exactions, I, through fear of God and the love which I have toward you all, in the first place make the holy church of God free, so that I will neither sell nor let out to farm, nor on the death of archbishop or bishop or abbot will I take anything from the church's demesne or from its men until the successor shall enter it. And I take away all the evil customs by which the kingdom of England was unjustly oppressed; which evil customs I here set down in part.

2. If any of my barons, earls, or others who hold of me [my tenants] shall have died, his heir shall not buy back his land as he used to do in the time of my brother, but he shall relieve it by a just and lawful relief. Likewise also the men of my barons shall relieve their lands from their lords by a just and lawful relief.

3. And if any of my barons or other tenants will to give his daughter, sister, niece, or kinswoman in marriage, let him speak with me about it; but I will neither take anything from him for this permission nor prevent his giving her unless he should be minded to join her to my enemies. And if, upon the death of a baron or other of my men, a daughter is left as heir, I will give her with her land by the advice of my barons. And if, on the death of her husband, the wife is left and without children, she shall have her dowry and right of marriage, and I will not give her to a husband unless according to her will.

4. But if a wife survives with children, she shall indeed have her dowry and right of marriage so long as she shall keep her body lawfully, and I will not give her (in marriage) unless according to her will. And the guardian of the land and children shall be either the

wife or another of the relatives who more justly ought to be. And I command that my barons restrain themselves similarly in dealing with the sons and daughters or wives of their tenants.

5. The common seigneurage [right to mint money], which has been taken through the cities and counties, but which was not taken in the time of King Edward, I absolutely forbid henceforth. If any one, whether a moneyer or other, be taken with false money, let due justice be done for it.

6. All pleas and all debts which were owing to my brother, I remit except my lawful fixed revenues and except those amounts which were covenanted for the inheritances of others or for those which more justly concerned others. And if any one had pledged anything for his own inheritance, I remit it; also all reliefs which had been agreed upon for just inheritances.

7. And if any of my barons or tenants shall grow feeble, as he shall give or arrange to give his money, I grant that it be so given. But if, being prevented by war or sickness, he should neither give nor dispose of his money, his wife, children or relations, and his lawful tenants shall distribute it for the good of his soul as shall seem best to them.

8. If any of my barons or tenants commit a crime, he shall not bind himself to a payment at the king's mercy as he has been doing in the time of my father or my brother; but he shall make amends according to the extent of the crime as he would have done before the time of my father in the time of my other ancestors. But if he be convicted of treachery or heinous crime, he shall make due satisfaction for it.

9. Also I pardon all murders committed before the day I was crowned king; and those which shall be committed in the future shall have satisfaction according to the law of King Edward.

10. By the common consent of my barons I have kept in my hands all forests as my father had them.

11. To those knights who render military service for their lands I grant of my own free will that the lands of their demesne be free from all payments, so that, having been released from so great a burden, they may more easily provide themselves with horses and arms and be better fitted for my service and the defence of my kingdom.

12. Also I impose a strict peace upon my whole kingdom and command that it be maintained henceforth.

13. I also restore to you the law of King Edward with those amendments with which my father improved it by the counsel of his barons.

14. If anyone, since the death of King William my brother, has seized any of my property or the property of any other man, the whole is to be quickly restored without fine; but if any one keep anything of it, he shall pay a heavy recompense for it.

Witnessed by Maurice bishop of London, William bishop-elect of Winchester, Gerard bishop of Hereford, earl Henry, earl Simon, Walter Giffard, Robert de Montfort, Roger Bigot, Eudo the steward, Robert son of Hamo, and Robert Malet. At Westminster when I was crowned. Farewell.

A. B. White and W. Notestein (eds), *Source Problems in English History* (1915)

Although we tend to think of the Magna Carta as a single document, it was in fact reissued no less than four times between the years 1215–25, with significant revisions each time. Additionally, while it is often regarded as a defining document securing human rights, in *Magna Carta*, Katherine Fischer Drew argues convincingly that it was unlikely that either the barons or King John knew just how important the originally unnamed charter would become; in fact, the barons' solution to the inherent difficulty of persuading King John to adhere to its specifications was 'to claim the right of feudal rebellion against an unjust lord'. Drew continues,

> In 1215 the solution had the barons select a group of 25 barons (one of whom was the lord mayor of London) who were to monitor the actions of the king and to receive complaints against him if he failed to observe the rights and liberties set out in the charter. If the king or his officers did not remedy the grievance within forty days, 'those twenty-five barons together with the community of the whole land shall distrain [seize property] and distress us in every way they can, namely, by seizing castles, lands, possessions and in other ways as they can' (Article 61, Magna Carta, 1215).

While the Magna Carta is undeniably important, for the City of London the right to finally elect their own mayor came before the Great Charter, just over a week before the barons captured the City when, between 7 and 9 May 1215, King John, taking refuge in Temple Church under the protection of the Knights Templar, at last issued a charter that granted its citizens the right to choose their own mayor:

> Know that we have granted, and by this our present writing confirmed, to our barons of our city of London, that they may choose to themselves every year a mayor, who to us may be faithful,

discreet and fit for government of the city, so as, when he shall be chosen, to be presented unto us, or our justice if we shall not be present.

It was, according to many, merely a bribe; but it was one which failed to work, for London continued to side with the barons, and while the City was in baronial hands John had little choice but to comply.

Thus, the City of London gained the right to elect its own mayor. Throughout the thirteenth century, the City's administrative structure continued to develop – much furthered by the efforts made by Gregory de Rokesle in his mayoralty between 1276 and 1277. His assizes, for instance, are recorded for posterity in the City's Letter-Book A, which outlines the rules of expected conduct for citizens.

Originally, many of the City's officials kept their own private records and it was only as the century progressed that complete records were kept of business, freedoms, apprentices, wills and deeds. City administration itself became more complex as the years wore on, and the matter of the City's hygiene was taken on by City officials, who were to rigorously punish any offending practice. By the thirteenth century this included taking pigs off the streets, which had hitherto been allowed to freely roam. In addition, building regulations became stricter, and regulations, of course, required enforcement. Despite the progress of the City's official structures (the post of City prosecutors began to appear at this time, as did the role of recorder), the City still suffered attacks from the Crown; despite all the promises of the charter of liberties, Henry III in particular continued to attack and undermine London's citizens. Says Woodcock:

The enmity of Henry against the city still continued, and various acts of persecution were carried on against the citizens. Some of these acts, however, were called for by the venality of the official functionaries. Gerard Batt who was re-chosen mayor in 1241, was rejected by the king for extorting money from the victuallers during a former mayoralty.

The harassments continued. Woodcock reveals that Henry's exactions from the citizens were renewed day by day:

> An ordinance came out about this time for covering houses with tiles or slates instead of straw, in order to prevent the ravages of fires which were of almost daily occurrence. The citizens were also ordered by the king to choose one of their best artists, as *custos cunii*, or keeper of the mint. In the same year, 1245, the corporation purchased, for the annual fee of £50 per annum, the farm of Queenhithe, in Thames Street from the Earl of Cornwall. The exhortations of the priests having, with those of the monarch, almost drained the mercantile community of its money, it was resolved at the Parliament held at Westminster, in 1247, to send letters to the popes and cardinals, humbly entreating them to consider the miserable state of the nation, and not to ruin the people entirely by their abominable exactions.

The scale of the Corporation was, says W. Woodcock, affixed to these letters by Parliament.

> The Parliament, in the following year, began to make a stand against the cruel exactions of the monarch. They refused to grant him any for his pecuniary aid. The king, incensed, dissolved the Parliament, but his poverty was such that he was obliged to sell his plate and

jewels. On being told he could find purchasers in the city of London, he replied, 'That if the treasure of Augustus were to be sold, the city of London could purchase it', adding 'that those clownish Londoners who call themselves barons and abound in all things, are an immense treasure of themselves', a fact he fully realised by the extent to which he had drained their coffers. Every scheme he could adopt to obtain money, whether of an insinuating character or *tout au contraire* he appears to have resorted to; at one time, trying to work upon their religious enthusiasm, by proposing a crusade; at another fermenting disturbances amongst them by his own domestics, that he might have the opportunity of mulcting them in fines for their unruly conduct. Remonstrance and prayers were vain. The sovereign was the greedy horse-leech, everlastingly crying, give, give.

By a subsequent charter given in consideration of receiving five hundred marks he again confirmed their ancient privileges and granted them the power of presenting their newly-elected mayor to the barons of the exchequer, in the absence of the king. As a proof of his insatiable rapacity, we find the following instances recorded, between the years 1254–6. In 1254 there was the tax for *aurum reginae*, or Queen's gold. In 1255 he accepted a gift of £100: and afterwards (because his majesty was not satisfied), a valuable piece of plate was presented to him. In the same year the city was fined three thousand marks for the escape of a prisoner. In 1256 a demand for a similar sum and a further sum of four hundred marks, for the restitution of the liberties which had been suspended for non-payment of the former sum; also, a further sum of one hundred marks in the same year.

London, one contemporary observer noted, was well-nigh ruined, and the hopes of its citizens must have been high when Edward I succeeded to the throne in 1272 after the death of his father in the Holy Land. Receiving him with great enthusiasm and ceremony, the City's optimism was not entirely unfounded – Edward's reign was to be recorded as one in which justice became a uniform right for all, although the City would find out in due course that his actions were often unscrupulous and aggressive.

2

REBELLION AND REVOLT
1300–1400

Tucked away in the south-western corner of London Bridge stands Fishmongers' Hall, home to a commanding statue of City hero Sir William Walworth. A prominent merchant and financially secure enough to advance personal loans to the king, in his lifetime Walworth was sheriff, alderman of Bridge Ward and twice Lord Mayor of London. However, it is not these credentials, impressive though they are, that earned him this lofty position on Holborn Hill, but the fact that in 1381 Walworth single-handedly (and wholly unexpectedly) put an end to one of the most brutal and bloody episodes in the City's history – the 1381 Peasants' Revolt.

Little is clear about Walworth's early life, save that his family came from Durham, but we do know that he became the apprentice of John Lovekyn of the Fishmongers' Guild and followed his example by becoming an alderman of Bridge Ward in 1368. His rise to prominence was thereafter relatively swift. By 1374 he had been elected Lord Mayor, but it was his second tenure, from 1380 to 1381, which secured his name in the City's history books, his deeds providing inspiration and recognition for the City's populace for years to come.

All might have seemed outwardly peaceful in the City of London when Walworth was re-elected in 1380, but in reality the cracks were starting to show. Despite the fact that the cogs of the City's industry – the trade and craft guilds – were prospering and beginning to recognise the benefits of organising themselves in efficient trading units, the City itself was recovering from a period in which it had suffered serious adversity. From 1348 to 1351, the Black Death, known at the time as the Great Pestilence, had travelled the length and breadth of Europe, killing around forty thousand people in the City of London alone. For those who survived, life was a horribly uncertain mix of labour shortages and famine – a situation which continued for some time. Reinforcing this suffering was an Ordinance issued by King Edward III on 18 June 1349 which stated that everyone under the age of sixty should be in employment and that workers should not receive wages higher than the pre-plague levels. A piece of legislation which was supposed to prevent workers from taking advantage of the shortage of labour by pushing up their wages actually resulted in extreme poverty and hardship. Prices had risen sharply since the Black Death took hold, and Edward's short-sighted and controversial edict meant that in reality the poor could hardly afford to buy the scarce amount of food that was on sale.

No matter how unpopular this legislation was, the fact remained that Edward was a strong and well-respected king. History tells us his was a firm and even hand, and his long reign was marked out as being particularly beneficial to commerce. The crown passed to his grandson when he died in 1377, and when the eleven-year-old

Richard II was crowned on 21 June of that year a great deal of uncertainty ensued. Although the young king's government was controlled by a series of councils, Richard himself was widely thought to be under the malign influence of his unpopular uncle, the 1st Duke of Lancaster, John of Gaunt. The City in particular was wary of the heavy-handed pressure John was said to inflict on his nephew. Desperate to obtain an official confirmation of Edward III's charter stipulating the City's rights with regard to commerce, the City's officials now appealed to the new king to uphold these vital privileges – particularly with regards to a clause which ordered that no foreigner should buy or sell to another foreigner within the liberties of the City. It was an overture that would remain unsuccessful until the point when the House of Commons became involved. By this time, the relationship between the City and the king's uncle was a less than cordial affair, owing to the arguably unlawful detention of a number of the City's citizens. However, the duke was subsequently persuaded to negotiate with the king for their release, and genial relations were once again restored.

It was a situation that was not to last. In 1378, a subsidy was granted in which every man was rated for taxation according to his station. The Lord Mayor was assessed at £4, the aldermen at £2 each (the same amount as the barons) and tradesmen and their wives and children over the ages of fourteen were to pay 4d a head. It was not a popular tax, and quickly became the source of frustration and much objection.

The king, however, was in dire need of finance. His coffers were all but empty thanks to the near-constant combat of the Hundred Years War, and he had been forced to turn to private individuals to fund the continuing battles against France. Even City officials donated – in 1379 John Philpot became Lord Mayor, contributing a large sum that was spent on a fleet of ships to assist the Duke of Brittany in his campaign against the King of France. For much of the rest of the population, though, the breaking point was near and when Richard, in a miscalculated attempt to raise further revenue, loaded the already struggling population of England with an additional costly tax, relations between Crown and country immediately soured. The poll tax was to be paid by everyone over the age of fifteen, regardless of their position, and it was this, along with the unremitting strictness and severity with which the unpopular tariff was collected, which proved to be the final straw. After various uprisings in rural parts of the country, two key figures emerged to spearhead a rebellion attacking Rochester Castle and Lord Chancellor Sudbury's Canterbury. On 12 June 1381, having raised substantial troops along the way, the discontented mob led by Wat Tyler and Jack Straw found themselves in London. Congregating on Blackheath, the hoarde was said to have been met by notorious preacher John Ball, who supposedly roused troops with the following words: 'When Adam delved and Eve span, who was then the gentleman?' This was a pointed allusion to the man-made divisions of a society in which the majority of the population was at the whim of a privileged few. Ball was keen to reiterate his point:

> From the beginning all men by nature were created alike, and our bondage or servitude came in by the unjust oppression of naughty men. For if God would have had any bondmen from the beginning he would have appointed who should be bond, and who free. And therefore I exhort you to consider that now the time is come, appointed to use by God, in which ye may (if ye will) cast off the yoke of bondage, and recover liberty.

It was with these rousing words in mind that the rebels made their final journey to the City, sacking and burning to the ground what was known as the finest nobleman's residence in the land, the Savoy Palace, then the London residence of John of Gaunt. Often referred to as the most dangerous event to have occurred in London, what happened next must certainly have been a horrifying experience for those who were the target of the rebels' crushing anger. The inmates of debtors' prison the Fleet (built on the eastern bank of the disappeared River Fleet) were freed and legal documents burned in fury. Bent on destroying their oppressors – whom they saw as being the nobility and the lawyers – the rebels set about finding and setting fire to the residences of lawyers and jurors, beheading those who fled. After the Savoy Palace was reduced to rubble, the Inns of Court around Temple were targeted, and from there the rebels divided themselves into three bodies. The first set out to St John of Jerusalem, a rich priory in Clerkenwell; a second headed to the Tower of London, where Lord Chancellor Simon Sudbury and Lord High Treasurer Sir Robert Hales were found at prayer, dragged to Tower Hill and decapitated; and the remaining third went to Mile End, where they boldly made their demands to the king: freedom of commerce, fixed rent for land, abolition of slavery and a general pardon. All demands were met.

Upon his return to the City, the king offered Wat Tyler the same terms as the Mile End party and a treaty was agreed. However, it seems as though this was merely a ploy to gain time. Another meeting was arranged between Wat Tyler and Richard at Smithfield, where events took a far more decisive turn. While accounts of this encounter vary, all are agreed that Tyler behaved with such insufferable arrogance that many of

Richard's party called for his immediate detention. The king gave his consent and commanded Walworth to make the arrest, whereupon Tyler tried to escape. Walworth then stepped forth, and in the scuffle that followed inflicted a near-fatal blow on Tyler, who fell wounded to the ground. Tyler's supporters were furious and on the verge of rebelling, but it was the quick thinking of the young king that averted further conflict. 'What, my lieges, will you then kill your king?' Richard is reported to have cried. 'Be not concerned for the loss of your leader, I myself will now be your general.'

Walworth's next act was also the result of quick, strategic thinking. Riding swiftly back into the City, he began to enlist help for the young ruler: 'You noblest of citizens, men who do what is pleasing and fear God, give help without delay to your king who is in danger of death. And help me, your mayor, for I am in the same danger. Or if, because of my faults, you decide not to help me, at least do not abandon your king.'

The citizens of London were quick to respond, and almost immediately a well-armed guard was appropriated to Smithfield. Thus, the rebellion was quashed and Walworth's place in the City's history books was assured, although in reality his work was far from over. As soon as Richard was satisfied that peace was fully restored, and shaking at the memory of his recent close encounter, the young king demanded that the revolt be investigated and the City be secured against the possibility of any further violence breaking out. Walworth and six others were appointed to bring the perpetrators of the rebellion to justice, and to do whatever was necessary to ensure that peace was maintained.

The City's officials were quick to enforce new safeguarding measures.

City hostellers were required to take responsibility for all those in their households, and all aldermen were obliged to take an oath of allegiance to the population of their various wards. If any person refused to take this oath there was to be no leniency – the offenders were to be immediately arrested. In the aftermath of the attack on the City of London, one thing that had surprised many of the City's officials was that the rebels had managed to get through the City's gates. It was assumed that they had been opened by citizens sympathetic to the peasants' cause and so extensive measures were adopted to ensure this couldn't happen again – including the arrangement that each ward would take charge of a certain gate on a pre-ordained day. It must have come as a shock to many to realise that there were sympathisers to the rebellion within the City; even a number of the City's aldermen were thought to have been involved. More than seventy City-dwellers believed to have colluded with the rioters found themselves hauled in front of the City's commissioners and forced to swear their loyalty and good behaviour.

While many heroic actions have been lost in time, the City does not forget its heroes easily. The story of Walworth, knighted for his decisive defence of the City, was to be told and retold for many centuries to follow. As is sometimes the case in the repeating of events, some of the original is lost and even in the sixteenth century we can see that the popular version of what happened on that seminal day was already being debated. In Stowe's sixteenth-century *Survey of London*, the London-born chronicler sought to rectify a popular theory that Walworth had, in addition, killed Jack Straw. He wrote, 'But Jack Straw being afterwards taken, was first adjudged by the said mayor and then executed by the loss of his head in Smithfield.' Stowe did, however, acknowledge that for some time it was widely believed that that brave Walworth had been knighted immediately on the battlefield along with three others:

> In reward of this service (the people being dispersed) the king commanded the mayor to put a bascinet (military helmet) on his head; and the mayor requested why he should do so, the king answered, he being much bound unto him, would make him knight: the mayor answered, that he was neither worthy nor able to take such an estate upon him, for he was but a merchant, and had to live by his merchandise only; notwithstanding, the king made him put on his bascinet, and then with a sword in both hands he strongly stroke him on the neck, as the manner was then; and the same day he made three other citizens knights for his sake in the same place; to wit, John Philpot, Nicholas Brembre and Robert Launde, alderman. The king gave to the mayor one hundred pounds land by year and to each of the other forty pounds land yearly, to them and their heirs forever.

Walworth, according to the Imperial Society of Knights Bachelor, became the first civilian to achieve knighthood.

On the impressively dominating statue of Walworth that stands within Fishmongers' Hall, the following inscription has been engraved:

> Brave Walworth, Knight, Lord Mayor yt slew
> Rebellious Tyler in his alarmes;
> The king, therefore did give in liew
> The dagger to the City armes,
> In the 4th year of Richard II, Anno Domini 1381

According to Stow, herein lies another oft-held but mistaken opinion – that the dagger which is part of the City's arms was added in honour of Walworth:

It hath also been, and is now grown to a common opinion, that in reward of this service done by the said William Walworth against the rebel, King Richard added to the arms of this City a sword or dagger … whereof I have read no such record but to the contrary. I find that in the fourth year of Richard II in a full assembly made in the upper chamber of the Guildhall, summoned by this William Walworth, then mayor, as well of aldermen as of the common council, in every ward, for certain affairs concerning the king, it was there by common consent agreed and ordained that the old seal of the office of the mayoralty of the city being very small, old, unapt and uncomely for the honour of the City should be broken and one other new should be had which the said mayor commanded to be made artificially and honourable for the exercise of the said office thereafter in place of the other; in which new seal, besides the images of Peter and Paul, which of old were rudely engraven, there should be under the feet of the said images a shield of the arms of the said city, perfectly graved with two lions, supporting the same, with two sergeants of arms; another part, one, and two tabernacles, in which above should stand two angels in between whom, above the said images of Peter and Paul, should be set the glorious virgin. This being done the old seal of the office was delivered to Richard Odiham, chamberlain, who brake it, and in place thereof was delivered the new seal to the said mayor, to use in his office of mayoralty, as occasion should require.

Stow gives further evidence against the new seal being made in honour of Sir William Walworth's actions:

This new seal seemeth to be made before William Walworth was knighted for he is not there intituled Sir, as afterwards he was; and certain it is, that the same new seale then made, is now in use, and none other in that office of the mayoralty; which may suffice to answer the former fable, without showing of any evidence sealed with the old seale which was the crosse, and sword of Saint Paul, and not the dagger of William Walworth.

While Sir William's eventful second tenure had been marked by insurrection, his successor, John de Northampton (1381 and 1382), wisely decided to leave nothing to chance. Northampton's time as chief magistrate was notable for his harsh crackdown on crime, and as though to punish the City's residents for the haste in which they had joined the resurrection he also decided to reform their morals. Such was the vigour in which he carried out his work that he actually drew the attention of the clergy, who strongly objected to him encroaching on their role. Crucially, he also managed to obtain a parliamentary Act which stated that no victualler should have judicial office in London, or any other city, unless there was no other suitably qualified person, in which case every such person was to completely abstain from that trade during their terms of office.

While Walworth's act had secured the City's favour with the young king, not all subsequent mayors were as demonstrative in their support. In fact, in the years following Walworth's tenure the relationship between Richard and the City turned into something of a struggle. Young, inexperienced and vulnerable to the malign influences of his ambitious uncle, we can see from the Calendar of Letter-Books of the City of London that, although initially the proud citizens of the capital were happy to call him the Londoner's king, it was a situation which was not to last. With many believing their monarch to be little more than a puppet in the hands of John of Gaunt, Richard's support in the City was irrevocably to divide. On one hand were those such as grocer Nicholas Brembre, who supported the king, while on the other John de Northampton came out in favour of John of Gaunt.

Only a few years earlier, the relationship between the City and the Crown had soured considerably with the very mayorship itself coming under threat when the Duke of Lancaster favoured a bill put forward in 1377 that decreed that the control of the City's government should be given to a member of the nobility – namely Henry Percy. Such a suggestion must have stung. Fractious arguments between the City and monarch had come and gone but to have the reigns of the City's governance in the hands of the nobility was a step too far.

It was a scheme that struck terror into the heart of the City's governance, particularly provoking John Philipot, who was untiringly vigorous in his opposition. That a group of the City's most prominent citizens, led by Philpot, decided to meet with Richard II – at that time a king-in-waiting – both to assure him of their support and also to downplay the recent hostilities caused by the proposal of the new bill, seems to have worked; there is not a trace more of its suggestion after 1377 and the death of Edward III. When Lord Mayor Adam Staple attended Richard's coronation on 16 July 1377, he did so promising to serve the king.

In the early days of Richard's reign, London's officials had been his constant advisors. It was Walworth and John Philipot whom Richard called upon to discuss how to proceed with the ongoing war with France (Spanish-French fleets had been spotted in the channel), and how to protect mercantile trade.

Both Philipot and Walworth sat at Richard II's first parliament while Brembre, Philipot and Walworth all loaned money to the king to help lift the country out of the financial black hole it was in – as did the City in its own right. In October that year, the City's position became secure once more when Richard issued, with backing from the House of Commons, his ample *inspeximus* charter, which ring-fenced the City's liberties, allowing no foreigner to buy from or sell to another foreigner with the liberties of the City. Privileges were further extended to the City's widows, who were freed from tallages or contributions to the government. Taking no chances, Brembre arranged for the terms of the charter to be publicly declared, but while the City's trading rights were thus secured, a different kind of trouble was brewing in its increasingly bitter relations with John of Gaunt, who was beginning to wager small but significant attacks on the City. It had happened that some of the Earl of Buckingham's servants were attacked while within the City walls, and on this account the earl's brother, who unfortunately happened to be John of Gaunt, waged his own personal battle against the City, summoning the Lord Mayor, Brembre, to answer for this occurrence, which he was sure was premeditated, before Parliament. Intending to cast an irredeemable slur on Brembre's character and therefore the City as a whole, it was a move calculated to spark hostilities between the Lords and the City – and it worked. By the time Philipot was Lord Mayor in 1378, this ongoing feud had resulted in many Lords leaving the City altogether. With them went the main source of income for the City's hostellers and vintners. Desperate to secure trade, the City officials met to agree a plan of action, raising money by subscription to bribe the Lords back. It was a thoughtful approach and one that worked – had it failed it would have been doubtful whether the king would have been able to successfully approach the City for money as he did again in early 1379. The Lord Mayor and aldermen negotiated between themselves, agreeing to loan Richard the substantial sum of £5,000, to be settled by November that year.

Richard, as previous monarchs had, relied heavily on the stability of the City for reasons of finance. Explains Caroline Barron in *London in the Later Middle Ages: Government and People, 1200–1500*: 'Financial wealth and expertise was increasingly concentrated among the merchants who traded in and out of London and the king needed their financial support.' Direct and indirect taxation were the principal means of raising money for a king who relied on the ability to quickly raise funds. But Richard wanted more: 'The king expected gifts, as well as loans in celebration of coronations, weddings or victories, and as bribes, or, occasionally, to ward off a dire threat to the security of the realm.'

When war was on the cards, the king expected even more from London:

> That the city in his realm would provide men to fight and ships to transport them across the Channel to foreign fields. It was also in London that the king might look to acquire the large number of bows and bowstrings, armour, harness, food supplies and all the accoutrements of war without which large numbers of men could not be converted into armies.

London was, for the Crown, more than its capital city:

> It was here that royal visitors were brought, such as the King of Armenia at Christmas 1385 and where jousts and tournaments

were held. Here royal triumphs and processions were played out and the appearance of the city was a matter of concern to the king. He wanted his capital city, his processional city, perhaps even his New Jerusalem to be clean and impressive. The king needed also a peaceful and orderly metropolis.

It was London's failure to be orderly that provoked Richard's sharp action against the City in 1392. If members of the king's Household and nobles and their retinues could not walk safely in the city streets then the king himself felt insecure and if city government had degenerated into a mass of squabbling factions and street fights, then London was failing to provide an appropriate ambience for the king's regality.

Richard II: The Art of Kingship by Anthony Goodman and
James L Gillespie

Despite Northampton's attempts to control London's citizens, his own reign as chief magistrate was striking primarily because of the number of disputes he got into and the high number of accusations levelled against him. Obstinate in character, he ruled the civic throne for two years and when his chief adversary, grocer Nicholas Brembre, was elected in 1383 (he was to serve for three years) he reportedly conspired continually with others to overthrow him. Brembre, aware of Northampton's ill feeling towards him, reported the matter to the king – an action which resulted in Northampton being bound to keep the peace to the sum of £5,000 on 22 January 1384. Northampton, however, could not remain idle for long and just a month later he and his brother Robert led a riot through Westchepe. Northampton was duly arrested, whereupon his supporters rioted further. Cordwainer John Constantyn was charged with leading the revolt since he had signalled for it to start by closing his shop. Making an example of Constantyn, Brembre immediately ordered his arrest and he was duly tried and beheaded. But this was not the end of the matter. The populace of London city had been at odds with itself ever since Brembre had taken his seat as Lord Mayor, and both Northampton and Brembre were cited as the cause. On 11 June, the Common Council, in an attempt to gain some degree of clarity in the matter, voted as to who the chief cause of the mischief was. All agreed it was Northampton, who now faced an uncomfortable trial.

On 18 August Northampton faced his one-time secretary, Thomas Usk, who had been brought into the courtroom by Brembre. Testifying against his former ally, Usk was the main witness against Northampton, who insisted Usk was a liar and challenged him to a duel. To no avail, Northampton asked the court to delay judgement upon him until his patron the Duke of Lancaster could be present, but this misguided suggestion served only to enrage the king, who swiftly condemned him to hang. At the intervention of the queen, Anne of Bohemia, Northampton's sentence was commuted to life imprisonment and he was first incarcerated in Corfe Castle and later at Tintagel. After this time Northampton was not allowed to come within a hundred miles of the City – a distance later reduced to eighty miles, thanks to the Duke of Lancaster's intercession. This might have quelled matters had Brembre's rivalry with Northampton not become a national issue. Northampton's policy, it seems, was to open up the City electorate and to try to make the City's governance more favourable to the smaller trades, such as craftsmen and shopkeepers who didn't have the benefit of overseas trade. But, says Goodman and Gillespie in *Richard II: The Art of Kingship,*

Of course these policies did not command universal support, but at first they seem to have been welcomed by the king. In October 1382 Richard wrote twice to the Londoners urging them to re-elect John Northampton as mayor ... Richard may have been moved to this course of action by Northampton's ability, as it seemed, to keep London under control. He was duly re-elected by his second mayoralty was much stormier than the first and Richard seems to have lost confidence in him and in his policies for in the following October, Nicholas Brembre was elected mayor '*rege favente*'. The election was virtually a riot and Northampton's refusal to accept the outcome led to his imprisonment, trial by the king and banishment from the City for the next seven years.

In the following October the king went further in his intervention in the mayoral election. He forbade the carrying of arms in the city and sent three members of his household, John lord Neville of Raby, Lord Fitzwalter and Sir Thomas Morieux, a Chamber Knight to act as 'observers' and to ensure that the election was conducted peacefully and according to custom. Although over 300 citizens were duly summoned, other 'persons of the middle sort' turned up uninvited, and protested when Brembre was re-elected. The king favoured Brembre's re-election but the protestors wanted the goldsmith, Nicholas Twyford ... The involvement of the Crown also became the norm; in October 1385 Brembre was re-elected for a third term '*rege annuente*'. Two years later Richard wrote to the mayor, aldermen and commons of the city, threatening them that if they did not choose a mayor 'who would govern the city well' he would refused to allow the barons of the Exchequer to take the oath.

At the Merciless Parliament of 1388, the king reiterated his demand that the City must elect a loyal, trustworthy and peaceful mayor.

Richard did not rely solely upon the mayor to impose order in the City, Goodman and Gillespie explains:

> He tried to make contact more directly with the citizens by demanding oaths of fealty. Such oaths in various different forms were to become one of the hallmarks of Richard's government. The use of oaths was not unique to the king. In 1377 all the members of fifty of the more powerful mysteries, whether masters, servants or apprentices had been sworn to keep the peace, obey mayoral summonses, put down conspiracies, keep the city's secrets, and only come to Guildhall if summoned. Similar oaths were demanded of all the 'good men' of the city in March 1382, February 11384 and May 1385. Presumably it was hoped that by these means the city would be fashioned into a giant fraternity bound together by mutual oaths. It was therefore no novelty for the Londoners to find themselves expected to swear to 'live and die' with King Richard against all rebels in the autumn of 1387.

The National Archives holds an interesting document which sheds light on what was happening in the City at this time. It was submitted by the bowyers, cutlers, fletchers, blacksmiths and spurriers to the king and Lords of Parliament in 1387, and cites misgovernment by Brembre and Extone. Among a number of complaints, are calls for Nicholas Exton to be removed from office as it is said he was unjustly elected by Brembre, and there is also a demand that an Anthony Cheyne and Hugh Fastolf also be removed. This is just one of several petitions made by disgruntled companies.

By the time Brembre's three-year reign came to an end in 1386 with the election of Nicholas Extone as Lord Mayor, the situation between the City and the Crown had changed dramatically. A commission for controlling the king's expenditure had been set up and the country was all but on the brink of civil war. The City was split between those who supported the king, and those who supported his advisors. Northampton's friends, meanwhile, were bent on getting him back into the City, and the citizens of the king took an oath from Brembre to uphold him against all enemies. Events escalated quickly. On 14 November, the Duke of Gloucester and his supporters – Arundel, Bolingbroke, Norfolk and Warwick (the Lords Appellant) – charged Richard and his supporters – Brembre, Archbishop Neville, the Duke of Ireland and Chief Justice Tresilian – with treason, and in 1387 they were tried by what became known as the Merciless Parliament. Wisely, by the time Parliament was called the accused had fled with the exception of Brembre, who remained to be charged with treason and to be hanged as 'the false London Knight'. Brembre remains, to this day, the only Lord Mayor to have been executed. Northampton's supporters, meanwhile, finally got their wish and in November 1390 Northampton was pardoned and his rights fully restored.

It was a bitter period in the City's history which showed how swiftly events can change, although throughout this period the reputation of Walworth, at least, still remained intact. Walworth died in 1385 and was buried at St Michael, Crooked Lane, a church to which he had contributed great sums to during his life, though it was destroyed in the Great Fire. It was rebuilt in 1687 by Christopher Wren but demolished in 1831 to make room for a larger approach to London Bridge.

An obvious choice to become the much-lauded hero of London City, he appeared in many popular tales, including Richard Johnsons's 'Nine Worthies of London' in 1592, in which Johnson celebrates leading figures in the time of Henry IV.

Containing a briefe rehearsall of the deeds of Chivalry, performed by the Nine Worthies of the world, the seauen Champions of Christendome, with many other remarkable Warriours. To the tune of List lusty Gallants

Was Smithfeeld, where his Maiefty did ftay,
An howre ere thefe Rebels found the way.
At laft the leaders of that brutifh rowt
Iacke Straw, Wat Tiler, and a number more,
Aproacht the place with fuch a yelling fhowt,
As feldome had the like been heard before:
The king fpake faire, and bad them lay downe armes,
And he would pardon all their former harmes.

I left him not, but ere I did depart,
I ftabd my dagger to his damned heart.
The reft perceiuing of their captaine flaine,
Soone terrified did caft their weapons downe,
And like to fheepe began to flie amaine,
They durft not looke on Iuftice dreadfull frowne.
The king purfude, and we were not the laft,
Till furie of the fight were ouerpaft.
Thus were the mangled parts of peace recurde;
The Princes falling ftate by right defended;
From common weale all mifchiefe quite abiurde,
With loue and dutie vertue was attended.
And for that deed that day before t'was night,
My king in guerdon dubbed me a knight.

Walworth's action proved an example to the citizens of London for many years to come – even in the dark days of the Civil War, he provided an example of bravery to that bold commander of armies General Monck:

> A speech
> Made to His excellency
> The Lord General Monck
> And the Council of State,
> At Fishmongers-Hall in LONDON.
> The Thirteenth of April, 1660.
> IS your Peace just? What Rock stands it upon?
> Conscience and Law make the best Union.
> If you gain Birthrights here by Bloud and Slaughter,
> Though you sing now, youl howle for ever after:
> Trust my Experience, one that can unfold
> The strangest truest Tale that ere was told,
> In my degree, few men shall overtake me,
> I was as great as Wickedness could make me;
> This heart, this habit, and this tongue to boot
> Commanded Forty thousand Horse and Foot,
> In three weeks time, My fortune grew so high
> I could have matchd my Fishers Family
> With the best Bloud in Naples: Right and Wrong,
> And Life and Death attended on my Tongue,
> Till (by a quick verticitie of Fate)
> I find too soon what I repent too late;
> And, though a Rebell in a righteous clothing,
> My glow-worm glories glimmerd into nothing.
> Thus fell that Fisher-man that had no fellow,

I am the Wandring Shade of Massianello;
Who, since I was into Perdition hurld,

Am come to preach this Doctrine to the world.

Rebels though backt with Power, and seeming Reason,
Time and Success, shall feel the fate of Treason.
But stay! what Pictures this hangs in my sight?
Tis valiant Walworth, the king-saving Knight:
That stabd Jack Straw: Had Walworth livd within
These four Months, where had Jack the Cobler been?
It was a bold brave deed, an act in Season,
Whilest he was on the Top-branch of his Treason.

He looketh up
to the Picture
of Sir William
Walworth (who
stabd Jack
Straw) that
hangeth over
the head of
my Lord Ge-
neral.
But from that Shaddow, dropping down My eye,
I see a Substance of like Loyalty.

To the Lord
General.
IF long renowned Walworth had the fate

To save a king, You have to save a State;
And, who knows what by Consequence? The Knight
By that brave Deed, gaind every man his Right:
And you, by this, may gain each Man his due,
Not onely Trusty Hearts, but Traitors too:
He drew bloud, you did not; tis all one sense,
Theres but a Straws breadth in the difference:
He savd the Town from being burnt, and You
Have rescued it from Fire and Plunder too:
He was this Companies good Benefactor,
And You have been their Liberties Protector;
For which, I heard them say, they would engage
Their States, and Blouds, and Lives against all rage
That shall oppose Your just Designes: And that
You are the welcomst Guest, ever came at
This Table; they say, All they can exhibit
Is not so much a Treatment as a Tribute:
They call you the First step to Englands Peace,
The True fore-runner of our Happiness:

A Parallel.

And, joynd with these great Councillors, You are
Our best Preservatives in Peace and War.
You have a Loyal Heart, a Lucky Hand,
Elected for the Cure of this Sick Land,
Who by Protectors and unjust Trustees,
Hath been Enslavd, and brought upon her Knees:

To the Council of State.

We humbly pray this may be thought upon
Before the kingdoms Treasure be quite gon:
And hope you will (though Envy look a squint)
When all is fit, Put a Just Steward int.

CHORUS.
Then may your fame out-live all Story,
And prove a Monument of Glory;
Kings and Queens (as Tribute due)
On their knees shall pray for you,
Whilst all True hearts confess with Tongue and Pen,
A Loyal Subject is the best of Men.

3

ALMS TO ARCHITECTURE
1380–1500

Today, on North London's Highgate Hill stands an ancient stone marker dedicated to one of the most legendary characters in the City's history. Surrounded by stout iron railings and accompanied by the figure of a cat, the monument is situated at the very spot from which it was famously said that Richard Whittington paused to hear the great bells of Bow church ring out the prophesy of his forthcoming good fortune. The now legendary chimes 'Turn again Whittington – Thrice Mayor of London' passed quickly into fable, along with many other aspects of Whittington's life, but what exactly are the facts behind the popular, often pantomime-esque portrayal of London's best-loved Lord Mayor?

Take a stroll across the City of London and you will find a number of clues. In the church of St Michael Paternoster, a luminous stained-glass window stands as an eternal dedication to the memory of a man who financed its building, attended its services and even conducted his business from within its hallowed walls. At St Bartholomew's Hospital, a similar epitaph once existed to serve Whittington's memory – this time a reminder of his extensive charitable donations. In the stately seat of the City's governance, the Guildhall, yet another depiction of London's most celebrated father hangs in a prominent siding on the edge of the Great Hall.

Whatever the fables and however far-fetched the myths, the fact that Whittington's likeness can still be viewed to this day in the administrative centre of a corporation he used to head, one of London's most prominent hospitals and at the church at which he worshipped tells us of the astonishingly generous yet very tangible contribution he made to his community during his long public life, and, in part, explains why his name is as familiar as ever – almost seven hundred years after his birth.

Born in the rural village of Pauntley in the 1350s, Whittington's background was not as humble as is popularly perceived. As the son of a Gloucestershire landowner he doubtless enjoyed a more secure upbringing than many in the economically uncertain late fourteenth century, but as he wasn't a first son he was unlikely to inherit, and so we find that by 1379 Whittington had already made his infamous journey to the City of London, drawn by the promise of potential wealth. At the time this was not an uncommon journey, and Whittington could easily have found himself in the same precarious position as the many other economic migrants who flocked to London, attracted by the diversity of trades in this burgeoning mercantile city. Undoubtedly, Richard was luckier than most. Becoming apprenticed to the well-respected Mercers guild, he found himself protected by the generous ordinances of an organisation which drew a tight ring of financial protection around its members. He also began to learn the ropes of a trade that would one day acquaint him with the most powerful men in the country.

It's unlikely that when Whittington first took the decision to join the Mercers he would have understood just how far this association would take him – though he may have had an idea. After all, in the late 1300s the Mercers were a highly organised and illustrious body of men who traded in expensive fabrics such as velvet, linen and silk, often imported from abroad. In terms of their merchandise, the Mercers were at the very highest end of the market, successfully peddling their luxurious wares even in a City still recovering from the merciless effects of the Black Death. But in the challenging times of early medieval life we only have to look at the wills of prominent citizens to see that, then as now, those of power and influence liked to dress well. Livery companies in particular exhibited their high status by frequently altering the colours of their dress, while the City's well heeled and wealthy went about their business resplendent in rich velvet tunics with silk-lined hoods, their garments often adorned with intricate embroidery in expensive gold thread. In this era, on particularly important occasions, many chose to follow the French fashion of having tiny bells sewn inside their hoods and sleeves – thereby giving off a gentle tinkle as they moved.

Certainly, the Mercers' trade was wholly tied up in status, underpinned by legislation to ensure it stayed that way. In 1363, a parliamentary bill reinforced the legalities of what cloth could be worn by whom: ermine and gold cloth were reserved for knights and for those holding lands worth more than 400 marks a year, while silk was only available for gentry worth 200 marks a year or for merchants whose goods were valued at £1,000.

The coarser, cheaper black and russet cloth and lamb's wool were reserved for the labouring classes – the agricultural workers, servants, yeoman and craftsmen – along with the less wealthy gentry, though this was not a static decree. The 1402 and 1406 parliaments conceded clothing rights to knights, mayors and to former Lord Mayors of London, York and Bristol, along with their wives, who could, from that point onwards, enjoy wearing furs and ornaments made from gold. It took much longer for the lower classes to enjoy the same privileges. In 1463 regulations were further relaxed when the fabrics available to gentlemen and esquires also became obtainable by sheriffs and aldermen, though inappropriately attired persons could still find themselves on the wrong side of disciplinary action. In the same year the regulations were introduced, several young men literally found themselves caught short when they were fined by their company (the Tailors) for wearing cloaks that weren't deemed to be long enough. Clothes were not the only matter for which apprentices could find themselves in disgrace. In 1479 the Mercers admitted a young man to their company with the stipulation that he must be of sound appearance, and the employee in question was ordered not only to smarten up his dress but also to cut his hair – 'that he sadly dispose hym and mannerly bothe in his arreye and also in the cuttynge of his here'.

Revealing a distinct gift for trade in the fast-moving cloth industry, Whittington soon began to make a name for himself, rising from his initial position as mercer's apprentice, to become master of the Company of Mercers not once but three times (1395, 1401 and 1408). In equal measure Whittington seemed able to combine natural business sense with the equally valuable trait of being able to cultivate and maintain lucrative business relationships, and his regular high-profile customers included Robert de Vere, childhood friend of Richard II, and Hugh, Earl of Stafford, to whom he supplied household goods for many years. The Duke of Gloucester,

Thomas of Woodstock, also became a client of Whittington's, as did his elder brother John of Gaunt and his son the future Henry IV. It was in 1389, though, that Whittington made what would turn out to be the most significant transaction of his career. Paying £11 for two cloths of gold, Richard II made his first purchase from the landowner's son – an arrangement that was long to continue. Receipts for royal expenditure show us that from 1392 to 1394, Richard II spent a small fortune on goods that had been supplied by Whittington – £3,475 to be exact – and by all accounts a friendship was born. In the days when allegiances could be short and terminated at any given moment, Whittington continued on good terms with Richard long after he failed to keep his crown, but he also didn't shrink in supplying his successor. For Henry IV he sourced countless items for the royal wardrobe, even providing materials for the wedding of Henry's eldest daughter, Blanche, to King Rupert of Germany's son Louis (the contract was signed on 7 March 1401, though the actual marriage didn't take place for a further year, on 6 July 1402) along with gold cloth and pearls for her sister Philippa's marriage to Eric of Pomerania, King of Denmark, Norway and Sweden.

From the very outset, Whittington's fast-accruing wealth meant that he became much more than a supplier of luxury goods. We can see that from 23 August 1388 to 23 July 1422 he made no less than fifty-nine loans to the monarchy (many of which were made jointly with other merchants). The largest of these loans was £2,833, while the smallest was £4.

It was in the June of 1392 that Whittington, along with twenty-four other prominent citizens, travelled to Nottingham on the invitation of the king to hear his damning speech about business misconduct in the City. Just a year later, his interest in civic affairs culminated in his appointment to the post of alderman. By the June of 1397, Whittington had risen further still, achieving the highest civic position a commoner could hope to attain in medieval England – the post of London's Lord Mayor.

Unusually, though, Whittington's accession to chief magistrate was not the result of an election. By 1397 the career of another influential and wealthy tradesman, this time belonging to the company of the Goldsmiths, was in its ascendancy. Adam Bamme had first become Lord Mayor in 1390, a tenure for which he was remembered with much gratitude since it was he who was responsible for agreeing the purchase of a substantial grain supply, which was promptly put into storage for London's citizens to use in times of shortage. For this he had negotiated a huge sum (around £400 from the Chamberlain's fund), an act for which the City's residents were unendingly grateful and one that also went a long way in securing him a second term in 1396. Sadly, Bamme died in office on 6 June 1397, and this time it was the king, Richard II, not the electorate, who decided his replacement – an act which left the barons of the Exchequer displeased.

It was a long-held tradition that all mayors who held office were put to the king *and* his barons for approval – a step which Richard, in this case, wilfully overlooked. The barons, in a fit of temper, refused to take Whittington's oath, but they were overruled by Richard, who received the oath himself. It was not an auspicious start.

Londoners, however, took a more pragmatic view. Recognising the benefits of Whittington's good standing at court, they were quick to approve the choice, while Whittington himself, thrust suddenly and without preparation into this most public and illustrious role, had little choice but to get on with the onerous job at hand. Ever aware of the pitfalls of discord, he personally took charge of the security arrangements during the first parliamentary session of 1397, recorded in *The Brut or the Chronicles of England* as follows: '[He] ordeined at euery yate and yn euery warde strong wacche of men of armez and of archers, and prinspally at euery yate of London duryng this same parlement.'

Within days he had negotiated with the king a deal which bought the City back its precious liberties, though for the not insubstantial sum of £10,000 (nearly £4 million today).

While history tells us that Whittington had a close and mutually beneficial relationship with Richard II, he was far from being the only merchant to receive favours from the Crown. At a time of burgeoning trade, merchants were not only becoming increasingly wealthy but also becoming ever more influential, though they generally tended not to aspire to the highs and lows of a career in politics. Whittington might have been a young man when he achieved success in supplying the royal wardrobe, but there were many other merchants who were doing the same. William Estfield, for instance, became a favourite of Henry VI for his generous loans to the royal purse (Estfield, in addition, was infamous at the time for selling a valuable stone known as The George to the king), while vintner Thomas Walsingham undertook so many duties for the Crown he found himself unable to continue his role as an alderman. Relationships between leading merchants and the Crown were both common and beneficial to both parties and had a wide and long-lasting impact on the nation's affairs – not least because many merchants were roped into diplomatic negotiations abroad, their acute business sense being particularly useful in state negotiations. While many of these merchants were not particularly interested in the uncertainties of the political area, it was, nonetheless, often in their best interests to remain involved. Throughout the fourteenth century the health of the nation's economy was intrinsically linked to the success of the wool trade – by far the country's largest export – and so the merchant's influence increasingly held some sway. At a time when parliaments could be held at various locations across the country, it was London's Lord Mayor and aldermen who in 1328 suggested to the king that a parliament ought to be held and that it should be based at Westminster – and there were sound economic reasons for this suggestion. A London-based assembly provided not only a good business opportunity for London's profit-orientated merchants, but also a golden opportunity to push their personal interests. One such case was the 1429/30 parliamentary session, when Lord Mayor William Esfield helped members to win the City's legal exemption from the restrictions that a recent statute had placed upon apprenticeships.

While all existing records point to a wealthy, astute and benevolent man, very little is known about Whittington's private life, although we can be sure that in 1402 he bought a sizeable property near the church of St Michael Paternoster Royal where he lived with his new wife, Alice, the daughter of Sir Ivo Fitzwarin of Wantage, Berkshire. By this time there can be little doubt that he had amassed a wealth far beyond anything he could have dreamed during his first uncertain days in the capital – his debtors included Sir Simon Burley, Earl of Somerset, John Beaufort and Sir Thomas Talbot, and he had already invested a substantial sum in the property market of London itself. He even lent money to Henry V to finance the 1415 invasion of France, which led to England's infamous victory at Agincourt.

Not always receiving direct repayment, on occasion Whittington was given financial remuneration in the form of a proportion of the wool tax which was collected at different ports, but as soon as he was able to export wool without paying duty he shrewdly furthered his interest in that area. While earlier on in his career Whittington struggled to raise enough money for investments (having loaned most of it out), by 1402 he was doing well enough financially to not only purchase his new London house but also to ship wool from London and Chichester.

Whittington was elected Lord Mayor again in 1406, and in the following year he held this post both in London and in Calais, but it was in 1416 that he involved himself in public affairs at an even higher level, becoming a Member of Parliament in 1416.

This was not a new path for the politically aware Whittington family – both his grandfather and his father sat in the Commons, in 1327 and 1348 respectively, while his brother Robert played a central role in local Gloucestershire politics, still finding the time to participate in six parliaments. Though there are a few similarities in their civic positions, Robert's career was very different to that of his famous brother's. From 1382 he played an active part in his local community, serving the various different posts of alnager (inspector of the quality and measurement of woollen cloth), sheriff, constable of the Forest of Dean, justice of the peace, coroner and escheator. In 1393 he was removed from his position as coroner, but only because his responsibilities as escheator were too numerous to carry out both roles at the same time. While there is no evidence to suggest that Richard and Robert were particularly close, they did have property interests in common and they both took legal action against James Clifford when a disagreement arose over land ownership. Richard was also present in Parliament in October 1416 when Robert petitioned the House seeking justice for the alleged wrongs inflicted upon him by one Richard Oldcastle in a matter recorded as a family feud.

Property and land, two ways in which many people realised wealth, were not ways in which Whittington preferred to operate. He did own some London property, and we can see that in 1412 this gave him an annual income of £25. His wife's family owned appreciable swathes of land, and although Alice sadly died before her father, Fitzwarn had settled property in both Wiltshire and Somerset which Whittington sold to John Chideok, his brother-in-law, for the sum of £340. When land did come into Whittington's hands it was generally in the form of security for the settlement of debts. A case in point is his loan of £500 to his uncle Philip Maunsell in February 1394. His uncle, unable to pay directly, eventually gave his manor Over Lyppiat in Gloucestershire to Whittington instead. A similar situation occurred in February 1397, with property being held by Whittington on the border of Oxfordshire until James Sparsholt and Richard Monmouth had repaid their debts.

For an individual who made his wealth providing loans to others, it may seem strange that he gave significant amounts away; but to understand the impetus behind Whittington's acts of charity we must first return to Whittington's London, perhaps to the tiny alley of Paternoster Row, where the clergy of St Paul's once trod the bare earth clutching their rosary beads and reciting the Lord's Prayer. The City might have been the beating heart of trade and commerce, but religion also played a central role in daily life, as evidenced by the number of churches within the square mile – at one time as many as three hundred. When Whittington attended services at St Paul's, it was the old St Paul's, begun in the time of William the Conqueror and remaining unfinished until the middle of the fourteenth century, when it stood proudly, revelling in its fame of being one of the longest churches in the world, having the tallest spire and also some of the finest stained glass. These noteworthy credentials, along with the fact that it was also home to the shrine of Saint Erkenwald, meant that it soon became a popular place of pilgrimage. Not only was this landmark building the seat of the Diocese of London, but it also came to be an important meeting place. What was known as Paul's Walk (the nave aisle) became the focal point of many a business transaction, as well as a guaranteed place to hear the latest London gossip. Within the grounds of St Paul's stood the infamous preaching cross and outdoor pulpit which was to become a hotspot for radical preaching, although in Whittington's time it was more of a site for public proclamations. It was from this very location that it was first announced, by a messenger of Henry III, that the new monarch wished London and its citizens well and that he desired them to be fairly governed and their liberties kept intact.

As with most citizens of medieval England, religion was a key influence, particularly the Christian duty of giving alms. At a time long before the welfare state, many of the City's churches, almshouses, prisons, hospitals, roads, drains and even urinals owed their existence to the munificence of wealthy benefactors. While the influence of religion was inescapable, perhaps it was also Whittington's own experiences as a mercer which impressed upon him the importance of looking after the basic needs of others. After all, the Mercers, like many of the ancient trade guilds, made it clear that acts of benevolence were not the exception but the rule. In the Mercers' own archives we can see records dating back to 1348 in which it is clear that the guild had a responsibility to provide alms to members who had fallen on hard times, whether by loss from debtors, loss at sea or bodily weakness which prevented attendance at work.

Long after his days as a mercer's apprentice were over, Whittington focused much of his energy on projects to enhance the welfare of the citizens of the City that had made him so rich. In 1411 he gave the Old Leaden Hall (which had started life as the site of a manor) to the City of London – a gift which in 1440 was passed on to London's citizens by Lord Mayor Simon Eyre, who by then had transformed the area by providing a public granary, chapel and school. Whittington also paid for unmarried mothers to have their own ward at St Thomas's Hospital and organised a large and much-needed public lavatory beside the Thames, with sixty-four seats for men and sixty-four seats for women.

While Whittington's name was known across the country, within his adoptive home his reputation could hardly have been greater; he is also associated with a number of more well-known projects, including the somewhat knotty financial arrangements of London Bridge. He also held a great deal of sway on a personal level, being thought of as a person of high influence. For instance, when a candidate was put forward to become gaoler of Newgate, the two clerks of the Privy Seal sought approval from both Richard Whittington and the Archbishop of Canterbury. Whittington was also strongly involved in the control of prices in the City of London for trade. When ale prices shot up, Whittington didn't hesitate to make his objections known and the Brewers' Company even paid fines for this misdemeanour in 1422. The aldermen were hesitant in collecting monies owed, saying it was 'bot for to plese Richard Whityngton, for he was the cause of alle the forsaid judgement'. Such was his untarnished reputation that he was also involved as judge in usury trials at around the same time. But for all Whittington's spotless reputation, he was not above going after what was rightfully his. The year 1404 saw a lawsuit brought in

October against a John Hert who was subsequently ordered to pay (bound by the statute of the Staple of Westminster) Whittington £651 within four months. The debt remained outstanding for eleven years, at which point John Hert's wife became possibly the only person to publically attempt to deprecate him when she claimed that it was in fact Whittington who owed money to her, as opposed to the other way round. This is the only recorded slander on Whittington's reputation – in June 1419 he was forced to (successfully) defend his reputation against it.

In the ancient London School for Boys on Queen Victoria Street stands a fine stone statue of one of Whittington's contemporaries and close friends, Thomas Carpenter, with whom Whittington undertook one of his least-known but most influential projects. Today the *Liber Albus* (White Book) is not a text of which much is commonly known, but its importance cannot be overstated. Written predominantly in Latin with some French, the *Liber Albus* is an exhaustive record of the laws and regulations of the City of London and is widely recognised as the very first book of English Common Law.

That Whittington became involved in this enormous undertaking is reflective both of his character and foresightedness. After all, Whittington was a merchant by training, deeply involved in political life but not necessarily legally experienced. But when John Carpenter the Younger, town clerk to the City of London, decided to approach the mammoth task of compiling all the City's records and asked for Whittington's help, the astute merchant willingly complied.

Today, the City of London's archive is astonishing in its range – and the same could be said of it in the early fifteenth century. Since the early piecemeal beginnings of the City's government, its defining records of civil authority, municipal law and ecclesiastical and military documents had remained largely unexamined and undocumented – providing a daunting and complex task to anyone who sought out the information they contained. Carpenter, in addition, had his own reasons to catalogue the City's most precious documents:

> Forasmuch as the fallibility of human memory and the shortness of life do not allow us to gain an accurate knowledge of everything that deserved remembrance, even though the same may have been committed to writing – more especially if it has been so committed without order or arrangement – and more so when no such written account exists, seeing too, that when, as not unfrequently happens, all the aged most experienced and most discrete rulers of the royal city of London have been carried off at the same instant, as it were by pestilence, younger persons who have succeeded them in the government of the city have on various occasions been often at a loss for the very want of such written information; the result of which has repeatedly been disputes and perplexity among them as to the decisions which they should give; it has long deemed necessary; as well by the superior authorities of the said City, as by those of subordinate rank, that a volume – from the fact of its containing the regulations of the City, it might be designated a 'Repertory – should be compiled from the more noteworthy memoranda that lie scattered without order of classification throughout the books [and] rolls, as well as the Charters of the said City.

Finally completed in the year of Whittington's last mayoralty, Carpenter widely acknowledged that the 'extreme laboriousness' of the project was almost certainly the reason it had never been attempted before, and he spoke justifiably proudly of his achievement.

> By favour of our Lord, is now at length compiled, in the mayoralty of that illustrious man, Richard Whityngton, mayor of the said City, that is to say in the month of November in the year of our Lord's incarnation one thousand four hundred and nineteen ... to the end that they may not be lost in oblivion hereafter, but also those noteworthy memoranda which have been committed to writing, but lie scattered in disorder in manner before-mentioned; that so by their being ascertained the superior authorities of the said City, as well as those of subordinate rank, may know henceforth with greater accuracy what in rare and unusual emergencies should be done, etc.

Carpenter's *Liber Albus* was enthusiastically received. Not only did it clearly lay out the changing City laws, but for the first time clear instruction was also provided as to the structure of governance within the City itself, even going as far as to explain how the mayoral role had originally come into existence:

> But it is in the Charter of King Henry, son of King John, that the chief officer of London begins to be called 'mayor'. In that charter it is written: 'Know ye that we have granted, and by this our present Charter have confirmed, unto our Barons of the City of London, that they may elect from among themselves their Mayor each year, who must be one trusty as towards us, discrete and fit for the governance of the City.'

In addition, the roles of the City's officers were clearly defined, and their duties past and present laid out for all to see:

And so it appears that in former times because a person was mayor he was chamberlain also of the City and Escheator of his Lordship the King; and because he was chamberlain he was coroner as well … receiving abjuration of felons, fugitives etc. taking indictments with the Sheriffs and sitting upon view of bodies *felo de se* and of person's killed etc.

The functional value of the *Liber Albus* to the City of London's governance was unquestionable even in Whittington's day, but now, more than five hundred years later, it also takes on the function of a highly prized tome for historical research. That fifteenth-century mayoral elections were an easy target for unrest is information that may not surprise, but in its detail and its scope we begin to see the London landmarks that were most significant to Whittington and his fellow fifteenth-century mayors. As a city which had taken St Thomas as its second patron saint (the first was St Paul), the monastery church of St Thomas was one of the pivotal sites of ceremonial importance to the custom-bound civic authorities. Built on the site of where St Thomas of Canterbury (Thomas à Becket) was born on Cheapside, this was where the Mercers, between the fourteenth and sixteenth centuries, met to discuss business in the absence of their own hall. Another site Whittington would have often visited was the Pardon churchyard, in use since the thirteenth century as a burial site for cathedral cannons. It was also associated with inclusivity, since those who died without the final sacraments or proper ritual oversight by a priest – for instance in times of plague – were buried there on the common understanding that their sins would still be forgiven. Gilbert Becket, father of Thomas, was also said to be buried in the churchyard along with his wife Anne. From 1406 to 1421 the Dean of St Paul's, Thomas More, enclosed the churchyard and renovated the Becket chapel, from which point on the churchyard became a popular resting place for the City's wealthy and powerful.

Within the pages of the *Liber Albus* we also learn that on the feast day of St Simon and St Jude (28 October), St Thomas's church became especially important to the new Lord Mayor of London, when, on the day of his election, he would ride in grand procession to Westminster where he would take his oath at the Exchequer and be formally accepted in the king's name. After returning to the City and feasting with aldermen and upper governor officers at his residence, the City's new chief magistrate would then process from the church of St Thomas of Acon, accompanied by the holders of various ceremonial and administrative offices plus his two sheriffs followed by the recorder and other aldermen, all keeping a respectful distance from the City's new governor. At Saint Paul's the procession would first stand between the two small doors in the nave to pray for the soul of Bishop William (who had obtained from William the Conqueror great liberties for the City of London); they would then continue to the churchyard where the bodies of the parents of Thomas, late Archbishop of Canterbury lay, saying the *De Profundis* for the repose of their souls before returning to St Thomas of Acon to make an offering. Subtle variations of this procession took place on numerous other feast days throughout the year, including 29 December (St Thomas), 1 November (All Saints), 25 December (Christmas), 26 December (St Stephen), 27 December (St John the Evangelist) and 6 January (Epiphany).

Many historians have drawn significance from the fact that civic processions culminated at Becket's tomb, thereby associating the mayoralty with a higher authority than that of the Crown. Then as now, new Lord Mayors were required to travel to Westminster to obtain the royal seal of approval. However, within the confines of the City, surrounded by its statues and its saints, London's governors did not have to be as submissive.

When Richard Whittington died in 1423, he ended a period of munificence the like of which Londoners would arguably never see again. But if the March of that year saw the culmination of a life of benevolence and charity, it was also the beginning of something that would last much longer.

During the months and years that followed as Londoners mourned their best-loved mayor, the name of Whittington began to obtain an almost legendary status. The Whittington arms began to emerge across the City, appearing on the Guildhall, a chantry chapel at St Paul's and on the south gate of St Bartholomew's Hospital near a stained-glass window depicting the seven works of bodily mercy.

Whittington's achievements also began to be remembered in writing: *The Libelle of Englyshe Polyce*, published in 1436, noted,

> And in worship nowe think I on the sonne of marchaundy Richarde of Whitingdone, That lodes starre and chefe chosen floure. Whate hathe by hym oure England of honoure, And whate profite hathe bene of his richesse, And yet lasteth dayly in worthinesse, That penne and papere may not me suffice Him to describe, so high he was of prise, Above marchaundis to sett him one the beste! I can no more, but God have hym in reste.

In this way, Whittington's name passed slowly into myth and the many stories we have become familiar with began to emerge. That he had a cat is certainly a possibility, but was it really true, for instance, that during his last mayoralty Whittington dined in the City with King Henry V and his queen, Catherine, and asked for a fire to be lit scented with cinnamon? It is widely told that he then threw bonds worth around £60,000 into the fire, thereby cancelling the debt of the king.

'Surely, never had king such a subject,' a grateful Henry was reputed to have said. Whittington's response was characteristically modest: 'Surely, sire,' answered one of the wealthiest self-made men in all the country, 'never had subject such a king.'

Fortunately for Londoners across the ages, the real legacy of Richard Whittington is much more tangible. Thanks to the generous provisions of his will (which can still be viewed at Lambeth Palace Library), the good works that Whittington committed himself to during his lifetime did not simply fade away after his death but continued, and do so to this day.

Around £7,000 was left to charity – equivalent to around £3 million today – an enormous sum that went a long way to financing a number of projects for municipal benefit, including the creation of some of the City's first drinking fountains, repair work to St Bartholomew's Hospital, the rebuilding of Newgate Prison, the creation of the first library in Guildhall along with the almshouses known as Whittington college and a hospital originally at St Michael's – now in Archway.

Whittington's executors were quick to carry out his wishes; by 1424 they had founded the hospital that housed thirteen citizens of London who were without means, built on the east side of the church of St Michael Paternoster Royal. Members of the Mercers' Company were the preferred choice for residents, who were expected to adhere to strict rules. Inhabitants could live separately in apartments in the house and eat meals together. They were only allowed to dress in cloth of a dark colour and in clothes of a 'seemly' nature. Daily duties were mainly religious – almsmen were to attend St Michael's Paternoster Royal on a daily basis, where they were to remember Whittington and his wife Alice in their prayers. After High Mass they were also required to adjourn to Whittington's tomb and recite the *De Profundis* (psalm 130, often used for the faithful departed). One of the people receiving these alms was known as the 'tutor', and it was his job to run the house, for which he received an extra 2*d* (16*d* instead of 14*d*) per week. Overall supervision, however, rested with the Lord Mayor, though in reality it was the wardens of the Mercers' Company who mainly did the work, receiving an inventory of the household goods each year and approving the use of the seal of the hospital. Remarkably, the almshouses survive though not in their original incarnation. In 1966 they were moved to Felbridge in Surrey, and they continue to this day to provide accommodation to those in need.

4

A KING CONDEMNED
1500–1680

In the early days of November 1642, Londoners were in a state of acute anxiety. King Charles I was riding with his army to attempt to secure the City for the royalist cause, and Londoners were preparing their defences. Under the orders of Lord Mayor Isaac Penington, the Trained Bands (the local militia) were heading up the guard, and with them a huge army of volunteers who had given up their paid daily duties – the men, women and children of London City – in a desperate attempt to fortify the City in preparation for imminent attack.

Bent on obtaining the gains to be had in controlling the City of London (particularly its deep mercantile purse), the royalist army finally made its approach, but, on being met by the Trained Bands at Turnham Green on 13 November 1642, Charles decided to withdraw – a decision which resulted in much criticism. While royalists felt the king had missed a crucial opportunity to end the war, many parliamentarians felt that they, too, missed their chance to defeat the king. Nonetheless, London's defence work continued. In the first instance guardhouses were erected and the streets were barricaded, but by the February of the following year it was decided that more comprehensive measures should be taken. Thus, the Court of Common Council approved Colonel Alderman Randall Mainwaring's proposals for an elaborate circuit of forts which were completed by mid-May 1643. Their efficacy, however, was to remain untested. Preoccupied by what turned out to be an indecisive battle at Edgehill in Warwickshire, Charles missed his chance to make a bid for the capital and London remained under parliamentarian control.

When Charles had acceded to the throne on 27 March 1625, the City of London had responded with its usual degree of celebratory fanfare. How was it, then, that seventeen years later it was taking every measure possible to defend itself against its king?

The core of the answer lies in Charles's belief that he was answerable to no one but himself – a conviction that formed the basis of many of his most contentious decisions. Perhaps the most damning of all was his presumption that he could rule without the input of Parliament and that he could impose as many taxes as he liked. This was a belief which had manifested itself in largely unjustifiable non-parliamentary taxation. While it was certainly true that Charles had inherited an unstable financial situation from his father, James I, his attempts to raise revenue were highly unpopular. Throughout his reign taxes became an increasingly thorny issue – particularly those he collected without parliamentary authorisation (tonnage and poundage or customs duties) – and criticism against this method of revenue raising was so vocal and so strong that by 1626 Charles was forced to raise money by other means. This time he resorted to forced loans, jailing those who refused to pay.

Behind it all, disagreements between Charles and Parliament had been simmering for several years. In 1628 an indignant Parliament, in an attempt to bring the king to heel, put forward the Petition of Right to resolve their grievances. The carefully worded petition drew heavily on rights granted in the time of Edward I and III, particularly with regards to taxation without parliamentary representation and the issue of forced loans:

To the king's most excellent Majesty.

Humbly shew unto our Sovereign Lord the king, the Lords Spiritual and Temporal, and Commons, in Parliament assembled, That whereas it is declared and enacted by a Statute made in the time of the Reign of King Edward the First, commonly called Statutum de Tallagio non concedendo, that no Tallage or Aid shall be laid or levied by the king or his Heirs in this Realm, without the good Will and Assent of the Archbishops, Bishops, Earls, Barons, Knights, Burgesses and other the Freemen of the Commonalty of this Realm; and by the Authority of Parliament holden in the Five and twentieth Year of the Reign of King Edward the Third, it is declared and enacted, that from thenceforth no Person should be compelled to make any Loans to the king against his Will, because such Loans were against Reason and the Franchise of the Land; and by other Laws of this Realm it is provided, that none should be charged by any Charge or Imposition called a Benevolence, nor by such like Charge; by which the Statutes before mentioned, and other the good Laws and Statutes of this Realm, Your Subjects have inherited this Freedom, that they should not be compelled to contribute to any Tax, Tallage, Aid or other like Charge not set by Common Consent in Parliament.

The fact that the king had, in addition to forcing his citizens to loan him money, imprisoned those who refused to pay was also directly addressed:

> Yet nevertheless, of late divers Commissions directed to sundry Commissioners in several Counties, with Instructions, have issued; by means whereof Your People have been in divers Places assembled, and required to lend certain Sums of Money unto Your Majesty, and many of them, upon their Refusal so to do, have had an Oath administered unto them not warrantable by the Laws or Statutes of this Realm; and have been constrained to become bound to make Appearance and give Attendance before Your Privy Council and in other Places; and others of them have been therefore imprisoned, confined, and sundry other Ways molested and disquieted; and divers other Charges have been laid and levied upon Your People in several Counties by Lord Lieutenants, Deputy Lieutenants, Commissioners for Musters, Justices of Peace and others, by Command or Direction from Your Majesty, or Your Privy Council, against the Laws and Free Customs of the Realm.

Charles had little choice but to agree to abide by the terms of the Petition and thus the following liberties were secured:

> That no freeman should be forced to pay any tax, loan, or benevolence unless in accordance with an act of parliament
> That no freeman should be imprisoned contrary to the laws of the land
> That soldiers and sailors should not be billeted on private persons
> Commissions to punish soldiers and sailors by martial law should be abolished.

Despite this the relationship between Crown and Parliament never really healed and on 10 March 1629 it reached a new low when Charles, angered by Commons passing a number of motions against the king's recent actions, dissolved Parliament in a fitful rage. Parliament would not meet again for eleven years – a period that became known as Personal Rule.

Charles further alienated himself by raising money in even less desirable ways. This included Ship Money – which provoked a new level of resistance. In essence, Charles turned an ancient law stating that all coastal counties should provide ships to the Crown into a way of gaining a substantial amount of funds from every county. By 1640, Charles, once more in need of funds, called what became known as the Short Parliament, hastily dissolving it when its members refused to comply with his demands. Later that year, still in desperate need of money, Charles tried again. The Long Parliament thus began its session by passing Acts to ensure that, not only was it to meet every three years, but also that it could not be dissolved without its own consent. Non-parliamentary taxation, including the controversial Ship Money, was also made illegal.

In a sense, it was too little too late. The relationship between all-powerful monarch and Parliament, who had become determined that Charles should not act alone, was ultimately incompatible with Charles's own belief in absolute rule. Adding religious tensions into the mix (particularly the introduction of a new Book of Common Prayer in Scotland which stressed ceremony as opposed to the more austere forms of worship that were becoming popular) only served to inflame matters further, and when in the summer of 1641 radical Protestants destroyed what they saw as idolatrous images in churches, relations broke down all together.

Parliament pitted itself against the king and Protestants rose up against the perceived threat to their creed. Now, all eyes were on London – would the wealthiest and most influential city in the kingdom stand behind its king?

In the City of London, hasty preparations were already being made to defend against the king. But if Charles's days on the throne were numbered, so were those of London's then Lord Mayor. For his unswerving support of the king, and for his execution of the king's commission of array (essentially Charles's call to arms), for which he remained resolutely unrepentant, Lord Mayor Richard Gurney found himself swiftly removed from the civic throne, recorded as a 'delinquent' and promptly impeached. *The Journals of the House of Commons, Volume 6* recorded the verdict of his trial as follows:

> The said Lords, having taken the said Charges into due consideration, do find, that the said Sir Richard Gurney, Lord Mayor of the City of London, guilty of causing the said Proclamation, for putting the Commission of Array in Execution to be published, tending to the Disturbance of the Peace of the Kingdom; and of not suppressing the said riots and misdemeanours; and of not calling a Common Council, as he was, by Order of Parliament, required; and for these Offences; the said High Court did award and judge, first, that the said Richard Gurney should be no longer Mayor of the City of London: Secondly, that he should be thereafter uncapable [*sic*] to bear an office in the City of London: Thirdly, that he should be uncapable to bear or receive any further Honours thereafter.

The unfortunate Gurney, knight and baronet, was unceremoniously committed to the Tower and his successor announced. Isaac

Penington, the radical parliamentarian, now directed all the City's resources into supporting the parliamentarian cause.

He didn't have to wait long for a result. On 4 January 1642, Charles I entered the House of Commons to arrest five of his most outspoken critics, but on finding they had already fled to the City he rode to the Guildhall and demanded their return. The Lord Mayor refused to cooperate, and just five days after this very public humiliation Charles left the capital. On 22 August, Charles raised his standard at Nottingham and the Civil War begun.

While many in the City had actively sought to topple the king from his throne, this was far from being the only item on their agenda. Many Londoners, particularly those unable to influence the City's governance, also wanted to reform the City's constitution, and as ripples of the 'new religion' spread far and wide across Europe, many wished to reform the Church, root and branch. Central to this was to be the end of the lavish imagery and accoutrements of what people saw, under Charles, as being an increasingly popish Church. As the country plunged into civil war, a different kind of quest took place. In line with the Long Parliament commission of 1641, Penington oversaw the removal of pictures, relics and idolatrous images within the City – a task resulting in previously unthinkable changes to the character of the City. Only with their chancels levelled, their communion rails, crosses and organs removed, and their statuary and inscriptions removed or defaced were the City's parish churches acceptable to the reformers' ideals. In the May of 1644, an Ordinance for the Further Demolishing of Monuments of Idolatry and Superstition was authorised and went one step further still – specifically targeting representations of God, angels and the saints:

The Lords and Commons assembled in Parliament, the better to accomplish the blessed Reformation so happily begun, and to remove all offences and things illegal in the worship of God, do Ordain, That all Representations of any of the Persons of the Trinity, or of any Angel or Saint, in or about any Cathedral, Collegiate or Parish Church, or Chappel, or in any open place within this Kingdome, shall be taken away, defaced, and utterly demolished; And that no such shall hereafter be set up, And that the Chancel – ground of every such Church or Chappel, raised for any Altar, or Communion Table to stand upon, shall be laid down and levelled; And that no Copes, Surplisses, superstitious Vestments, Roods, or Roodlons, or Holy-water Fonts, shall be, or be any more used in any Church or Chappel within this Realm; And that no Cross, Crucifix, Picture, or Representation of any of the Persons of the Trinity, or of any Angel or Saint shall be, or continue upon any Plate, or other thing used, or to be used in or about the worship of God; And that all Organs, and the Frames or Cases wherein they stand in all Churches or Chappels aforesaid, shall be taken away, and utterly defaced, and none other hereafter set up in their places; And that all Copes, Surplisses, superstitious Vestments, Roods, and Fonts aforesaid, be likewise utterly defaced; whereunto all persons within this Kingdome, whom it may concern, are hereby required at their peril to yield due obedience.

To many within the City, it must have seemed as though nothing was safe from the disapproving Puritan gaze. The churches of the City guilds were targeted and offending images removed, while many of the City's ancient landmarks were demolished or defaced. In line with the Protestant oath to defend the true religion against 'popery and popish innovation', the Strand's maypole was dismantled and those great tributes to Queen Eleanor, Charing Cross and Chepe Cross were lost to the City forever. Even St Paul's Cathedral could not escape reform. With Isaac Penington at the helm of a committee charged with removing all offensive items from St Paul's so that the Lord Mayor and his deputies might comfortable attend Sunday service, all religious imagery was removed while 'superstitious' items such as a mitre and a crosier staff were also taken out. St Paul's cross, which marked a spot where political sermons took place outside the cathedral, was also dismantled and taken away.

Did Penington go too far? Many of his contemporaries thought so. It was said that 'churches, parishes and even the apostles were unsainted during his mayoralty' – a situation that continued until the year 1660.

Public opinion, meanwhile, as was often the case in conflicted times, found itself an outlet in the verse of popular song. This broadside ballad laments the pulling down of the ancient Charing Cross, which, along with Cheapside Cross, fell foul of the new religion:

> Undone! undone! the lawyers are,
> They wander about the towne,
> Nor can find the way to Westminster
> Now Charing-Cross is downe:
> At the end of the Strand they make a stand,
> Swearing they are at a loss,
> And chaffing say, that's not the way,
> They must go by Charing-Cross.
>
> The Parliament to vote it down
> Conceived it very fitting,

For fear it should fall, and kill them all
In the House as they were sitting.
They were told god-wot, it had a plot,
Which made them so hard-hearted,
To give command it should not stand,
But be taken down and carted.

Methinks the Common-council should
Of it have taken pity,
'Cause, good old cross, it always stood
So firmly to the city.
Since crosses you so much disdain,
Faith, if I were as you,
For fear the king should rule again
I'd pull down Tiburn too.

The uncertainties of the Civil War continued to drag on, disrupting almost every aspect of daily life in London. Scarcity and shortage was the reality of living in a continual state of conflict – food supplies were intermittent and when the parliamentarians blockaded Newcastle in the early days of the war, even the coal supplies dried up. Not only did Londoners face a worrying lack of victuals but they were denied the basic comfort of keeping warm. On top of this, many of the capital's men had left the City to fight in battles across the country, and the City's finances were left much reduced when the royal court left London. It was hardly surprising, then, that divisions developed within the parliamentary party, split between the Presbyterians, who wanted to quickly end the war and were willing to enter into talks with Charles for this purpose; and the

Independents, who would settle for nothing less than subjecting their terms upon a fully compliant king.

Having officially started on 22 August 1642 when Charles I raised his standard at Nottingham, the conflict didn't end until May 1646, nearly a year after the king had been taken prisoner after the Battle of Naseby in Northamptonshire on 14 June 1645.

Even at this crucial point, Charles had refused to give up hope. From captivity he desperately tried to negotiate his return to London, convinced that now, at last, he would be able to win the support of its citizens. This wasn't as unrealistic as it might have seemed. Within the boundaries of the City walls, support for the parliamentarians had become distinctly fractured – the problem being that there were so many factions that few could agree. Radicals, Puritan Independents and the Levellers were broadly in favour of a republic, but those associated with the Presbyterian Puritans and those with more moderate views were hoping for the restoration of the king and a Presbyterian Church. As this broadside ballad, written in 1645, shows, there were many who simply wanted peace:

> I love my King and country well,
> Religion and the laws;
> Which I'm mad at the heart that e'er we did sell
> To buy the good old cause.
> These unnatural wars
> And brotherly jars
> Are no delight or joy to me;
> But it is my desire
> That the wars should expire,
> And the king and his realms agree.

I never yet did take up arms,

And yet I dare to dye;

But I'll not be seduced by phanatical charms

Till I know a reason why.

Why the king and the state

Should fall to debate

I ne'er could yet a reason see,

But I find many one

Why the wars should be done,

And the king and his realms agree.

I love the king and the Parliament,

But I love them both together:

And when they by division asunder are rent,

I know 'tis good for neither.

Whichsoe'er of those

Be victorious,

I'm sure for us no good 'twill be,

For our plagues will increase

Unless we have peace,

And the king and his realms agree.

The king without them can't long stand,

Nor they without the king;

'Tis they must advise, and 'tis he must command,

For their power from his must spring.

'Tis a comfortless sway

When none will obey;

If the king han't his right, which way shall we?

They may vote and make laws,

But no good they will cause

Till the king and his realm agree.

A pure religion I would have,

Not mixt with human wit;

And I cannot endure that each ignorant knave

Should dare to meddle with it.

The tricks of the law

I would fain withdraw,

That it may be alike to each degree:

And I fain would have such

As do meddle so much,

With the king and the church agree.

We have pray'd and pray'd that the wars might cease,

And we be free men made;

I would fight, if my fighting would bring any peace,

But war is become a trade.

Our servants did ride

With swords by their side,

And made their masters footmen be;

But we'll be no more slaves

To the beggars and knaves

Now the king and the realms do agree.

Certainly, the City paid a high financial price for the conflict. London was forced to pay a new tax, 'the monthly assessment', along with a new excise tax on consumer goods. These were wildly unpopular with London's merchants, who squealed at the impact on their trade. On 15 February 1647, after many months of unrest, public ill feeling culminated in a major anti-excise riot in Smithfield, which the Lord Mayor, Sir Thomas Adams, and his sheriffs were forced to attend to in person. In his text, *Excise Taxation and the Origins of Public Debt*, D'Marris Coffman explains that the confrontation arose when 'a guard attempted to stop a buyer, who had refused to pay the excise on the livestock he had purchased. The crowd, led by a butcher, came to the customer's defence, and returned later to burn down the Excise Office.' It was a shocking protest, but one that had an effect. On 11 June 1647, the excise on salt and flesh was subsequently removed.

After years of disarray, it was the conflict in Ireland which set in motion an unexpected chain of events. The parliamentary Presbyterians now wanted the army (which had been largely unpaid) to be sent to Ireland; however, on hearing this, the army marched to London to demand its pay while the City closed its gates in fear. By the July of 1648, the City fathers had had enough and demanded of Parliament that control of the Trained Bands should be theirs. Unfortunately, what they had in boldness they lacked in popular support, and on 4 August the army entered the City, taking the Lord Mayor Sir John Gayer and aldermen Adams, Langham, Culham and Bunce back to Parliament, where they were accused of high treason and committed to the Tower. Serjeant Glyn, the Recorder, also lost his office. This unfortunate occurrence provided the City's ballad writers with a wealth of material, and it wasn't long before the unfortunate episode appeared in song:

To the tune of 'London is a fine town and a gallant city'

Why kept your train-bands such a stirre?
Why sent you them by clusters?
Then went into Saint James's Parke?
Why took you then their musters?
Why rode my Lord up Fleet-street
With coaches at least twenty,

And fill'd they say with aldermen,
As good they had been empty?
London is a brave towne,
Yet I their cases pitty;
Their mayor and some few aldermen
Have cleane undone the city.
The 'prentices are gallant blades,
And to the king are clifty;
But the lord mayor and aldermen
Are scarce so wise as thrifty.
I'le pay for the apprentices,
They to the king were hearty;
For they have done all that they can
To advance their soveraignes party.
London, etc.
What's now become of your brave Poyntz?
And of your Generall Massey?
If you petition for a peace,
These gallants they will slash yee.
Where now are your reformadoes?
To Scotland gone together:
'Twere better they were fairly trusst
Then they should bring them thither.
London, etc.
But if your aldermen were false,
Or Glyn, that's your recorder!
Let them never betray you more,
But hang them up in order.
All these men may be coach't as well
As any other sinner

Up Holborne, and ride forwarde still,

To Tyburne to their dinner.

London, &c.

God send the valiant General may

Restore the king to glory!

Then that name I have honour'd so

Will famous be in story;

While if he doe not, I much feare

The ruine of the nation,

And (that I should be loth to see)

His house's desolation.

London, etc.

Next, early in December 1648, came Pride's Purge – the expelling of all except the most radical members of Parliament by Colonel Thomas Pride and his army. Charles did see his beloved City again, but this time it was under heavy guard. In the January of 1649 the Rump Parliament charged its king with subverting the fundamental laws and liberties of the nation, the crux of their case being that it was treasonable offence for the king to wage war upon his subjects. He was subsequently charged with the following offences:

> That the said Charles Stuart, being admitted King of England, and therein trusted with a limited power to govern by and according to the laws of the land, and not otherwise; and by his trust, oath, and office, being obliged to use the power committed to him for the good and benefit of the people, and for the preservation of their rights and liberties; yet, nevertheless, out of a wicked design to erect and uphold in himself an unlimited and tyrannical power to rule according to his will, and to overthrow the rights and liberties

of the people, yea, to take away and make void the foundations thereof, and of all redress and remedy of misgovernment, which by the fundamental constitutions of this kingdom were reserved on the people's behalf in the right and power of frequent and successive Parliaments, or national meetings in Council.

Of the myriad events to have taken place in the Palace of Westminster up to the fateful year of 1649 – the coronations, the weddings and the state funerals – none were as significant as the trial of Charles I. In the painted chamber, accompanied by the sound of trumpets and drums, Charles faced both the public and his accusers early that year when he faced the ultimate humiliation of standing in the makeshift courtroom, accused of tyranny and treason – the first of four appearances the king was obliged to make in which he persistently disputed the court's right to try him as a 'tyrant, traitor and murderer; and a public and implacable enemy to the Commonwealth of England'.

Of the 135 commissioners who were invited to sit on the trial of the king, around fifty declined to participate, in addition to which a small number withdrew once the trial had begun. Among those who remained to sit in judgement of their king were Sir Isaac Penington, Sir Thomas Atkins and Sir Robert Tichborne, who listened solemnly to the following charges:

he, the said Charles Stuart, for accomplishment of such his designs, and for the protecting of himself and his adherents in his and their wicked practices, to the same ends hath traitorously and maliciously levied war against the present Parliament, and the people therein represented, particularly upon or about the 30th day of June, in the year of our Lord 1642, at Beverley, in the County of York.

It was a decision all three would come to regret. When Charles was found guilty and executed on a side street of Banqueting House, Whitehall, on 30 January 1649, shockwaves spread across the City. Many were appalled at the murder of the king, including that year's Lord Mayor, Abraham Reynardson, who declined to proclaim that the monarchy had been abolished. On 29 March he held civic court for the last time, standing before the Bar of the House on 2 April to give his explanation. Saying that he couldn't go against his mayoral oath – his conscience wouldn't allow it – he was removed from his post, fined and sent to the Tower for two months.

We can see from the Aldermen's records that the punishments were carried out immediately:

From the special Court of Aldermen, held 2 April 1649. Present – Wollaston, Atkin, Andrews, Fowkes, Foote, Kendrick, Culham, Edmonds, Park, Dethicks.

Item: in obedience to an order of the Commons assembled in Parliament, made the 2nd day of this instant month, it is ordered by this Court that the Livery of the several Companies of this City shall be summoned according to ancient custom to meet in the Guildhall tomorrow in the afternoon, by 2 of the clock for the election of a new Lord Mayor, in the place of Abraham Reynardson, late Lord Mayor, and that the sword and all ensigns and ornaments of state belonging to the Lord Mayor of this city be forthwith sent for to the use and purpose in the said order mentioned.

In 1657, a document entitled the Humble Petition and Advice was drawn up which offered Oliver Cromwell the crown. Its first incarnation, the Humble Address and Remonstrance, had been taken before the Second Protectorate Parliament in 1657 by former Lord Mayor Sir Christopher Packe, but Cromwell had refused this version, which alluded to a royal title. The revised document, expressing gratitude to Cromwell for his efforts, as below, was finally adopted on 25 May.

To his Highness the Lord Protector of the Commonwealth of England, Scotland and Ireland, and the dominions thereto belonging; the Humble Petition and Advice of the Knights, Citizens and Burgesses now assembled in the Parliament of this Commonwealth.

We, the knights, citizens and burgesses in this present Parliament assembled, taking into our most serious consideration the present state of these three nations, joined and united under your Highness' protection, cannot but in the first place, with all thankfulness, acknowledge the wonderful mercy of Almighty God in delivering us from that tyranny and bondage, both in our spiritual and civil concernments, which the late king and his party designed to bring us under, and pursued the effecting thereof by a long and bloody war and also that it hath pleased the same gracious God to preserve your person in many battles, to make you an instrument for preserving our peace, although environed with enemies abroad, and filled with turbulent, restless and unquiet spirits in our own bowels, that as in the treading down the common enemy, and restoring us to peace and tranquillity, the Lord hath used you so eminently, and the worthy officers and soldiers of the army (whose faithfulness to the common cause, we and all good men shall ever acknowledge, and put a just value upon): so also that he will use you and them in the settling and securing our liberties as we are men and Christians, to us and our posterity after us, which are those great and glorious ends which the good people of these nations have so freely, with the hazard of their lives and estates, so long and earnestly contended for: we consider likewise the continual danger which your life is in, from the bloody practices both of the malignant and discontented party (one whereof, through the goodness of God, you have been lately delivered from), it being a received principle amongst them, that no order being settled in your lifetime for the succession in the Government, nothing is wanting to bring us into blood and confusion, and them to their desired ends, but the destruction of your person; and in case things should thus remain at your death, we are not able to express what calamities would in all human probability ensue thereupon, which we trust your Highness (as well as we) do hold yourself obliged to provide against, and not to leave a people, whose common peace and interest you are intrusted with, in such a condition as may hazard both, especially in this conjuncture, when there seems, to be an opportunity of coming to a settlement upon just and legal foundations: upon these considerations, we have judged it a duty incumbent upon us, to present and declare these our most just and necessary desires to your Highness.

Cromwell finally accepted a revised version of the document and was installed as Lord Protector on 26 June 1657 – a title which was his for life, and gave him the privilege of choosing his own successor. The ceremony of his investiture and installation took place on 26 June 1657 at Westminster Hall, when he was enthroned and seated on the chair of state with Lord Mayor Tichborne, in his arms the sword of London City, on his left-hand side.

If the City's officials thought their problems with money were over then they had a lot to learn. While Charles I had recklessly abused the City's purse in 1640, he had also seized the gold from the Royal Mint – in the process all but destroying public confidence that this was the best place to keep their money. When the country descended into war, the kingdom's entire financial system fractured, leaving Parliament without access to the funds it needed to continue fighting. It therefore, like Charles, sought revenue from the governors of the City of London and through individual loans, with Sir Thomas Vyner, Sir Christopher Packe, Sir Thomas Andrews, Sir John Dethicke, Sir Thomas Foote and Sir John Ireton all lending between £3,000 and £4,000 each. In July 1658 the City's aldermen were approached by Cromwell and managed to raise further funds.

The City, though far wealthier than any other in the kingdom, complained stridently about paying taxes. In November 1642 Parliament had arranged a loan from the City, with lenders being promised 8 per cent interest. This, however, proved not to be enough to maintain the parliamentarian army, and the Committee for the Advance of Money pushed for a direct weekly tax for three months, followed by a second weekly assessment which exempted London. On 21 February 1645, the first monthly assessment of £21,000 was introduced, in time becoming the preferred method of raising revenue in the Interregnum governments.

In Guildhall, the seat of the City's government, many conversations both whispered and aloud took place as to the unfair nature of these burdensome taxes, the inescapable fact being that the City was greatly in arrears. Sir Christopher Packe attempted to address the problem at the Court of Aldermen, pointing out on 28 April 1654 that not only was the City paying more than its fair share but that trade had suffered so greatly during the Civil War that the City was simply not in a position to be able to pay these vastly inflated sums. A petition was duly drawn up to be sent to Parliament which complained that 'although the City stretches only from Temple to

Aldgate and from Bridge to Bishopsgate, it pays one-fifteenth of the total assessment of England and Wales'. It was decided to omit all mention of arrears. Sadly, Parliament dissolved and nothing came of it until the Second Protectorate Parliament was in session, the request being changed and a remission for arrears placed at the front. This time Parliament took note, and City officials were called upon to explain why they hadn't paid their debt. The City countered that it had still not received money from previous loans back from Parliament. According to Maurice Ashley in his text *Financial and Commercial Policy Under the Cromwellian Protectorate*, from the end of the Civil War to the establishment of the Protectorate, the figure of £1,440,000 had been demanded overall for the monthly assessments – a sum which alone exceeded the total revenue of Charles I – but there was little the governors of London could do; as long as the army was required, the taxes had to be paid.

It has long been argued that the sheer scale of public debt was influential in the failure of the Protectorate, and this indeed seems to be the case. When Cromwell died on 3 September 1658, it was said that his son and successor, Richard, had to borrow money from France simply to pay for the funeral. Richard renounced his powers just nine months after his succession which led to a leadership crisis, and none of the regimes that followed in rapid succession in 1659–60 – the army and the Rump, the army without the Rump and the Rump without the army – proved capable of resettling the nation.

It was an anxious and unsettling time. Ever fearful of military intervention, those who dwelt within the City walls took to their streets to make their dissatisfaction known. But the arrival in February 1660 of General George Monck (the ranking commander in Scotland) in London with 7,000 soldiers changed everything. He demanded that the Rump Parliament call an immediate election and that the moderate Presbyterian parliamentarians be allowed to take their seats. The City, at last, could rejoice – the Corporation lent £60,000 in support of the interim regime and bonfires were lit and rump steaks cooked on the flames. Pepys himself, after visiting the Guildhall to see if Monck and the Lord Mayor had arrived, described the scene as joyous. In his diary he described the scene on Saturday 11 February 1660:

> Thence we took coach to the City for Guildhall, where the Hall was full of people expecting Monck and Lord Mayor to come thither, and all very joyful ... In Cheapside there were a great many bonfires, and Bow bells and all the bells in all the churches as we went home were a-ringing. Hence we went homewards, it being about ten o clock. But the common joy that was everywhere to be seen! The number of bonfires! There being fourteen between St Dunstan's and Temple Bar, and at Strand Bridge I could at one view tell thirty-one fires. In King Street seven or eight; and all along burning, and roasting and drinking for rumps. There being rumps tied upon sticks and carried up and down ... Indeed, it was past imagination, both the greatness and the suddenness of it ...

On Tuesday 21 February 1660 Pepys further noted:

> In the morning going out I saw many soldiers going towards Westminster, and was told that they were going to admit the secluded members again. So I to Westminster Hall, and in Chancery Row I saw about twenty of them who had been at White Hall with General Monk, who came thither this morning, and made a speech

to them, and recommended to them a Commonwealth, and against Charles Stuart.

But it wasn't long after this that the Convention Parliament (so called because it convened itself without royal assent), almost wholly royalist in sympathy, was called and Charles Stuart (son of Charles I) was invited to return as king. Charles issued the declaration of Breda, assuring the House of Commons that he held Parliament in the highest esteem.

> We do assure you, upon our Royal Word, that none of our Predecessors have had a great Esteem of Parliaments, than we have in our Judgement, as well as from our Obligation: We do believe them to be so vital a Part of the Constitution of the Kingdom, and so necessary for the Government of it that We well know neither Prince nor People can be in any tolerable Degree happy without them; and therefore you may be confident, That we shall always look upon their Counsels, as the best we can receive; and shall be as tender of their Privileges, and as careful to preserve and protect them, as of that which is most dear to Ourself, and most necessary for our own Preservation.

Crucially, he also promised that 'no Crime whatsoever committed against us, or our Royal Family, before the Publication of this, shall ever rise in Judgment or be brought into question, against any of them, to the least indamagement of them, either in their Lives, Liberties or Estates, or (as far forth as lies in our Power) so much as to the Prejudice of their reputations'.

By the August of 1660, the monarchy was restored and the Act of Indemnity and Oblivion was passed as a gesture of reconciliation. Under the Restoration settlement a free pardon had been granted to everyone – all treasons and political crimes between 1 January 1637 and 24 June 1660 – who supported the Commonwealth and Protectorate, but in the new Act there were some notable exceptions: those who had directly participated in the trial and execution of King Charles I.

By October 1660, the regicides who had been brought into custody were put on trial, with ten being sentenced to death and nineteen facing the grim prospect of spending the rest of their days in the impenetrable fortress of the Tower. The most notable of these was the unfortunate Robert Tichborne, who had become Lord Mayor in 1656. A dedicated and active supporter of the parliamentary party, Tichborne's star reached its peak when, as a favourite of Oliver Cromwell, he was knighted. His fortunes reversed sharply on the Restoration, and when questioned in court as to his role in the trial of Charles I he was forced to desperately plea for his life; in *The High Court Justice: Comprising Memoirs of the Principal Persons who sat in judgement of Charles I and signed his death warrant* by James Caufield, he is reported to have said,

My Lord, it was my unhappiness to be called to so sad a work, when I had so few years over my head; a person neither bred up in the laws, nor in parliaments where laws are made. I can say with a clear conscience, I had no more enmity in my heart to his majesty than I had to my wife that lay in my bosom. My Lord, I shall say nothing; after I was summoned; I think truly I was at most of the meeting; and I do not say this that I did not intend to say it before but preserving that salvo to my own conscience, that I did not maliciously and knowingly do it, I think I am bound in my conscience to own it. As I do not deny but I was there, so truly I do believe I did sign the instrument; and had I known that then which I do now (I do not mean, my Lord, my afflictions and sufferings; it is not my sufferings make me acknowledge) I would have chosen a red hot oven to have gone into as soon as that meeting ... I do acknowledge the matter of fact and I do solemnly protest I was led into it for want of years.

Although Tichborne was sentenced to death, the sentence was never carried out. He received a reprieve following reports that he had saved the lives of condemned royalists during the Protectorate and he spent the rest of his life in prison, dying in the Tower in July 1682. He was buried in the chapel of Saint Peter-ad-Vincula in the Tower.

Considering the high degree of influence Penington exerted and the fact that he was involved in the Parliamentarian cause, it is surprising that he escaped with his life and did not end his days with the ignominy of execution at Tyburn. Instead, Penington, too, swapped the court room for the Tower of London, though it was likely that his plea of ignorance was not what saved him: 'My sitting amongst them,' said he, 'was out of ignorance; I knew not what I did; therefore I hope you will believe there was nothing of malice in anything I did: I was misled in it.'

To those who knew him, this must have been hard to swallow – having been placed in the seat of London Lord Mayor by the parliamentarians, thereby ousting the more royalist Lord Mayor Richard Gurney, Penington had been active in his support for the parliamentarian case. It was he who was in the magisterial seat when the indecisive Battle of Edgehill took place, and it was under his command that London's fortifications were built. He had also been at the forefront of the drive to remove idolatrous images from the City of London, had supervised the destruction of Cheapside Cross and had insisted that St Paul's Cathedral be made fit for a new era of worship. Moreover, his accession to the position of Lord Mayor was actually the culmination of many years of public activity. In the December of 1640 he had presented the citizen's petition against the rites of the Church, and he also acted as a speaker between Parliament and the City. He came to hold a number of prestigious positions; not only was he Lord Mayor, he was also Lieutenant of the Tower, a Member of Parliament and a militia and committee man for London. As one of the commissioners on the trial of Charles I, Penington had also, along with Thomas Andrews, proclaimed the Act for abolishing kingly power. Despite all this, his life was spared – not because of his pleas of ignorance, nor due to his claims that he was 'drawn into it'. Despite, being petitioned many times, Penington's saving grace was that he hadn't signed the death certificate. He was therefore committed to the Tower, where he died the next year.

It wasn't just London's Lord Mayors who found themselves answerable to the new king on the charge of regicide. William Goffe, a freeman of the Grocers, took perhaps the wisest route in escaping to New England at the first sign of trouble. His fellow freeman John Jones stayed put and ended his life being hanged, drawn and quartered.

Alderman Thomas Andrews had also been one of Charles's judges, had been in attendance when the sentence was pronounced and had signed the death certificate. A favourite of the republicans, who made him treasurer of the money and plate sent to Guildhall, treasurer at war and commissioner for the ground belonging to St Paul's church, he had been in the position of Lord Mayor when the Scots had tried to put Charles II on the throne but had been defeated. Dying before the Restoration, he was fortunate in escaping the torturously painful punishment of many of the other regicides, though an Act of Attainder took all of his possessions. He was also fortunate in that his burial site was left unmolested, whereas the bodies of other regicides – John Bradshaw, Henry Ireton and Oliver Cromwell – were exhumed and their heads stuck on pikes.

Only time would reveal that the return of the monarchy was not everything that had been hoped for, and that once again relations would sour over the issue of money.

From Walter Thornbury's *The Lord Mayors of London in Old and New*, we see that the City, refusing to loan the new monarch £100,000, found twenty of its principal citizens seized and imprisoned, while four aldermen were imprisoned for not disclosing the names of their friends who refused to advance money to king. Ignoring their rights still further, Charles II forbade the City officials from petitioning for redress of this grievance and in so doing, created a new wave of bitter protests directed at the monarchy.

5

TERROR AND TUMULT
1660–1700

On 22 October 1663, London's Lord Mayor, Sir John Robinson, was to be found searching intently through the Corporation's records contained in that voluminous tome *Liber Albus*, desperate to find guidance as to how to deal with the possibility of plague. Just four days earlier, the king's secretary William Morrice had informed Robinson that the pestilence had broken out in Europe and needed to know what measures had been taken in the past to prevent infection from reaching the City.

The Lord Mayor was at a loss; while he had found paper upon paper referring to methods used to halt the infection at home, he could find nothing useful to prevent it entering the City from abroad. Consulting with the Court of Aldermen, he finally penned his reply – ships arriving from infected countries should be allowed only as far as Gravesend, where their cargo should be unloaded and held to be aired for forty days. After further consultation, it was decided that ships should stop further from London, at Moll Haven, and that a guard be appointed to prevent communication with persons on shore. In the event of an infected vessel arriving, a list should made of everyone on board and if anyone passed away the body should be thrown overboard. If the ship proved to be free of contagion after an isolation period of forty days had passed then it would be allowed to make 'free commerce'. If, on the other hand, it was found that a ship came from an infected port, it should be sent immediately back to sea. As a further safeguard, it was further suggested that Charles II 'issue a manifesto to his allies informing them that no ships or vessels would be allowed to enter the Port of London unless they brought with them a certificate from the port authorities whence they came'.

The measures, however, proved ineffective. Before long the fearful symptoms of this devastating disease were to be found in the parish of St Giles-in-the-Fields, just outside the City walls, while in Westminster three people exhibiting plague-like symptoms suddenly passed away. In less time still, the rumours began to circulate. In seventeenth-century London it was widely believed that the plague visited the City every forty years or so – and since it had last struck in 1625, the citizens began to fear that an outbreak was now inevitable. It was a notion that gained credence with the predictions of the numerous astrologers who, by interpreting planetary alignments, alarmed the City's residents with their sinister visions of doom. The City's apothecaries, meanwhile, saw a sharp uptake of business as an agitated populace hastily armed itself with remedies. As winter turned to spring, the Bills of Mortality showed an unquestionable rise in deaths from the plague and the citizens began to panic in earnest. 'Fear quickly began to creep upon people's hearts, terrifying and confounding men of all religions and professions,' wrote Gideon Harvey in *The City Remembrancer*.

Great alarms and discourse began to spread about the plague and all cast in their minds whither they should go, if the distemper should increase – yet when the next week's bill signified to them the decrease from nine to three, their minds were something appeased; discourse of that subject ceased; fears were hushed, and hopes took place, that the black cloud did but threaten and give a few drops, but the wind would drive it away. When, in the next bill, the number of the dead by the plague amounted from three to fourteen; in the next to seventeen; in the next to forty-three; and the disease not only increased but dispersed, a dreadful consternation fell upon all, and fearful bodings of a desolating judgment: every one began to look about and think into what corner of the world they might try to hide themselves.

Over the following weeks, the Lord Mayor struggled to respond to all the requests he received to leave the City and there was reportedly no getting to his door without the greatest of difficulty: 'The hurry was much increased by false rumours that the government had ordered turnpikes and barriers on the roads to prevent people's travelling, and that the towns on the roads would not suffer any from London to pass ... it looked as though the whole City was running away.'

The outbreak officially began in the City in the February of 1665, but had any regulations been published before then the effect, Harvey pointed out, would have been terrifying – 'especially such as would pretend to dispose of the people otherwise than they would dispose of themselves, it would have put city and suburbs into the utmost confusion'. But it seems that John Lawrence, Lord Mayor (1664–5) and his officials acted with the utmost tact and consideration: 'The magistrates widely caused the people to be encouraged; made very good laws for regulating the citizens, keeping good order on the streets and making everything as eligible as possible to all sorts of people.'

The Lord Mayor and City officials did, indeed, distinguish themselves that terrible year. While the king, the gentry and most of the City's wealthy citizens fled, the Lord Mayor, sheriffs and aldermen made public their resolution not to leave the City, assuring the terrified citizens that they would remain to provide good order and justice and to discharge their duties to the best of their abilities. It was not an easy task, but according to Harvey's Remembrancer it was one they fulfilled as pledged:

> The Lord Mayor and Sheriffs were continually in the streets and at places of the greatest danger; and though they did not care to have too great a resort of people crouding about them, yet in emergent cases they never denied the people access and heard with patience all their grievances and complaints; the Lord Mayor had a low gallery erected on purpose in his hall, where he stood a little removed from the croud, when any complaint came to be heard; that he might appear with as much safety as possible. The aldermen and sheriffs constantly attended in their wards and stations; the Lord Mayor's officers and serjeant, received orders from the aldermen so that justice was executed in all cases without interruption.

The Lord Mayor also held daily councils to hear dispositions for preserving public peace – no easy task in the time of plague. Once again, Lawrence and his City officials exerted themselves for the good of all those who remained – so much so that it was later said that 'the people were used with all possible gentleness, tenderness and clemency; but presumptuous rogues, thieves, house-breakers, plunderers of the sick or dead were duly punished and severe declarations were continually published'.

On 1 July 1665 the Lord Mayor's orders finally came into force, though they did not immediately halt the spread of plague. The City's mortality bills show that 267 Londoners died from plague in the week before the orders were issued, while in the last week of July the number had risen to 1,843.

Nonetheless, the regulations, drawing as they did on the modus operandi of the Italian authorities – a country more than familiar with the ravages of the plague – were as sophisticated as they could be, putting in place a number of official posts for searchers, watchmen and examiners who would variously seek out plague victims, ensure the houses of infected persons were closed up and that no one entered or left, and record the numbers of victims and houses of those infected.

All of these were unenviable tasks which also carried the grave risk of exposure to infection. However, the work was vital and so the positions, overseen by the aldermen and Common Council, were made compulsory on pain of imprisonment. In addition, each post holder was obliged to stay in his position for a period of two months.

In this way, London's Lord Mayor managed the City's needs in the best way he knew how. Two watchmen were sworn to oversee and attend to the needs of every affected household; the first watch took place from 6 a.m. until 10 p.m., whereupon the night watchman would then take over. Women searchers were employed to seek out the bodies of those who had died and give true and honest reports to the best of their knowledge as to the cause of death, and physicians were also appointed to cure and to help prevent infection, in addition overseeing the work of the searchers.

Animals were widely thought to be carriers of infection, and with this in mind men were employed to kill dogs and cats (estimates suggest around sixty thousand animals were disposed of in this way). In order to stop groups of possibly infectious persons gathering together City orders decreed that from 9 p.m. meeting places such as taverns would be closed, and that street entertainment was prohibited, to discourage crowds from gathering in public. To prevent hidden, and thus unrecorded, internments taking place, burials could now only be carried out in daylight hours and gatherings at plague graves were prohibited.

Despite these thorough and fulsome regulations, the number of plague deaths only continued to rise, and by the end of July, just weeks after the orders were first brought into being, more Londoners than ever found themselves succumbing to the plague. Many of these had found large, hard lumps about their person and, sweating profusely, had died within two days. Others, in retrospect the luckier ones, experienced no noticeable symptoms and simply dropped down dead on the streets.

No matter how hard the Lord Mayor and his colleagues tried to ensure that the plague orders were enforced, it seemed an impossible task to contain the spread of infection. To begin with, it was simply not possible to shut up all the houses of contaminated persons because the infection spread too far and too quickly. It wasn't unknown for entire streets to be infected, and it was certainly the case that many died before they even realised they were infected. Another problem was that of human nature – many citizens who discovered they had plague symptoms simply ran away in preference to being shut up in their houses. Indeed, many considered the shutting up of houses as unthinkably cruel and made bitter remonstrances to the Lord Mayor. It was a practice, they argued, that only engendered despair. At the first sign of any symptoms the head of the household was required to report to the authorities, but this wasn't always carried out. The City, it seems, was already full enough of the laments of those who, confined to their houses and shut away from their friends, resorted to shouting their despair from their windows.

During these piteous months of misery and desolation, Lawrence received many complaints. Not only was the practice of shutting up houses a source of widespread discontent, but it soon came to light that the watchmen, tasked with ensuring the confined households had food and medicine, along with any other comfort they might require, had been neglecting their duties. Many simply failed to attend to their allotted sufferers, and when they did it was often reported they were either uncivil or resoundingly drunk. Thus, the vigilance of the Lord Mayor was sorely tested, but Lawrence also had other matters on his mind. Realising the importance of keeping the economy as stable as possible, he took great pains to keep the price of bread affordable and the ovens continued baking on pain of losing the freedom of the City. Another of the vital tasks the Lord Mayor carried out was to ensure that the freedom of the market was kept, and to this end a city official, often the Lord Mayor himself, would attend the market each day to ensure that those bringing in their provisions from outside London were not dissuaded from entering the City. Key to this was the rather gruesome task of ensuring that any dead bodies from those who had died suddenly on the streets were either taken away or covered up. Later, the Lord Mayor would encourage the country folk to simply stop before the entrance to the City, which they did in places such as St George's Fields in Southwark, while the Lord Mayor and magistrates sent officers and servants for provisions.

It was said at this time that only the poor remained in the City of London, and one of the many difficulties associated with the exodus of the metropolis's richer citizens was the mass of servants, journeymen, footmen, maidservants and cooks they left behind, now homeless in addition to being without employment. Charitable giving was now their only lifeline, and the Lord Mayor and City officials who remained provided the most desperate cases with money and employment, such as watchmen and nurses.

Lawrence's stalwart efforts during London's terrible plague earned him considerable praise and attention, and his considerate management of the City's affairs was widely observed as Harvey notes:

> Everything was managed with so much care and such excellent order observed in the whole city, and suburbs, that London may be a pattern and example to all cities of the world for the good government and excellent order that was everywhere kept even in the most violent infection and when the people were in the utmost consternation and distress.

Eventually the plague began to loosen its deadly grip on the City and the death rates recorded on the Bills of Mortality at last began to fall. But, as the City Remembrancer records, the London left behind was very different to the City the plague had entered:

> The great street in Whitechapel is one of the broadest and most public streets in London; all the side where the butchers lived was more like a green field than a paved street; toward Whitechapel church the street was not all paved, but the part that was paved was

full of grass; the grass grew in Leadenhall Street, Bishopsgate-Street, Cheapside, Cornhill and even in the Royal Exchange: neither cart nor coach was seen from morning to evening, except country carts with roots, beans, pease, hay and straw to the market and those very few: coaches were scarcely used but to carry people to the pest-house or hospitals; or some few to carry physicians; coaches were dangerous, sick infected persons sometimes dying in them.

As the pressure on the City began to lessen, the Lord Mayor now turned his attention to the actions of his ancient predecessor, who had governed during the harrowing episode of the great plague of 1348. At that time it was the rapid action of the civil authorities which decreased the impact of the economic turmoil that had so swiftly ensued. So severely and so quickly did the outbreak of plague decimate the City's population that it seemed the economics of the City changed almost overnight. Women and children were to be found working in positions previously held by men, while both night-time employment and working on public holidays became such an issue that King Edward III and his council felt obliged to act with force. This they did, issuing the Ordinance of Labourers 1349, a policy designed to keep wages to their pre-plague levels while also ordering mayors and bailiffs across the kingdom to prevent sellers of victuals from artificially raising their prices. We can see from the Calendar of the Plea and Memoranda Rolls of the City of London that it was an edict which kept the London's Lord Mayors busy for a number of years. On 18 July 1349 William de Osprenge, John Chaumpeneys and John de la Maneys were among a number of bakers' servants who were indicted for demanding double or triple the amount of their former wages, for which they were all duly fined. Similarly, on

14 November 1349 a number of cordwainers complained before the Lord Mayor and aldermen about their servants, whom they charged with entering into a conspiracy not to serve them except by the day and on their own terms (a contravention of the masters' right to rule the trade). When examined in court the servants confessed as charged, throwing themselves on the mercy of the Lord Mayor and aldermen. On being further questioned they gave up the names of several others who had joined their group and were henceforth consigned to Newgate, where they were released on the Thursday after the Feast of Saint Katherine, 25 November, promising to work for the same wages as formerly and to maintain future good behaviour.

Such cases were far from being the exception. Later that year, on 2 December, John Baltrip and Geoffre le Cordwainer of Bassieshaw were committed to prison for selling shoes to Adam de Leynthale and Margaret Condal at the unlawful price of 8*d* a pair.

Even in the following year the examples do not abate. On the Monday after the Feast of St Barnabas, 11 June, John Natus, Walter de Lyncoln, Thomas Shrousbury, John de Holne, Stephen de Cobham and William Combe, belonging to the 'mistery of Shearmen', were committed to prison for refusing to work except at double wages. Surety was accepted for their future good behaviour.

The same day John Adam, spicer, paid to Thomas de Walden, the chamberlain, a fine because his servant John Coumbe sold a gallon of wine by his orders at a price contrary to the proclamation.

It was hardly surprising that such situations arose. For the first time in their lives, the general working population of London found themselves in a position of power. Not only did a shortage of labour mean they could charge extra for goods, but workers were understandably liable to suddenly desert their employers if they were offered higher wages elsewhere. The City's archives are crammed with cases of employees selling their skills to the highest bidder (and it would seem there were plenty of bidders to choose from). In *The History of King's Works, Vol, 1: The Middle Ages*, we see that 'the men hired to build the palace at Westminster abandoned their monarch because working conditions were better in the capital'. This greatly displeased the king, who concluded that the laws were not being properly enforced in the City, and when the first parliament after the contagion gathered in the February of 1352, Edward wasted no time in making his displeasure known in the Statute of Labourers:

> Whereas late against the malice of servants, which were idle, and not willing to serve after the pestilence, without taking excessive wages, it was ordained by our lord the king, and by the assent of the prelates, nobles, and other of his council, that such manner of servants, as well men as women, should be bound to serve, receiving salary and wages, accustomed in places where they ought to serve in the twentieth year of the reign of the king that now is, or five or six years before; and that the same servants refusing to serve in such manner should be punished by imprisonment of their bodies, as in the said statute is more plainly contained: whereupon commissions were made to divers people in every county to inquire and punish all them which offend against the same: and now forasmuch as it is given the king to understand in this present parliament, by the petition of the commonalty, that the said servants having no regard to the said ordinance, but to their ease and singular covetise, do withdraw themselves to serve great men and other, unless they have livery and wages to the double or treble

of that they were wont to take the said twentieth year, and before, to the great damage of the great men, and impoverishing of all the said commonalty, whereof the said commonalty prayeth remedy: wherefore in the said parliament, by the assent of the said prelates, earls, barons, and other great men, and of the same commonalty there assembled.

When dealing with the harrowing effects of the City's seventeenth-century plague, Lawrence had plenty of examples to follow. Not only do we find in the City's archives material from Italy on how Milan had responded to the outbreak in 1576–7, but we also see suggestions from the City's own experiences of yet another outbreak in the late sixteenth century. For instance, the January of 1582 saw Lord Mayor Sir James Harvie busily engaged in compiling a detailed catalogue of the number of infected persons who had visited inns, ale or victualling houses in the preceding two months. This was then printed onto a general bill which was posted in prominent spots around the City.

If we look through the records of the *Remembrancia* 1579–1664 we can see numerous additional examples of the types of precautionary measures London's Lord Mayors took to guard the citizens against infection.

On 3 April 1582, for example, Harvie wrote to the Lords of the Council with the news that he had taken steps to halt the spread of plague by putting an end to burials in the churchyard of St Paul's. In part this was because the churchyard was already reaching its limit. Twenty-three parishes were currently using the consecrated space, a number which the Lord Mayor intended to reduce to thirteen. Those parishes which were to be excluded from using the area would be able to use a new site provided by alderman

Sir Thomas Rowe, advised the missive, until such time as other churchyards could be built or bought.

Conscious of the adverse reaction his intended actions might provoke, the Lord Mayor, while desiring the council to issue directions to the authorities of the cathedral accordingly, was quick to point out that his reasons were not intended to prevent any person of honour or worship being buried there but only to halt the 'pestering of the churchyard with whole parishes'.

Just months later, on 1 September 1582, the Lord Mayor again received a letter from the Lords of the Council asking him to have a 'better regard for his duty'. Advising that the number of plague deaths had greatly increased in the previous week, it was pointedly suggested that the reason for this rise was that the City was not being kept clean enough, and that in addition the Lord Mayor had been neglecting to paint the required red cross on the doors of houses where the plague was found and to subsequently shut up the dwellings.

The Lord Mayor responded immediately, assuring the Lords of the Council that every care had been taken in the execution of the council's orders, that the streets had been cleansed every second day and that the parish clerks had been overseeing the closing of infected houses and had put papers on the doors. As a further precaution, the Lord Mayor had also appointed officers to patrol the City to ensure his orders had been carried out.

The possibility of infection, meanwhile, affected every aspect of London life.

On 8 October 1582, Oxford's mayor wrote to London's Lord Mayor asking him to direct the City's citizens away from their forthcoming fair. It had become customary for Londoners to attend what was known as the Frideswide Fair with their merchandise, but this year a vital trading opportunity was to be lost. Just a week later, the Lords of the Council issued a similar edict – that the Lord Mayor should prohibit any merchant, victualler or retailer from resorting or sending into the towns of Hertford, Ware, Hodston or Standstead any kind of merchandise, stuff, bedding, victual or suchlike upon pain of imprisonment, Her Majesty's high displeasure and disfranchisement.

Such measures, stringent though they were, did little to halt the spread of the pestilence. By the early spring of 1583 the infection had started to spiral and the Lord Mayor, this time Sir Thomas Blancke was, once again, reminded of his duty to contain the spread; the dwellings of all those afflicted, the council insisted, were to be shut up and provision made to feed and maintain the increasing numbers of sick persons within. All infected houses were to be marked with either a red cross or the words 'Lord have mercy', the streets thoroughly cleansed and a 'sufficient number of discreet persons appointed to see the same done'.

To gain a more detailed picture of how the City was affected during these plague years we need to look further than the City's archives, to accounts of those who also lived through these dark days. One of these was Thomas Vincent, Minister of Maudlins on Milk Street, who in 1667 wrote the following telling account in his pamphlet entitled 'God's Terrible Voice in the City', reprinted in 1832:

Now the citizens of London are put to a stop in the career of their trade; they begin to fear whom they converse withal, and deal withal, lest they should have come out of infected places. Now roses and other sweet flowers wither in the gardens, are disregarded in the markets, and people dare not offer them to their noses lest with their sweet savour, that which is infectious should be attracted;

rue and wormwood are taken into the hand: myrrh and zedoary into the mouth; and without some antidote few stir abroad in the morning. Now many houses are shut up where the plague comes, and the inabitants shut in, lest coming abroad they should spread infection. It was very dismal to behold the red crosses, and read in great letters, LORD HAVE MERCY UPON US, on the doors and watchmen standing before them with halberts; and such a soliture about those places, and people passing by them so gingerly and with such fearful looks as if they had been lined with enemies in ambush that waited to destroy them.

Now rich tradesmen provide themselves to depart; if they have not country-houses, they seek lodgings abroad for themselves and families and the poorer tradesmen, that they may imitate the rich in their fear, stretch themselves to take a country journey …

Now the highways are thronged with passengers and goods, And London doth empty itself into the country; great are the stirs and hurries in London by the removal of so many families.

While Sir John Lawrence is remembered as the Lord Mayor who laboured tirelessly to alleviate the citizens' suffering during the desolation of the plague, the name of Thomas Bludworth, Lord Mayor of London during the fateful year of 1666, is spoken of in a very different way. It was he who, on being summoned to a fire in the Billingsgate ward of the City in the early hours of Sunday 2 September, deemed the flames to be too insignificant to warrant the remedial action of pulling down dwellings to halt the spread – instead, he impatiently uttered the infamous words 'Pish! A woman might piss it out', and promptly returned to his home. Within hours of this proclamation the ancient ward of Billingsgate had all but been reduced to ashes. Houses had burned to the ground, shops stood in ruins and the mighty Fishmongers' Hall was damaged beyond repair. The decision to leave the flames unchecked was one that would haunt Bludworth not simply for the rest of his mayoralty but for the remainder of his life. To be fair, though, others in the City had been equally blasé. The great seventeenth-century diarist Samuel Pepys wrote that night,

> Some of our maids up late last night to get things ready against our feast to-day. Jane called us up about three in the morning, to tell us of a great fire they saw in the City. So I rose and slipped on my nightgowne, and went to her window, and thought it to be on the backside of Marke-lane at the farthest ... I thought it far enough off; and so went to bed again and to sleep.

In this way, without any great alarm being raised, the fire raged unabated through the night, consuming Garlick-hithe in Thames Street and most of Cannon Street. Waking the next morning at 7 a.m. to hear that, far from the flames having burned themselves out, the fire had now reached Fish Street by London Bridge, burning three hundred houses along the way, Pepys immediately set out to survey the scene:

> So I made myself ready presently and walked to the Tower and there got up upon one of the high places, Sir J. Robinson's little son going up with me; and there I did see the houses at that end of the bridge all on fire, and an infinite great fire on this and the other side the end of the bridge ... So down with my heart full of trouble, to the Lieutenant of the Tower who tells me that it begun this morning in the king's bakers house in Pudding Lane and that it hath burned down St Magnes Church and most part of Fish Street already.

Taking a boat on to the Thames, Pepys next recorded the following chaotic scenes: 'Everybody endeavouring to remove their goods, and flinging into the river or bringing them into lighters that lay off. Poor people staying in their houses as long as till the very fire touched them, and then running into boats or clambouring from one pair of stair by the waterside to another.'

Having stayed a good hour without witnessing any attempts to put the fire out, Pepys then made haste to Whitehall, where his account of the catastrophe was said to have dismayed both the Duke of York and the king: 'They seemed much troubled,' he later wrote, 'and the king commanded me to go to my Lord Mayor from him and command him to spare no houses but to pull down before the fire every way.'

Pepys did so, returning to the burning City to seek out its chief magistrate: 'At last met my Lord Mayor in Canning Street, like a man spent, with a handkercher about his neck. To the king's message, he cried like a fainting woman. "Lord, what can I do? I am spent! People will not obey me. I have been pulling down houses. But the fire overtakes us faster than we can do it!"'

The City's fire engines now proved useless against the scale of the blaze and it seemed as though the raging flames could not be overcome. The combination of largely wooden residences, a hot, dry summer (which the City had welcomed since the heat, it was thought, would help to eliminate the plague) and a strong easterly wind proved to be a deadly combination.

As the day progressed, the damage worsened – flames ran through the broad streets of Cornhill, devouring the magnificent structure of the Royal Exchange, and then to Cheapside and St Paul's, where the heat proved so intense that the lead reportedly melted and ran down in rivers from the roof. Paternoster Row succumbed next as destruction spread to the Old Bailey and on to Fleet Street.

The noise was said to be horrendous – not simply the roaring of the vehement flames, but the sound of the houses falling against each other as they crumpled to the ground. The sound of the families, too, as they fled the City wailing their remonstrances to the Lord, their carts and coaches filled with whatever they had been able to save as they made their way to nearby fields, the only place now for them to stay.

Amid fears of riot and looting, the City armed its Trained Bands and sent them out on to the streets to keep guard. The Earl of Craven (who had proved himself magnificently in the plague year, helping to keep order) was sent by the king along with several companies of his guard to help Bludworth in whatever way possible, while nobles and gentry alike were to be seen on the streets assisting in pulling down houses to stop the fire. Those houses in the City which were known to contain stores of gunpowder were immediately pulled down, and supplies of explosives were removed from the Tower, where the naval supplies were kept. In carrying out the king's specific orders, Bludworth now sent as many provisions as he could muster into the fields where the homeless citizens were taking refuge. On finding the supply of bread much diminished, it was then arranged for the Navy's store of sea biscuits to be distributed.

But if Monday's flames had brought havoc on an unparalleled scale to the City, then the fire that raged through the streets the following day was worse still, destroying the largest part of the City thus far. The sight of a burning Guildhall was described as a 'fearful spectacle which stood the whole body of it together in view for several hours after the fire had taken it without flames, (possibly because the timber was such solid oak) in a bright shining coal as if it had been a palace of gold, or a great building of burnished brass'.

At last, on Tuesday night, the wind abated. On meeting with brick buildings at the Temple, the fire began to lose its force so that on Wednesday hope was restored. On the Thursday, the *London Gazette* wrote,

> By the blessing of God it was wholly beat down and extinguished. But so as that evening it burnt out afresh at the Temple, by the falling of some sparks (as it supposed) upon a pile of wooden buildings; but his royal highness, who watched there the whole night in person, by the great labour and diligence used, and especially by applying powder to blow up the houses about it, before day happily mastered it.

By the Thursday of that week the fire was all but extinguished, and Bludworth and his officials, exhausted by the events of the preceding days, began to assess their losses.

All in all, 436 acres had been affected, most of the old city had burned to the ground, 87 parish churches and 44 of the livery halls were lost, along with the City's gates. Public buildings had fared no better. Hospitals, schools and libraries were all damaged as was the Royal Exchange; Newgate; the Old Bailey; Custom House and St Paul's Cathedral along with the seat of the City's Corporation, Guildhall. Worse was the fact that when the City's officials surveyed the ruins they estimated that 13,200 houses had been lost, with the appalling result that up to 10,000 citizens were now homeless.

In the confusion that prevailed in the aftermath of this destructive event, one question was heard loud and clear – how had the fire got so out of control? After all, the City wasn't unacquainted with the possibility of fire – it had a history littered with many notable instances. The years 1077, 1087 and 1092 had all seen the City threatened by flames while a fire in Southwark in 1212, soon after the new stone London Bridge was finished, took the lives of around three thousand people who became trapped by fire at both ends of the structure.

Neither was the City unprepared. Fire engines had been in use in London as early as 1625 and the City's livery companies, owners as they were of impressive guildhalls, were well acquainted with the use of their firefighting supplies. In London, as was the case in many towns and cities of the time, buckets, ladders and firehooks were kept, along with brass squirts. In the early 1640s the twelve great livery companies were also appealed upon to keep three dozen buckets, two ladders, two great hooks with chains, pickaxes, spades and shovels. Fire protection became one of the chief duties of the night watchmen.

With an exceedingly hot summer just passed, it perhaps wasn't surprising how quickly the flames spread, considering that the fire wells were almost dry and the conduits all but empty. The amount of highly inflammable materials held within the City walls also had a part to play. Not only were many of the houses of wooden construction with thatched roofs, but many people's cellars contained stocks of gunpowder. In addition to this, fires were everywhere – in the ovens of bakers, the furnaces of blacksmiths – open fires were kept for cooking, lighting and heating right across the square mile. Fuel was often kept close by, and the hay and straw from horses' stables did little to help matters. Neither did the problem of overcrowding and the popular habit of smoking.

In this respect, the habits of the citizens of the City of London were closely watched by its authorities. Fire hazards were reported and the offenders instructed to remove or correct the fault, with fines

Above: 1. In 1215, London Mayor William Hardel became the only commoner to witness King John agree to the terms of the great charter of liberty, Magna Carta. This copy is one of two held at the British Library. (Courtesy of the British Library)

Right: 2. The moment London Mayor Serlo le Mercer opened the City's gates to the barons, a turning point in the negotiations with King John was reached. This resulted in the draft settlement known as the Articles of the Barons. (Courtesy of British Library)

3. Baynard's Castle was home to leader of the rebel barons, Robert Fitzwalter, who led the negotiations with London's Lord Mayors against King John. (Wellcome Library, London)

Wat Tyler slain.

4. Sir William Walworth, Lord Mayor of London, killing the leader of the Peasants' Revolt, Wat Tyler, in Smithfield, 1381. From Samuel Goodrich's *Pictorial History of England.* (Author's collection)

Opposite: 12. Many of London's mayors have followed the example of Richard Whittington and donated sizeable sums to St Bartholomew's Hospital. (© Ben Hatfield)

Right: 13. Leadenhall Market was given to the City of London by Richard Whittington. (© Ben Hatfield)

Below: 14. Letters patent incorporating the Guild of Clothworkers in the City of London. (With kind permission of the Worshipful Company of Clothworkers)

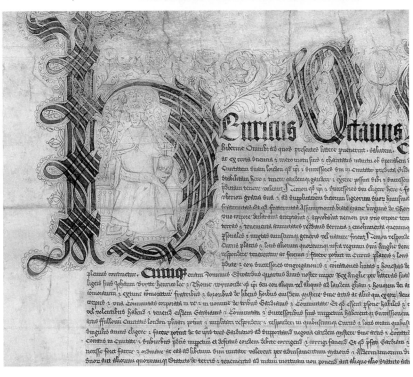

15. The Clothworkers' coat of arms. (With kind permission of the Worshipful Company of Clothworkers)

VIEW OF CLOTHWORKERS' HALL.—Mr. SAMUEL ANGELL, Architect.

16. Engraving of the proposed Mincing Lane facade of the Victorian Clothworkers' Hall. (With kind permission of the Worshipful Company of Clothworkers)

Grocers' Hall.

Fishmongers' Hall.

WHITTINGTON'S COLLEGE, COLLEGE HILL.

Above left: 24. Grocers' Hall and Fishmongers' Hall as they were in 1820. (Author's collection)

Above right: 25. Whittington's Almshouses on College Hill, 1850. (Wellcome Library, London)

Below: 26. The Guild Hall and Merchant Taylors' Hall, 1820. (Courtesy of the British Library)

27. It was Lord Mayor Isaac Penington who agreed to the destruction of Charing and Cheapside Crosses during the 1643 Maypole season. The crosses, said to be the location of spiritual fornication and idolatry, were torn down in 1647 (Courtesy of the British Library)

28. Baynards' Castle was burned to the ground by King John in 1213 in revenge for the City's opposition to his rule. (Courtesy of the British Library)

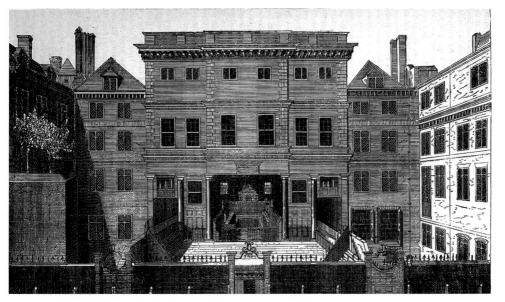

29. This image is of the Old Bailey's Session House in 1750, the same year in which an epidemic of typhus broke out in the courthouse, killing Lord Mayor Sir Samuel Pennant. (Wellcome Library, London)

Above left: 30. The arms of Richard Whittington. (Wellcome Library, London)

Above right: 31. This map shows the land granted to the Virginia Company by James I's charter of 1609. (Author's collection)

Next page: 32. Generous to the last, Lord Mayor Richard Whittington bequeathed money towards the rebuilding of the City's notorious Newgate prison. (British Library)

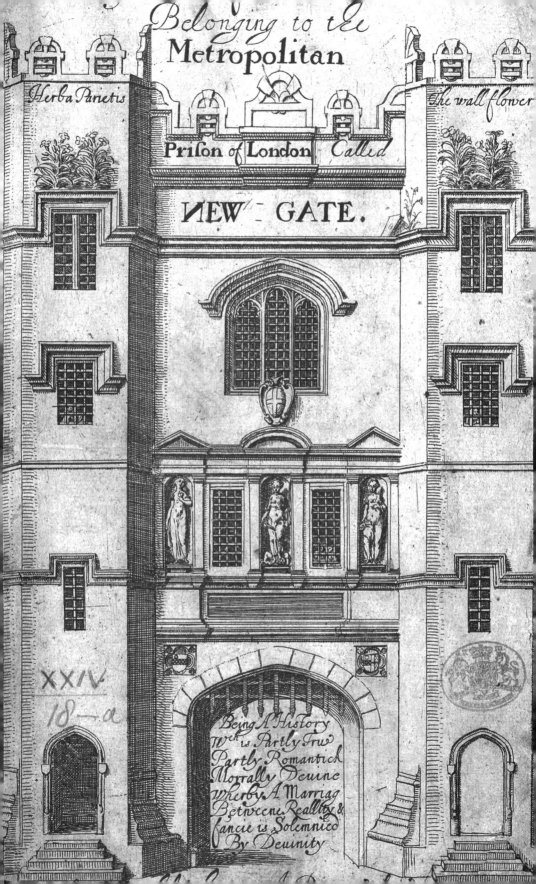

Belonging to the
Metropolitan

Herba Parietis

The wall flower

Prison of London Called

NEW - GATE.

Being A History
Wch is Partly Trw
Partly Romantick
Morrally Deuine
Wherby A Marriag
Betwcene Reallity &
fancie is Solemnied
By Deuinity

XXIV
18 - a

imposed on those who did not comply. Among other infringements of the bye-laws, says Stephen Porter in *The Great Fire of London*, 'householders in Cornhill Ward were reported for throwing out cinders, using a hot press, drying boards and storing wood chip in a room where fires were lit and constructing dangerous chimneys'.

In the aftermath of the great fire, there were many conflicting opinions as to why the blaze had occurred. King Charles referred to the calamity as 'God's Judgment', while the speaker of the House of Commons Sir Edward Turner agreed: 'We must forever with humility acknowledge the justice of God in punishing this whole nation by the late, dreadful conflagration of London,' he said. The Common Council joined in what was now becoming the official line, putting forth the opinion that 'the fire was, by all, justly resented as a most sad and dismal judgment of heaven'. The Privy Council concluded that the fire was the result of a combination of 'the hand of God, a great wind and a dry season'.

Not everyone agreed. Some suggested the blaze was a furtive act of war by the Dutch and French, while others favoured a conspiracy of the Jesuits and papists (memories of the Gunpowder Plot of 1605 and the Irish Rebellion of 1641 being still fresh in the collective mind.) Amid the spiralling rumours, one particularly troubling report appeared to give new strength to the insurrection theories – this was when a house on Fetter Street was set on fire purportedly by the servant Elizabeth Oxly, who was duly sent to prison. She, confessing to the fact, said she had been paid £5 to do it by the papist Stubbs, who was then questioned and declared it 'was no sin to burn the houses of heretics'. There were many who were now utterly convinced that London was burned by papists.

In a city still recovering from the shock, Charles II, having previously been criticised for leaving Londoners to their fate during the devastating years of the plague, now visited frequently with his attendants to ensure everything possible was being done to provide aid to the people. Declaring that a fast would be carried out on 10 October throughout the kingdom, he also called upon Bludworth to administer a fund for relief, calling upon Christians across the land to give what they could towards it.

Bludworth himself, now inundated with requests by citizens to rebuild their homes, carried out the king's prescriptive but highly necessary orders:

> That the Lord Mayor and court of aldermen cause an exact survey to be made of the ruins, that it may appear to whome the houses and ground did belong, what term the occupiers were possessed of, what rents were paid and to whom the reversions and inheritances did appertain, for satisfying all interests, that no mans right be sacrificed to the public convenience. After which a plot and model shall be framed of the whole building which no doubt may so well please all persons as to induce them willingly to conform to such rules and orders as shall be agreed to.

Up and down the City, residents and workers were deciding how to proceed – a question which the merchants wasted no time in addressing: Wrote Pepys:

> This day our Merchants first met at Gresham College, which by proclamation is to be their Exchange. Strange to hear what is bid for houses all up and down here – a friend of Sir W Riders having 150*l* for what he used to let for 40*l* per annum. Much dispute where the Custome house shall be; thereby the growth of the City again to be forseen. My Lord Treasurer, they say, and others, would have

it at the other end of the town … A proclamation us come out for markets to be kept at Leadenhall and Mile end greene and several other places about the town, and Tower Hill and all churches to be set open to receive poor people.

In 1667 the Act for rebuilding the City of London was passed and in the days and weeks that followed the Lord Mayor and the City officials and aldermen were tasked with rebuilding the public areas of the City. The Lord Mayor in 1668–9, Sir William Turner, was heavily involved in the reconstruction; through his dedication and perseverance, the City, in four short years, was rebuilt and he was much honoured for his work, so much so that he was chosen again for the Lord Mayor's post but refused it. In order to reduce the possibility of fire spreading as quickly as it had recently done – many regulations had to be followed – houses built in by-lanes could not exceed two stories, with three along the river and four on the high streets. Also highly regulated were party walls and windows, while there was to be no more easy fuel for the fire – all structures were to be built in brick and stone. The many building regulations meant the result was certainly more satisfactory than it had been before, with its irregular narrow streets with many-storeyed wooden houses leaning perilously close to houses on the opposite side of the road. Streets were widened in order for the 'sweet air' to circulate – a way of also ensuring the good health of the citizens and of preventing the plague. The City responded with incredible efficiency and, by 1669, eight livery halls and 1,600 houses were rebuilt. In 1672, Newgate and the Royal Exchange were finished, as was nearly all the housing.

The City's shock at what had happened and the way in which it dealt with it is forever engraved in the monument which stands not only as a memorial of the fire itself but also as testament to the way in which the citizens of London and the officials of the City responded. Located on the corner of Fish Street Hill and Monument Street, Sir Christopher Wren's vision was erected in 'perpetual remembrance of this dreadful visitation'. The Lord Mayor and aldermen decided on the inscriptions and it is sited as near as possible to where the fire began. On the west side is depicted the City itself in flames, with its inhabitants appealing to the Gods to appease their sufferings, along with pictorial depictions of liberty, imagination, contrivance, art and industry – all being the attributes which allowed the City to so successfully repair itself. The north side vividly describes the event of the fire itself, lamenting the speed in which it devoured the City:

In the year of Christ 1666, the second day of September, eastwards from hence, at the distance of two hundred and two feet (the height of this column) a terrible fire broke out, which, driven by a high wind, not only wasted the adjacent parts, but also places very remote, with incredible noise and fury ... To the estates and fortunes of the citizens it was merciless, but to their lives, very favourable. The destruction was sudden, for in a small space of time the same city was seen most flourishing, and reduced to nothing. Three days after, when this fatal fire had baffled all human counsels and endeavours, in the opinions of all, as it were by the will of heaven, it stopped, and on every side was extinguished.

Transcribed from Latin, the east side reads,

This pillar was begun, Sir Richard Ford, knight, being Lord Mayor of London, in the year of 1671, carried on in the mayoralties of Sir

George Waterman, knight; Sir Robert Hanson, knight, Sir William Hooker, knight, Sir Robert Viner, knight, Sir Joseph Sheldon, knight, and finished Sir Thomas Davis, Knight, being Lord Mayor in the year 1677.

The words on the south side of the monument give praise to the ability and the efforts of those who enabled the City to transform itself and rise again out of the ashes, particularly to Charles II, who, after the fire, remitted the citizens' taxes and took note of the requests of City officials and Parliament, ensuring that the rebuilding of the City was no modest affair: 'that public buildings should be restored to greater beauty ... that churches, and the cathedral of St Paul's should be rebuilt from their foundations with all magnificence; that bridges, gates and prisons should be made new, the sewers cleansed; the streets made straight and regular'.

Ultimately, the City was reborn and began to thrive, the twin disasters of plague and fire gradually forgotten. 'People do all the world over cry out of the simplicity of my Lord Mayor in general,' wrote a no doubt frustrated Pepys at the time of the Great Fire. But perhaps the last word should rest with the Lord Mayor of London himself, who ultimately had no authority to pull down houses without the king's consent unless he wanted to be personally liable for the cost of rebuilding them: 'Never was a man so sorely tested,' said the merchant and Member of Parliament who remained, according to parliamentary records, 'a zealous person in the king's concernments and willing, though it may not be very able, to do great things in the City'.

6

POMP AND PAGEANTRY
1600–1700

In April 1606, the City's investors were abuzz with the news of a promising venture. A charter had been granted to the Virginia Company by King James I, who was anxious to begin the settlement of America. He therefore granted a 'licence to make habitacion, plantacion and to deduce a colonie of sondrie of our people into that parte of America commonly called Virginia, and other parts and territories in America either appertaining unto us or which are not nowe actuallie possessed by anie Christian prince or people'. The land to be settled was 'all along the sea coastes between fower and thirtie degrees of northerly latitude from the equinoctial line and five and fortie degrees of the same latitude and in the maine lande betweene the same fower and thirtie and five and fourtie degrees, and the ilandes thereunto adjacente or within one hundred miles of the coaste thereof'.

In a bid to raise as much money as possible for the new venture, James I decided to state a strong preference for the type of individual he wanted to invest:

And to that ende, and for the more speedy accomplishemente of the saide intended plantacion and habitacion there are desirous to devide themselves into two severall colonies and companies, the one consisting of certaine knights, gentlemen, marchanntes and other adventurers of our cittie of London and elsewhere, which are, and from time to time shall be joined unto them which doe desire to begin their plantacions and habitacions in some fitt and conveniente place.

Virginia, at this time, was not an entirely unknown destination. Sir Walter Raleigh's third venture there had included men, women and children with the explicit purpose of forming a colony. Forced to leave what he had hoped would be called the City of Raleigh in Virginia to raise more money to keep his venture going, Raleigh had been unable to raise the necessary funds to send out a ship until midway through 1590. When the crew arrived, no trace of Raleigh's settlers could be found.

The fate of what became known as the Lost Colony served as an important lesson for English investors, who now knew that sustained finance was the key to successful colony-building. When the Anglo-Spanish Wars finished in 1604 (although war had never been officially declared, these were a series of battles which had continued for nearly twenty years), England could once again concentrate on building its empire abroad, and at this time attention towards the North American settlements was renewed with much vigour. Two competing companies, the Virginia Company of London and the Virginia Company of Plymouth, both operating on different territories, now came together to form the Virginia Company to which James granted his carefully worded charter.

Enjoying a potentially lucrative monopoly of trade as long as business was conducted through English ports, the company could manage the colony as it pleased. The only stipulations were that the colonists adhered to English laws and that any further explorations had to be approved by the king. All who partook in this new venture were obligated to swear their allegiance to the Crown and the Church.

On 20 December of that very same year, and with the hope of bringing back the valuable commodities of timber, tar, glass and sassafras, 104 settlers gathered on the banks of the Thames to board three ships: the *Susan Constant*, captained by Christopher Newport; the *Godspeed*, which had Gosnold at the helm; and the aptly named *Discovery*, of which John Ratcliffe took charge. After a comparatively straightforward journey, the party reached Chesapeake Bay on 26 April the next year and shortly afterwards set up their camp on the James River. The first official act the men undertook was opening a sealed box which contained the seven names of those who were to become the first councillors of Virginia. Included on this list was Captain John Martin – son of Richard Martin, once Master of the Mint and Lord Mayor of London in 1593–4. Vocal and highly opinionated, John Martin was to constantly clash with his fellow councillors, alleging corruption and mismanagement of the settlement from the moment the ship docked. Nonetheless, little more than a week after the camp at Jamestown had been built and just under two months since the adventurers had first set foot in the new world, Christopher Newport sailed back to England bearing a letter from Virginia's new councillors to the governors of the Virginia Company, updating their masters with upbeat and positive pronouncements of the success of the colony to date: 'Within lesse then seaven weekes, wee are fortified well against the Indians. We have sowen good store of wheate. We have sent yow a taste of Clapboard. We have built some houses, wee have spared some hands to a discoverie and still as god shall enable us with strength wee will better and better our proceedings.'

The Virginia Company's council was rightly careful to keep interest high in the fledgling colony, especially in regards to its financial possibilities:

Wee are sett downe 80 miles within a River, for breadth, sweetness of water, length navigable upp into the contry deepe and bold Channell so stored with Sturgion and other sweete Fishe as no mans fortune hath ever possessed the like. And as wee think if more maie be wished in a River it will be founde, The soile [is] most fruictfull, laden with good Oake, Ashe, walnut tree, Popler, Pine sweete woodes, Cedar and others, yet without names that yeald gummes pleasant as Franckumcense, and experienced amongst us for greate vertewe in healing greene woundes and Aches, wee entreate your succours for our seconds with all expedition leaste that all devouringe Spaniard lay his ravenous hands upon theas gold showing mountains, which if we be so enhabled he shall never dare to think on.

The councillors finished the letter by asking the king's hands to bless their labours so that they may proceed with strength.

Although they were at the time unaware of this, the colonists had arrived at the start of what was to become the driest period in more than seven hundred years. In the months and years that followed they would need all the blessings they could get.

It wasn't until 1609 that the Virginia Company, having recognised the need to significantly reorganise itself, began to appeal in earnest

for fresh funds. It now released new subscription opportunities
to coincide with James's second charter to the company, which
in the same year was renamed the Treasurer and Company of
Adventurers and Planters of the City of London for the first
Colony in Virginia. Detailing the 'success, good desires and good
worke, much pleasinge to God and profitable to oure kingdom',
James's second charter appealed for help for the adventurers of the
first colony in their efforts to establish the plantations:

> Nowe, forasmuch as divers and sondrie of oure lovinge subjects,
> as well adventurers as planters, of the said First Collonie (which
> have alreadie engaged them selves in furtheringe the businesse
> of the said plantacion and doe further intende by the assistance
> of Almightie God to prosecute the same to a happie ende) have
> of late ben humble suiters unto us that, in respect of their great
> chardeges and the adventure of manie of their lives which they have
> hazarded in the said discoverie and plantacion of the said countrie,
> wee woulde be pleased to graunt them a further enlargement and
> explanacion of the said graunte, priviledge and liberties, and that
> suche counsellors and other officers maie be appointed amonngest
> them to manage and direct their affaires [as] are willinge and readie
> to adventure with them; as also whose dwellings are not so farr
> remote from the cittye of London but that they maie at convenient
> tymes be readie at hande to give advice and assistance upon all
> occacions requisite.
>
> We, greatlie affectinge the effectual prosecucion and happie
> successe of the said plantacion and comendinge their good desires
> theirin, for their further encouragement in accomplishinge so
> excellent a worke, much pleasinge to God and profitable to oure
> kingdomes, doe, of oure speciall grace and certeine knowledge and

meere motion, for us, oure heires and successors, give, graunt and confirme to oure trustie and welbeloved subjects.

It was a successful approach. James's second charter attracted significant investment for the company, although he had been forced to turn to London's Lord Mayor, Sir Humphrey Weld, for help. In the March of 1609 James sent Weld a letter inviting him and others to invest 'to ease the city and suburbs of a swarme of unnecessary inmates as a contnyual cause of dear and the very originalle cause of all the Plagues that happen in this kingdome'. Weld responded quickly, making a direct appeal to potential subscribers. He approached fifty of the City companies, among whom many, including the Mercers, Grocers, Drapers, Fishmongers, Goldsmiths, Skinners and Merchant Taylors, provided funds. Weld himself, along with other high-profile figures including Oliver Cromwell and Sir Francis Bacon, also decided to invest.

While the Virginia Company needed investment, it was also in need of settlers and it was in this that Weld's talents as a salesman really came to the fore. Purchasing three bills of adventure himself, he then induced the City's population to consider the chance of a new life in America, with the promise of their own homes and gardens. It was a tactic which could not fail to entice. Hundreds of the City's workers, employed in every imaginable trade (masons, butchers, bakers and shoemakers), now bought the chance of a new, seemingly more secure way of life than they had in London, while King James added his own enticements to the merchants by allowing the Virginia Company to 'shipp and carrie awaye such goods and merchandizes' as the colony needed without the government levying 'anie custome impost or other duties'.

All in all, more than 659 individuals bought into the dream of sailing to a new England, but it wasn't simply the encouragement from London's chief magistrate that had been the source of their persuasion.

Much literature was published at this time which glorified life in the new colony. Robert Johnson's *Nova Britannia*, 'offering most excellent fruits by planting in Virginia', describes the new land as an 'earthly paradise' and, significantly, propounds a commonly held view that colonisation is necessary to the continuation of the courage and glory of the English people across the globe.

It is known to the world, and cannot be forgotten that the days and reign of Queen Elizabeth brought forth the highest degree of wealth, happiness and honor that ever England had before her time, whereof to let pass the particular praises as impertinent to my purpose, I do only call to mind our royal fleets and merchant ships (the jewels of our land); our excellent navigators and admirable voyages, as into all parts and round about the globe with good success; to the high fame and glory of our nation, so especially their aim and course was most directed to the new found world; to the mainland and infinite islands of the West Indies; intending to discover with what convenience to plant and settle English colonies in places not already possessed and inhabited by subjects of other Christian princes, wherein after many tedious and perilous adventurers, howsoever strange seas and miserable famine had devoured and distressed ships and men of inestimable value yet were not the remnant escaping, swallowed up of despair not their heart and spirits daunted with fear; but daily armed afresh with invincible courage and greater resolution, scorning to sit down by their losses, made new attempts, not enduring to look on while so huge and spacious countries, the fourth part of the world, and the greatest and wealthiest part of all the rest, should remain a wilderness, subject, for the most part, but to wild beasts and fowls of the air and to savage people which have no Christian nor civil use of anything ...

The question of religion was an enduring point. In its own 1609 campaign for funds the Virginia Company had assured the nation that investment was not only a glorious opportunity to build another England, but also that it was God's will. The idea that the settlement of America was in some way the divine will of the maker was a long-held belief that had formed a core part of James's original charter, which had propagated the idea that native Americans were living in darkness and were desperately in need of missionary assistance:

> Wee greatly commending and graciously accepting of theire desires to the furtherance of soe noble a worke which may, by the providence of Almightie God, hereafter tende to suche people as yet live in darknesse and miserable ignorance of the true knowledge and worshippe of God and may in tyme bring the infidels and salvages living in those parts to humane civilitie and to a settled and quiet governmente doe by theise our letters patents graciously accepte of and agree to theire humble and well-intended desires.

Certainly, among the first subscribers on the initial round was the clergyman Richard Hakluyt, who in 1589 had edited *The Principall Navigations, Voyages, and Discoveries of the English Nation*. He was, perhaps, more convinced than anyone of America's potential and by 1609 many of London's clergymen agreed. Appeals to the public were made from many a city pulpit by clergymen united in espousing the benefit of settling the American lands for the 'Christian purpose'.

The promise of saving souls might have given the intrepid subscribers an acute sense of purpose as they set off on their voyage, but it was strictly with profit in mind that the newly appointed governor Sir Thomas Gates left England in June 1609 with instructions from the government to find silver, gold and as many human resources as practically feasible. Eight other ships followed Gates, some of which had been financed by Weld, with around five hundred passengers. Two of these vessels sank, while Gates's ship, the *Sea Venture*, was blown to the Bermudas. Building two new craft out of the wreckage, which they named *Patience* and *Deliverance*, the survivors arrived in the new world in the May of 1610 to find that only ninety of four hundred colonists had survived the preceding winter. It was a bitter blow, seriously affecting the confidence of all involved.

There was no hiding the tragic news in London, and the adventurers then had the greatest difficulty in collecting those subscriptions they had initially agreed could be paid in instalments. Forced to try and create a new wave of enthusiasm the company published *A True and Sincere Declaration of the Purpose and Ends of the Plantation Begun in Virginia*, which disputed many of the criticisms that had begun to be levelled against it.

Upon which Grounds, we purpose to deliver roundly and clearly, our endes and wayes to the hopefull plantations begun in Virginia; and to examine the truth, and safety of both, to redeeme our selves and so Noble an action from the imputations and aspertions, with which ignorant rumour, virulent envy or imious subtilty, daily callumniateth our industries and the successe of it:wherein we doubt not, not only to satisfie every modest and well affected heart of this kingdome: but to excite and kindle the affections of the Incredulous and lazy and to coole and asswage the curiousity of the jealous and suspitious & to temper and convince, the malignity of the false and treacherous.

If Piety, Honour, Easinesse, Profit not Conscience cannot provoake and excite, then let us turne from hearts of stone and iron and pray unto that mercifull and tender God who is both easie and glad to be intreated, that it would please him to blesse and water these feeble beginnngs and that as he is wonderfull in all his workes, so to nourish this graine of seed, that it may spread till all people of the earth admire the greatnesse and seeke the shades and fruite thereof. That by so faint and weake indevors his great Councles may bee brought forth and his secret purposes to light, to our endlesse comforts and the infinite Glorye of his Sacred Name. Amen.

They ended their plea with a list of thirty-four occupations that were needed in the colony. Once again London's Lord Mayor found himself in the position of asking the City companies for their assistance and, somewhat surprisingly, an additional 150 recruits were raised for the colony.

From 1609, a major turning point in the colonists' propaganda towards convincing the public of the viability of the Virginia plantations was stating that it was the drive for individual profit that was the cause of the colony's apparent decay.

In his map of Virginia, published in 1612, John Smith claimed that, from his own experience, the Jamestown colony was full of men who never did anything apart from 'devoure the fruits of other mens labours'. In reality, one of the colony's main problems was the fact that many of its first settlers had more of an interest in striking it rich than in making a profit for others. An additional and seemingly insurmountable problem was that the Virginia settlement did not have a large enough supply of labourers to export the quantities of goods the investors expected.

Undoubtedly it had been a troublesome few years, but in 1612 James granted his third charter to the company, which significantly extended the company's territories to include Bermuda, where part of the expedition of 1609 had been shipwrecked:

Now for asmuchas we are given to undestande that in these seas adjoyning to the said coast of Virginia and without the compasse of those twoe hundred miles by us soe grannted unto the said Treasurer and Companie as aforesaid, and yet not farr distant from the said Colony in Virginia, there are or may be divers islandes lying desolate and uninhabited, some of which are already made knowne and discovered by the industry, travell, and expences of the said Company, and others allsoe are supposed to be and remaine as yet unknowen and undiscovered, all and every of which itt maie importe the said Colony both in safety and pollecy of trade to populate and plant, in regard where of, aswell for the preventing of perill as for the better comodity and prosperity of the said Colony, they have bin humble suitors unto us that we wold be pleased to grannt unto them an inlardgement of our said former lettres patent, aswell for a more ample extent of their limitts and territories into the seas adjoyning to and uppon the coast of Virginia as allsoe for some other matters and articles concerning the better government of the said Company and Collony, in which point our said former lettres patents doe not extende soe farre as time and experience hath found to be needfull and convenient ...

We doe by theis presents, give, grannt and confirme unto the said Treasurer and Company of Adventurers and Planters of the said Citty of London for the First Colony in Virginia, and to their heires and successors for ever, all and singuler the said iselandes [whatsoever] scituat and being in anie part of the said ocean bordering upon the coast of our said First Colony in Virginia and being within three hundred leagues of anie the partes hertofore grannted to the said Treasorer and Company in our said former lettres patents as aforesaid, and being within or betweene the one and fortie and thirty degrees of Northerly latitude, together with all and singuler [soils] landes, groundes, havens, ports, rivers, waters, fishinges, mines and mineralls, aswell royal mines of gold and silver as other mines and mineralls, perles, precious stones, quarries, and all and singuler other commodities, jurisdiccions, royalties, priviledges, franchises and preheminences, both within the said tract of lande uppon the maine and allso within the said iselandes and seas adjoyning, whatsoever, and thereunto or there abouts both by sea and land being or scituat; and which, by our lettres patents, we maie or cann grannt and in as ample manner and sort as we or anie our noble progenitors have heretofore grannted to anie person or persons or to anie Companie, bodie politique or corporate or to any adventurer or adventurers, undertaker or undertakers of anie discoveries, plantacions or traffique, of, in, or into anie foreigne parts whatsoever, and in as lardge and ample manner as if the same were herein particularly named, mencioned and expressed: provided allwaies that the said iselandes or anie the premisses herein mencioned and by theis presents intended and meant to be grannted be not already actually possessed or inhabited by anie other Christian prince or estate, nor be within the bounds, limitts or territories of the Northerne Colonie, hertofore by us grannted to be planted by divers of our loving subjects in the northpartes of Virginia. To have and to hold, possesse and injoie all and singuler the said iselandes in the said ocean seas soe lying and bordering uppon the coast or coasts of the territories of the said First Colony in Virginia as aforesaid, with all and singuler the said soiles, landes and groundes and all and singular other the premisses heretofore by theis presents grannted, or mencioned to be grannted, to them, the said Treasurer and Companie of Adventurers and Planters of the Cittie of London for the First Colonie in Virginia, and to their heires, successors and assignes for ever, to the sole and proper use and behoofe of them, the said Treasurer and Companie and their heires, successores and assignes for ever; to be holden of us, our heires and successors as of our mannor of Eastgreenwich, in free and common soccage and not in capite, yealding and paying therefore, to us, our heires and successors, the fifte part of the oare of all gold and silver which shalbe there gotten, had or obteined for all manner of services, whatsoever.

While James's charter had included new territories, the Virginia Company still found it difficult to shake off the bad image the colony had gained. In the public's view, the company's enticements to leave England were verging on the profane. The company extensively advertised the many benefits of moving to the New World, glossing over the realities of hardship and even starvation, but the public were not to be persuaded. In 1622, a broadside appeared warning those who were considering joining the new colony of the possible dangers which lay ahead.

'The inconveniences that have happened to some persons which have transported themselves from England to Virginia without precautions necessary to sustain themselves has greatly hindered the progress of that noble plantation,' advised the cautious editorial, before giving extensive lists of necessary apparel which included victuals, arms, tools and household implements.

By the 1650s, as the new cash crop tobacco began to flourish, several more ballads appeared, this time of a satirical nature to counteract the Virginia Company's own invitations to London's women to take advantage of the glorious new work opportunities abroad:

> Come all your very merry London girls
> That are disposed to travel
> Here is a voyage now at hand
> Will save your feet from gravel
> If you have shooes you need not fear
> For wearing out the Leather
> For hwy you shall on shipboard go
> Like loving rogues together
> Some are already gone before
> The rest must after follow
> Then come away and do not stay
> Your guide shall be Apollo
>
> Then why should those that are behind
> Slink back and dare not venture
> For you shall prove the sea-men kind
> If once the ships you enter
> You shall be fed with good strong fare
> According to the season
> Bisket salt-beef and English beer
> And Pork well boyld with Peason
> And since that some are gone before
> The rest with Joy may follow
> To bear each other company
> Conducted by Apollo

When you come to the appointed place
Your minds you need not trouble
For every groat that you here
You shall have three times double
For there are gold and silver mines
And treasures much abounding
As plenty as Newcastle coales
At some parts may be founding
Then come away make not delay
All you that mean to follow
The ships are ready bound to go
Conducted by Apollo

The reason as I understand
Why you go to that nation
Is to inhait that fair land
And make a new plantation
Where you shall have good ground enough
For planting and for tilling
Which never shall be taken away
So long as you are living
Then come brave lasses come away
Conducted by Apollo
Although that you do go before
Your sweet-hearts they will follow

An additional ballad from around the same time can be found in the University of California's English Broadside Ballad Archive that portrays a more realistic view of life in the Virginian colony. It is entitled 'The Trappan'd Maiden or the Distressed Damsel':

Give ear unto a Maid
That lately was betray'd
And sent into Virginny o
In brief I shall declare
What I have suffered there
When that I was weary
Weary, weary, weary o

Five years served I
Under Master Guy
In the land of Virginny o
Which made me for to know
Sorrow, grief and woe
When that, etc

When my Dame says Go
Then I must do so
In the land of Virginny, o
When she sits at meat
Then I have none to eat
When that, etc

So soon as it is day
To work I must away
In the land of virginny o
Then my dame she knocks
With her tinder-box
When that etc.

A thousand Woes beside

That I do here abide
In the Land of Virginny, o
In misery I SPEND
My time that hath no end
When that etc

Then let Maids beware
All by my ill-fare
In the land of Virginny, O
Be sure thou stay at home
For if you do here come
You will all be weary etc

By the 1620s, the future of Virginia was clear. Its fortune could now be made, not from sassafras, gold or silver, but from the humble Indian tobacco plant. However, by 1623 relations between the Virginia Company and the Crown had broken down so completely that a *quo warranto* was issued through the Privy Council which questioned the company's legal right over the colony. The colony now came under Crown control. This, along with the increasing demand for tobacco, meant that the Virginia settlement now began to flourish.

It had taken a lot longer than anyone had expected. But the importance the City of London made to the fledging settlement is clear. The London connection was so much more than just the monetary contribution of affluent City officials, merchants and gentry/nobles – it provided a new patriotism and nationalism that was to fuel an empire-building frenzy right across the globe.

In 1609 the City of London was offered another investment opportunity when, yet again anxious to attract the riches of the guilds, James I submitted a uniquely targeted document entitled 'Motives and Reasons to induce the City of London to undertake the Plantation in the North of Ireland' to the City's Lord Mayor. Essentially a prospectus detailing the opportunities to be had in investing in the newly acquired lands in the north of Ireland, the king's brochure suggested an extensive swathe of land could be acquired and planted to the profit of all.

> The City of Derry upon the Foyle, and one other place at or near the Castle of Coleraine upon the Bann, do seem to be the fittest places for the City of London to plant ... These towns his Majesty may be pleased to grant unto not only Corporations, with such liberties and privileges for their good government, &c, as shall be convenient, but also the whole territory and country betwixt them, which is above twenty miles in length, bounded by the sea on the north, the river Bann on the east and the river Derry or Lough Foyle on the west, out of which 1,000 acres more may be allotted to each of the towns for their commons, rent free, the rest to be planted with undertakers as the City of London shall think good for their best profit, paying only for the same the easy rent of the undertakers.

Given that the fate of a large part of the Ulster province was now in the hands of the Crown, James was sure to make it clear that he was acting in the best interests of the nation by bringing in investors to manage the land.

> Whereas the greatest part of the Province of Ulster being escheated and come to the Crown, upon view whereof his Majesty, of his princely bounty, not respecting his own profit, but the public peace and welfare of that kingdom, by the civil plantation of those

unreformed and waste countries, is graciously pleased to distribute
the said lands to such of his subjects as, being of merit and ability,
shall seek the same with a mind not only to benefit themselves, but
also to do service to the Crown and Commonwealth, not to such
as intend their private profit only, and not the advancement of the
public service.

London's Lord Mayor, George Bolles, having been informed
of James's intentions, was now obliged to pass James's plea for
investment on to the Common Council – a copy of which still
survives in the Irish Letter-Book:

> Whereas, I have lately received from the Lords of his Majesty's
> most honourable Privy Council a project for a plantation in Ireland,
> the Copy whereof, together with a printed book, you shall receive
> hereunto annexed with intimation of the king's most gracious
> favour and love to the city of London to grant us the first offer of
> so gracious an action, which is likely to prove pleasing to Almighty
> God, honourable to the City and profitable to the undertakers ...

On first glance, James's propaganda might have seemed enticing
enough for the City companies to have no doubt as to the lucrative
prospects that lay ahead. After all, in his 'reasons and motives' the
king had supplied ample information on the abundance of natural
resources the land in Ireland held:

> 1. The country is well watered and supplied with fuel either of trees
> or turf [peat]. 2. It supplies such abundance of provisions as may
> not only sustain the plantation, but may furnish provisions yearly to
> the city of London, especially for their fleets, as beeves, pork, fish,

rye, bere, peas, beans and in some years will help the dearth of the city and country about, and the storehouses appointed for the relief of the poor. 3. It is fit for breeding of mares and for cattle and thence may be expected store of hides, tallow &c. 4. The soil is suited for English sheep and if need were, wool might be had cheaply out of the west of Scotland. 5. It is fit in many parts for madder, hops and wood 6. It affords fells of red deer, foxes, sheep and lambs, cony, martens, squirrels etc 7. It grows hemp and flax better than elsewhere, and thus might furnish materials for canvass, cables and cordage, and such like requisites for shipping. Also for thread, linen cloths and stuffs made of linen yarn which is finer there and more plentiful than in all the rest of the kingdom. 8.Timber, stone, lime and slate, and building materials are to be had; and the soil is good for making bricks and tiles. The goodliest timber in the woods of Glanconkein and Killeitragh may be had, and may compare with any in his Majesty's dominions, and may be brought to the sea by Lough Eagh and the Bann. Fir masts of all sorts may be had out of Loughnaber in Scotland more easily than from Norway. 9. All materials for building of ships (except tar) is there to be had in great plenty and in countries adjoining. 10. There is wood for pipe staves, hogshead staves, barrel staves, hoop staves, clap boards, wainscot, and dyeing ashes, glass and iron-work; copper and iron-ore are there found abundantly. 11. The country is fit for honey and wax.

With sea fishing seemingly plentiful (particularly with regards to herring and eel), plus an abundance of seafowl and rivers that were described as holding great stores of fish, there seemed to be much to induce the City to commit. But James was still sure to make the financial possibilities of the northern lands abundantly clear, and in this way he made his own expectations known:

If multitudes of men were employed proportionally to these commodities, many thousands would be set at work, to the great service of the king, the strength of his realm and the advancement of several trades. It might ease the City [London] of an insupportable burthen of persons which it might conveniently spare, all parts of the city being so surcharged that one tradesman is scarce able to live by another; and it would also be a means to free and preserve the city from infection, and consequently the whole kingdom which of necessity must have recourse hither, and being pestered or closed up together can never otherwise or very badly avoid infection.

On 8 July 1609 George Bolles called the City companies together, asking them to assemble 'a competent number of the most grave and substantial men of your company to consider advisedly of the said project'. The nominated men were to

make their appearance at the Guildhall, upon Wednesday next, by eight of the clock in the forenoon, then and there further to consult with four of every other company; and to set down in writing such reasons and demands as are fit to be remembered, required, or considered of, in the undertaking of so great and honourable an action. And that the said four persons by you named, and the four of every other company, bring the same in writing to the Guildhall, upon Friday morning, by eight of the clock, there to confer with me and thy brethren upon the same, wherein you are not to fail.

By 15 December 1609, a committee had been chosen and the named members conversed with the Privy Council. From this meeting came the following recommendations: that cities should be built in Derry and Coleraine, that rents should be proposed for various divisions of land, and that 'a company be instituted in London, of persons to be selected for that purpose, and Corporations to be settled in Derry and Coleraine: but all things concerning this Plantation and undertaking to be managed and performed in Ireland, by advice and direction from the Company in London'.

All in all, it had taken the City companies a long time to react. After all, it had been as far back as July when the Lord Mayor had called for action and yet the committee itself wasn't in a position to meet with the Privy Council until more than five months later. So why had it taken the City so long to reach a decision? According to some historians, it is clear that the project didn't elicit as much interest as was initially hoped. Architectural historian Professor James Steven Curl, in an essay on the plantation for the BBC, explains that many of the London livery companies thought it would be exceedingly foolish to meddle in the Irish lands and that it was only when several respectable citizens had been gaoled, fined and threatened that the City of London felt obliged to yield itself to the will of the Crown.

Certainly, when James had first mooted the idea of investing in Ulster, many of the City of London companies were well aware of the difficulties they could face – particularly with regards to hostilities from the indigenous population. In the aftermath of the bloody Nine Years War (1594–1603), the northern earls had inexplicably fled in 1607, and in 1608 what became known as O'Doherty's Rebellion – an eleven-week affair – had culminated in Sir Cahir O'Doherty capturing the British settlement at Derry and burning it to the ground. However, now unable to extract themselves from the schemes of the domineering king, the City companies grouped together in order to provide the requisite funds. Often unable to contribute as a single entity, many of the companies joined with others in order to raise the required amount. For example, the Fishmongers joined together with the Basket Makers, Plasterers, Musicians, Glaziers and Leathersellers, while the Tallow Chandlers were the associates of the Drapers, who bought them out in the early days.

For all that the City companies were persuaded into business by the king, they still took pains to check out the true resources and potential of the land. Many of the companies sent agents out to the settlement to find out the real state of the rivers and fisheries, which places in particular were good for planting and what areas were covered by woodlands. By and large, the agents' findings fitted with the original reports:

> The said country is most fit for breeding of all kinds of cattle as horses, mares, kine, goats, sheep, hogs &c., the kine as fair and likely as the ordinary cattle of England. Swine are there both plentifully bred and fed. The land is apt for all kinds of husbandry and where is well manured, yields increase answerable to the ordinary sort of lands in England, will produce store of butter, cheese, tallow and hides; all sorts of grain, as wheat, barley, beare, oats &c and also of madder, hops, wood, coal, rape, hemp and flax. There is a store also of red deer, foxes, sheep, lambs, conies, martens, otters and squirrels.

In the woods of Glankonkayn and Killatrough it was said there existed a 'great store of goodly oaks, fit for all manner of building, ash also, with elm of great bigness. The country in every place is plentiful of stone, apt for any uses; clay and sand in divers places thereof for making brick and tile; limestone is there also in great abundance, and in the river of Loughfoyle great and plentiful shoals of sheaves whereof the inhabitants for the more easy charge, make a sort of good lime.'

The reports also give details of a sort of slate that is 'not very good or plentiful' but points out that the inhabitants 'easily supply themselves with an excellent sort of that material out of the islands of Scotland, the coasts of Wales and the Isle of Man'.

Despite its wealth of natural resources, ultimately the plantation project was slow to fulfil its alleged potential, and on 21 December 1612 the king wrote a letter of complaint about the settlement's lack of progress: 'It is well known unto you how great a revenue we might have raised to our Crown by our escheated lands if we had not preferred the reformation of that disordered country by a civil plantation to be made therein, before the private profit which we might have reaped.'

It was to be the first of many letters of reproof. Numerous surveys were carried out on the City companies' lands and it became increasingly obvious to the disenchanted monarch that, far from being widely populated with a full quota of labourers working the land, the settlements were, in fact, incomplete and that many of the manor houses had not even been completed. When Charles I came to the throne in 1625, matters only got worse. Forcing the City of London to pay substantial amounts towards his wars with France and Spain, the impatient king decided that the City had not fulfilled its obligations within its Articles of Agreements, at which point its Irish estates were taken away and the company was fined. By 1641 the situation was rectified when it was found in the English House of Commons that the City had been treated incorrectly. However, the plantation now faced a very different kind of assault – that of rebel Catholics who attacked Protestant settlers in the rebellion of 1641, which in fact continued for nearly ten years.

Despite all this, the efforts of the City companies continued until the late nineteenth century, when the Clothworkers decided to sell their portion in 1871, with the Grocers' Company following suit in 1877. According to Curl, the Drapers fell into financial trouble during the land agitation of the 1880s and the Fishmongers experienced considerable hardship when their tenants refused to pay rent.

The nineteenth century also saw further disagreements which culminated in the Skinners initiating legal proceedings against the Irish Company itself as it fought for its share of the fisheries' profit:

> My Lord, the prayer of the bill is that it may be declared that the plaintiffs and the other Companies who contributed to the expenses of the said new plantation in Ulster aforesaid, and to whom, and for whose benefit, the said lands and hereditaments were allotted and conveyed as aforesaid are beneficially entitled to the rents and profits of the said ferries, fisheries and town lands, subject only to the payment of the said yearly sums to the Bishop of Derry and the Governor of Culmore Castle,and to the charges, if any, to which the same are subject under the said articles of agreement, and the said charters respectively, and that it may be declared that the said Irish Society of London are trustees of the same rents and profits, subject as aforesaid, for plaintiffs and the said other Companies.
>
> 'The Skinners' Company against the Honourable the Irish Society', the Corporation of London and others commencing
>
> 9 February 1838

Despite its conflicts, internal and otherwise, it is clear that the London companies were an integral part of the development of Ulster. As Dr Éamonn Ó Ciardha, University of Ulster historian and a leading organiser of the Plantation of Ulster conferences concludes, 'The Ulster Plantation may have been four hundred years ago but its impact is still being felt at home and abroad. It effectively copper-fastened the English and British conquest of Ireland, and transformed Ireland's physical, demographic, socio-economic, political, military, religious and cultural landscapes.'

7

AN EXPANDING EMPIRE
1600–1700

On 29 October 1616, Londoners and visitors alike gathered together to witness an extraordinary spectacle. There, on the crowded streets of the City, a series of magnificent pageants were taking place, and the jubilant onlookers gaped in awe as a highly stylised drama unfolded before their eyes. First to be wheeled along the narrow thoroughfares was a Dutch-style fishing boat bearing the distinctive nautical emblem of the Fishmongers' Company. The next offering, an enormous crowned dolphin, was, in turn, followed by a golden leopard from which a character dressed as the King of the Moors threw ingots of silver and gold into the outstretched arms of a bellowing crowd. A pelican, perched on a fruiting lemon tree, followed soon afterwards, accompanied by five children, each dressed to embody one of the five senses. An eagle represented sight, a hart symbolised hearing, a spider was touch, an ape tasting and a keen-nosed dog embodied the sense of smell. The fifth and most widely anticipated item on the programme that year was the effigy of City hero Sir William Walworth, whose progress through the thronging streets was accompanied by six trumpeters whose triumphant sounds loudly proclaimed the City's conquest of good over evil. Close behind rode a glowing angel on horseback whose role in this glorious vision was to 'awaken' Sir William from his long sleep.

Standing among the cheering crowd, struggling perhaps to hear the speeches, it would be easy to think that the climax of the day's entertainment had now been reached. After all, what could possibly better the almost religiously styled resurrection of the saintly Walworth? But this was the Lord Mayor's Show – a once-yearly opportunity to demonstrate all that was splendid and unique about the City and its guilds. And so the parade continued, with shimmering mermaids and mermen – a nod to the Worshipful Company of Fishmongers, to whom that year's City Father Leman belonged. Later another incandescent angel appeared, this time hovering protectively over a likeness of Richard II, beneath whom sat figures dressed as the virtues of Truth, Morality and Conscience busily engaged in defeating Treason and Mutiny in a highly allegorical expression of kingly virtues.

The Lord Mayor's Show of 1616 was later deemed to be one of the most gorgeous of all pageants thus far performed – high praise indeed when you consider the stiff competition. Often pageants, or 'triumphs' as they were known, were an elaborate, high impact opportunity to showcase the splendour and wealth of the City. Usually incorporating trumpets, drums and flutes, Sir Christopher Draper's show of 1566 went further, resulting in a bill of £700 for gunpowder alone. Certainly, as the sixteenth century progressed the show's tenders became evermore fantastic, promising to display the might of the City in increasingly elaborate ways. From knights riding seahorses to camels, elephants and griffins, the inclusion of two giants, now widely known as Gogmagog and Corineus, must have seemed tame by comparison.

The third pageant of Sir Thomas Davies' inaugural show of 1676 was 'Fortunes Bower', which took the form of an enchanted goddess processing serenely through the streets in the company of Gladness, Prosperity, Plenty, Honour, Peace and Riches. In 1672 new mayor Sir Robert Hanson from the Grocers' Company was treated to the classical figures of Apollo, Flora, Peace, Ceres, Justice, Fame and Aurora. By the time of vintner Sir Samuel Dashwood's magisterial reign, pageants had become thrilling to the point of exotic. As Dashwood made his way back from Westminster he found himself in the company of twenty dancing satyrs enthusiastically wielding tambourines along with the chariot of Ariadne, drawn by panthers.

All in all, these pageants were the highlight of the City's festive calendar, but who was actually behind these extraordinary displays? By the late 1500s the writing of the Lord Mayor's pageant was a highly lucrative business and one in which only the most experienced wordsmiths could hope to be employed. Authors such as Anthony Munday, Thomas Middleton, Thomas Heywood, John Webster and Thomas Dekker were some of the most accomplished playwrights of the day but no matter how critically acclaimed their work was by the pundits of London's theatres, the chance to write a pageant for the ever-popular Lord Mayor's Show was an enviable opportunity not to be missed.

Of those who successfully pitched their ideas to the City's commissioners during this competitive period, by far the most prolific was Anthony Munday. Starting his working life as a printer before progressing to writing pamphlets, translations and finally plays, Munday's first involvement in a Lord Mayor's Show is evident in the City's accounts for the year 1602, where he is listed as working on speeches and props. However, his natural talent for the intricacies of pageantry did not remain undiscovered for long. It was Munday himself who was responsible for the aforementioned pageant of 1616, the detailed drawings of which can still be found among the company's papers in their archive at Fishmongers' Hall. He also penned such epics as the 1609 show for Thomas Campbell, entitled *Campbell: The Ironmongers Faire Field*; the 1615 show for the John Jolles, *Metropolis-Coronata*; and the 1618 show for Sebastian Harvey, *Sidero-Thriambos*. However, had Munday not exercised an unusual abundance of diplomacy in the early days of the seventeenth century, his career as pageant writer might never have got off the ground.

When Elizabeth I died in 1603, it fell upon London's Lord Mayor, Robert Lee, along with other state officers and nobility, to invite James of Scotland to take the throne – an accession which saw pageantry begin to thrive. While Elizabeth had been well known for her very public love of theatre, James I, conversely, stood his distance. But, ironically, in the gulf that opened up between the City's celebrations and the Crown, pageantry took a new form in which it celebrated the power and particularly the independence of an increasingly wealthy metropolis. The exception to this was Sir Leonard Holliday's 1605 pageant – the first since James's accession – in which Munday took great care to applaud unification. *The Triumphes of Re-united Brittania*, therefore, took an enthusiastic view of the new king and of a new, united country.

Troya Nova
Then you fair swans in Thamesis that swim
And you choice nymphs that do delight to play

On Humber and fair Severn, welcome him
In canzons, jigs, and many a roundelay
That from the north brought you this blessed day
And in one tuneful harmony let's sing
'Welcome King James, welcome bright Britain's king!'

While extremely supportive of the new king's intentions, Munday's enthusiasm for a wholly joined state turned out to be premature. Thanks to an indecisive Parliament it took until the year 1707 before Scotland, England and Wales became a single state.

By the early seventeenth century, another pageant writer, Thomas Middleton, had caught the eye of the City's band of commissioners. A contemporary of William Shakespeare, after Shakespeare's death in 1616 it was to this highly accomplished and much-praised playwright that the Shakespeare Company turned to adapt the Bard's plays. In 1624, the celebrated Globe Theatre that staged the first performance of Middleton's *A Game of Chess*, which quickly became one of the most watched plays of its time, before being shut down by King James for its political transgression of likening the act of censorship to castration. Subsequently spending a short time in prison did little to harm Middleton's career – with a talent said to encompass a vast array of literary forms including, but not limited to, prose, verse, satire and poetry, Middleton continued to receive support from the City of London. His most lauded pageants, *The Triumphs of Honour and Industry* (1617) and *The Triumphs of Honour and Virtue* (1622) were very different in style to those of his contemporaries. Their appeal, as far as the City commissioners were concerned, was the glorified portrayal of the inner workings of the great metropolis – its endowments, its majestic buildings and its bequests. Central to all of this was the theme which linked industry to wealth and showed that London was proud of its place in the global economy. When Middleton penned the well-received *Industry* he not only paid homage to the guild of George Bolles, the Grocers, but also answered some of the City's fiercest critics, who linked the growth of the City with the decline of the countryside. Subsequently, commissioners took great pains to promote the benefits of trade as they planned future mayoral inaugural shows. Munday's *The Island of Lemnos*, for the Worshipful Company of Ironmongers' Sebastian Harvey (1618), portrayed the many benefits of mining ore – to create implements of navigation, commerce and war – while in 1613 the recently established forts of the East India Company were vividly represented for grocer Sir Thomas Myddelton by five islands artfully garnished with the valuable new culinary commodity – spices – in cinnamon, nutmeg and cloves.

While Middleton's shows were costly to produce – *The Triumphs of Truth*, his 1613 pageant, holds the dubious credit of having been the most expensive of all the renaissance Lord Mayors' Shows (£1,300), his depictions of a City as a sea of business-related prosperity and wealth were in direct contrast to the more pastoral pageants of Thomas Heywood. In the 1630s, six out of seven of the commissioned pageants were given to Thomas Heywood, who chose to link the ideals of the seventeenth-century capital back to earlier classical themes, invoking the myths and traditions of England in the process. For his first pageant of this decade, Heywood reiterates the theme of Elizabeth I's coronation pageant for Lord Mayor George Whitmore in 1631 – a beautiful woman dressed like Summer, sitting underneath a 'faire and flourishing tree', attended by the three theological virtues of

Faith, Hope and Charity. The background to this tableau is the archetypal green and pleasant hill on which is pinned the motto '*Civitas bene Gubernata*' – a city well governed. This linked in splendidly with a former pageant of 1591 for Sir William Web – George Peele's *Descensus Astraeae*, which was primarily concerned with reaffirming the City's love of the Queen, royal glory and ceremonial magnificence.

With romantic depictions of landscapes filled with towers, temples and triumphal arches, the Lord Mayor's earlier pageants embraced a natural wilderness filled with leopards, camels and unicorns; however, as the sixteenth century progressed, the City's pace began to change and this was reflected in its pageants. While the art of pageantry had always been a balancing act – generally speaking between the City and the Crown as the City became more at ease with itself – the context of its pageants also began to shift. Not only was London more at ease with the products of its trades, but it was now able to celebrate itself – its myths, its legends, its heroes and its landscape.

Symbolic, sentimental and striking, the illustrious mayoral pageants of the sixteenth and seventeenth centuries were far from being idle entertainment. For all the elaborate visual spectacle that attended the accession of the new Lord Mayor, the myth and symbolism, particularly when it came to portraying the physical elements of the landscape, were clear for all to see. In the pageant of 1620 for Sir Francis Jones, *The Tryumphs of Peace*, Oceanus paid tribute to the Thames as follows:

> My care that shall be for ever to attend
> Your wealthy bottoms to your coasts apace
> And this my promise I will never end

Water pageants, popular throughout much of this period, were also an ideal way to honour the City's hard-working waterway, and though the exact date this custom began is disputed, we do know that in 1453 Sir John Norman personally bore the cost of building his own barge on which to process from the City to Westminster.

The public, more used to seeing the greying waters of the Thames filled with working vessels, flocked to the waterside to catch sight of the grand mayoral procession, while the watermen of the Thames, well pleased with their unexpected rise in income, wrote the following opening lines to a song in praise of London's imaginative new Lord Mayor:

> Row thy boat Norman.
> Row to thy Lemnan.

In this way water pageants were successfully established, becoming such a popular part of Lord Mayor's Day that skirmishes often broke out as to the order in which the guild barges should progress. It soon became obvious that a strict order would have to be enforced and the following roll was put in place: The Lord Mayor's; the Lord Mayor's Company; Mercers; Grocers; Drapers; Fishmongers; Goldsmiths; Skinners; Merchant Taylors; Haberdashers; Salters; Ironmongers; Vintners; and Clothworkers.

Just as the land pageants had done, the water pageants also became more elaborate as time went on. In 1661, an onlooker to Sir John Frederick's show noted that the water pageant was finer than any that had gone before, with the Lord Mayor processing along the river with a dolphin-drawn sea chariot on which sat the sea-nymph Galatea, behind which followed two pipe-playing

Tritons riding on sea lions. The trend for water pageants continued unabated until 1816, when the popular Sir Matthew Wood opted to return from Westminster in his coach.

Behind all this activity, underscoring the festivals, ceremonies, even the position of Lord Mayor itself, a greater force was at work; behind every Lord Mayor was the successful and influential guild to which the Lord Mayor belonged.

Today there are more than a hundred livery companies in the City of London, but in the earlier days of the City's history much of the wealth within the City was generated by the most influential twelve guilds – namely the Mercers, Grocers, Drapers, Fishmongers, Goldsmiths, Merchant Taylors/Skinners (alternate years), Haberdashers, Salters, Ironmongers, Vintners and Clothworkers. In turn, it was these companies who bore the often weighty expense of organising the pageants – each pageant's content being weighted towards the particular guild to which that year's new Lord Mayor belonged. Increasingly, as the seventeenth century progressed, the City's institutions began to come under attack, particularly from those who believed the City's wealth came at the expense of the rest of the country. To add to this, the City itself suffered an internal schism as the rivalry between the newly powerful merchant citizens and gentry created a vast, insurmountable divide. A period of intense renegotiation of the City's inner relationships followed and increasingly it was the gentry who found themselves side-lined as the tradesmen and the guilds, in their eyes, monopolised the City's affairs. Economically it was the tradespeople, not nobility, who began to negotiate influential positions within London's civic government and who began to benefit from royal concessions; and as the merchants made the City their home, becoming in time dutiful aldermen and Common Councilmen, they gradually came to be seen as positive role models for what an ordinary citizen could achieve. The nobility, meanwhile, moved west. It was a breakdown of relationships that was to be echoed across the country, and in Sir Maurice Abbot's inaugural pageant of 1639, *Londini Status Pacatus*, written by Thomas Heywood, there was an unapologetic cry for peace:

> War, the the unexperienc'd, pleasant showes,
> But they who in the Progessse and the Close
> Shall trace it, know it horrid; 'Tis a time
> Destin'd, to the revenge, and scourge of Crime:
> ... And such a Time is War, and such the throwes
> Our neighbour Nations travel now in; woes
> Quite desperate of delivery; whilst calme Peace
> Prosperity and Plenty, with increase
> Of all concatenated Blessings smile
> With cheerfefull face on this sole-happy Isle.

Though none could have known it at the time, *Londini Status Pacatus* was the last pageant to be shown before the country sunk into the depths of civil war.

In a period when the City's calendar was regularly punctuated by holy days and festivals, the Lord Mayor's Show was far from being the only occasion to provide the City's residents with entertainment. In his 1603 *Survey of London*, contemporary chronicler John Stowe vividly describes the vibrant early-summer celebrations as being a time when bonfires were made, meat, sweet bread and drink were plentiful, and friends and neighbours gathered together to enjoy the festive mood:

In the months of June and July, on the vigil of festival days, and on the same festival days in the evenings, after the sun-setting, there were usually made bonefires in the streets, every man bestowing wood or labour towards them. The wealthier sort, also, before their doors, near to the said bonefires, would set out tables on the vigils, furnished with sweet bread and good drink; and on the festival days, with meat and drink, plentifully; whereunto they would invite their neighbours and passengers also, to sit and be merry with them in great familiarity, praising God for his benefits bestowed on them. These were called Bonefires, as well of good amity amongst neighbours, that being before at controversie, were there by the labours of others reconciled, and made of bitter enemies loving friends; as also for the virtue that a great fire hath to purge the infection of the air. On the vigil of Saint John Baptist, and on Saint Peter and Paul, the apostles, every man's door being shadowed with green birch, long fennel, St. John's wort, orpin, white lillies, and such-like, garnished upon with beautiful flowers, had also lamps of glass, with oyl burning in them all the night. Some hung out branches of iron, curiously wrought, containing hundreds of lamps, lighted at once, which made a goodly show.

If the pomp and pageantry of the Lord Mayor's Show was a flamboyant method of welcoming in the new Lord Mayor while simultaneously showcasing the wealth and splendour of the City, then the Midsummer Watch, while also a much anticipated spectacle in its own right, was also a device through which City officials could demonstrate their power, this time as a conduit through which they kept law and order. While the earliest watches on record date back to the thirteenth century, these appear to have been carried out to protect the City against the annual threat of potentially devastating midsummer fires. As Sheila Lindenbaum explains in *City and Spectacle in Medieval Europe*, 'The mayor's announcement of a ceremonial watch was still accompanied by an order to place a tub of water outside each house in the City.' But if the founding watches were originally a way of mitigating the risk of fire, then, under the command of the Lord Mayor, they soon began to serve the additional function of guarding the City's residents against the threat of criminal activity. Under the command of the mayor, City officials began nightly to send their men to patrol the streets, ensuring that no wrongdoings were being committed. From these early origins, what came to be termed as the 'standing watch' eventually generated a processional 'marching watch', so memorably described by Stowe:

> Then had ye besides the standing watches, all in bright harnes in euery ward and streete of this Citie and Suburbs, a marching watch, that passed through the principal streets thereof, to wit, from the litle Conduit by Paules gate, through west Cheape, by ye Stocks, through Cornhill, by Leaden hall to Aldgate, then backe downe Fenchurch streete, by Grasse church, aboute Grasse church Conduite, and up Grasse church streete into Cornhill, and through it into west Cheape againe,and so broke up. The whole way ordered for this Marching Watch extended to 3,200 taylors' yards of assize. For the furniture whereof, with lights, there were appointed 700 cressets, 500 of them being found by the Companies, the other 200 by the Chamber of London. Besides the which lights, every constable in London, in number more than 240, had his cresset; the charge of every cresset was in light two shillings four pence; and every cresset had two men, one to bear or hold it, another to bear a bag with light, and to serve it; so that the poor men pertaining to

the cressets taking wages, besides that every one had a strawen hat, with a badge painted, and his breakfast.

Perhaps inevitably, given the City's predisposition for being colourfully entertained, it wasn't long before pageants came to dominate the marching watch, giving the City's twelve great livery companies yet another opportunity to showcase their creative talents. Morris dancers, hobby horses, jugglers, gunners and trumpeters were all employed at some point in the processional watches, while in 1522 visiting dignitary Emperor Charles V was duly impressed by the representations of authority and kingship in the Drapers' spectacular pageant of the popular Greek myth of the Golden Fleece. A fable with strong resonance for the Drapers, a ceiling painting of Jason and the Golden Fleece was added to the court dining room of Drapers' Hall on Throgmorton Avenue when renovations took place there in 1869.

If the Holy Roman Emperor was captivated by the City's interpretation of the Golden Fleece, he could not fail to be impressed by the size of the show. According to Stowe, the marching watch incorporated no less than two thousand men, many of whom were captains, sergeants, corporals, gunners, archers and pikemen who processed in a highly ordered configuration around the City's streets.

Waytes of the City, the Mayors Officers, for his guard before him, all in a Liuery of wolsted or Say Iacquets party coloured, the Mayor himselfe well mounted on horseback, the sword bearer before him in fayre Armour well mounted also, the Mayors footmen, & the like Torch bearers about him, Hench men twaine, vpon great stirring horses following him. The Sheriffes watches came one after the other in like order, but not so large in number as the Mayors, for where the Mayor had besides his Giant, three Pageants, each of the Sheriffes had besides their Giantes but two Pageants, ech their Morris Dance, and one Hench man their Officers in Iacquets of Wolsted, or say party coloured, differing from the Mayors, and each from other, but hauing harnised men a great many.

No matter how well attended or entertaining, neither the City's standing watch nor its processional version ever came to completely cast off its prime military function, and the City's turbulent history is littered with occasions when the watch was called for defensive reasons. One of these times was after the execution of the Duke of Buckingham on 17 May 1521, which resulted in many protests from the duke's supporters in the City. In the same month, London's Lord Mayor, Sir John Bruge, found it necessary to urgently call the watch again in an attempt to mitigate the actions of Cardinal Wolsey, who, at the suggestion of Pope Cardinal de Medici, had engaged in the highly provocative and disastrously divisive action of burning Luther's books in the churchyard of St Paul's Cathedral.

While the benefits of keeping law and order in the City were obvious, this did not always stop the Crown from asserting its authority, and from time to time even interfering in the schedule of the midsummer festivities. Frustrated at the City's ever-increasing authority and ideological portrayals of its might, Henry VIII cancelled the Midsummer Watch on a number of occasions in order that entertainments of his own choice could take priority.

The 1539 show is a prime example. Lord Mayor Sir William Hollyes had been due to lead that year's offering but Henry cancelled the event and ordered an assembly of troops in St James' Park instead. London's citizens were denied their midsummer entertainment for another nine long years; it wasn't until Henry VIII died and Edward

VI entered his second year on the throne that at last Lord Mayor Sir John Gresham gave the instruction for the much mourned Midsummer Watch to be revived. This wasn't the first or the last time the Crown was to interfere in the City's arrangements; more cynically, in 1618, Sir Walter Raleigh's execution was purposefully scheduled for the same day as the Sir Sebastian Harvey's show in order that the majority of people's attention might be elsewhere when the ill-fated explorer met his inglorious end.

While England's monarchs often resented the City's grandiose displays of authority, they nonetheless leaned heavily on the City's ability to add weight and dignity to an occasion, requiring the Lord Mayor and City officials to entertain visiting dignitaries, to formally receive royalty from both home and abroad and also to provide grand processions and imaginative pageants (at their own expense) to give colour and a strong civic presence to state occasions. Anne Boleyn's coronation was one such event – though she was very far from being the most popular of Henry's consorts, 29 May 1533 was a day which promised such finery and grandeur that few Londoners could resist gathering on the crowded banks of the Thames to witness the procession. Even by the standards of City dwellers, hardly unfamiliar with the glories of pageantry, the procession for England's new queen must have been a truly memorable sight – the typically dark, greying waters of the Thames became suddenly alive with an abundance of vibrantly coloured flags and banners bearing the immediately recognisable insignia of the guilds. The golden-spotted lions of the Drapers and the Mercers' Maiden both had their part to play, but it was the enormous, fire-blowing dragon (a representation of the red dragon of the Tudor arms) that really stole the show. In keeping with the tradition of royal occasions, the Lord Mayor's barge was covered in red cloth (instead of its usual blue), alongside which sailed the Bachelors' Barge, carrying the most talented music makers of the day. To complete the scene was a crowned white falcon perched atop a golden rock from which were hung bunch upon bunch of red and white roses.

It was in this exalted manner that London's Lord Mayor Sir Stephen Peacock accompanied England's new queen to the Tower, where City chronicler Edward Hall tells us she was received by Henry to the sound of over a thousand guns being fired at the Tower, at Limehouse and from other ships along the Thames.

If we study the activities of London's early medieval Lord Mayors we will find them engaged in many similar activities. In 1236, Andrew Buckerell took his place in the procession of Henry III and his consort Eleanor of Provence as they rode through the thronging streets of the City and into Westminster, escorted by aldermen and no less than 360 citizens, each bearing a cup of either gold or silver, representing the ancient duty of the Lord Mayor to officiate as chief butler at the queen's coronation. In the December of 1381, Lord Mayor John Northampton, along with representatives from the livery companies, rode in ceremonial style to Blackheath to greet Anne of Bohemia, the future wife of Richard II. It is widely documented that Anne was particularly fond of London – could this have been a result of the enthusiastic response to her arrival in the City? According to Vide Herbert's seminal work on the livery companies, the future queen was greeted with an unparalleled number of pageants of great splendour. A large castle formed part of the pageant carried out in Cheapside, while seven minstrels were also employed. Years later, in 1415, Henry V made a triumphant return to the City from Agincourt, where he had successfully fought the final battle of the Hundred Years War in 1415. French captives in tow, he too was met with a magnificent display, this time at the gate tower of London Bridge. Two giants bearing the City keys greeted the jubilant king while artistic depictions celebrating the decisive victory of the Hundred Years War included an antelope holding a sceptre out towards the king, while a majestic lion held aloft the banner of the king. An effigy of St George completed the spectacle – the head of his armour-clad figure adorned with laurel and gems, the widely recognised symbols of victory and wealth. Once again, in the November of 1429 it was Lord Mayor William Estfeld who, along with the City's alderman, rode to Westminster to present the newly crowned Henry VI with the not insubstantial sum of £1,000 to celebrate his coronation. But if London's Lord Mayor's played a pivotal role in the City's religious celebrations, its victories and its royal successions, then they were also a part of its mourning. On 7 January 1806 Lord Mayor Peter Perchard, the aldermen and livery companies of the City sombrely took their places in the magnificent water procession which brought the body of one of Britain's most celebrated figures, Admiral Lord Nelson, from Greenwich to burial at Saint Paul's, accompanied by the sober sound of minute-gun salutes.

Whether the lavishly styled pageants of Lord Mayor's Show, the solemn weight of the coronation, the jubilant return of a triumphant monarch or the simple act of greeting foreign dignitaries into the kingdom, the order in which the City representatives processed was of high importance. In 1575 Haberdasher William Smith recorded in exacting detail the Lord Mayor's return journey from Westminster to the City as they processed by horse from Paul's Wharf. Passing through Cheapside (which had been cleared by beadles), the standards of the City and the Lord Mayor's own company led around eight hundred poor men, marching in twos wearing gowns of blue. Music was supplied by a cornucopia of instruments including drums, flutes and trumpets, and after the pageant had passed came the bachelors, who were to wait on the Lord Mayor. The sheriff followed, as did the Lord Mayor's officers – the common serjeant and the chamberlain. On this occasion, Smith records that around a thousand people attended Guildhall for the customary feast, after which the city officials attended evening prayers at St Paul's – a tradition which was abandoned after the Great Fire of London.

From at least the date of 1585, when George Peele wrote the *Device of the Pageant borne before Woolston Dixie*, to around 1702, it became fashionable to issue a printed account of the Lord Mayor's Show, either as a record of the day's events or possibly as a souvenir, and though rare, some of these still exist. However, these aren't the only physical reminders of the celebrations. Quite often verses appeared in broadside ballads (single pieces of inexpensive paper on which rhymes were printed), which today make for fascinating reading since they offer an unusually candid portrait of the City's chosen mayor and his inaugural ceremony. Traditionally, these were a story in song, and the verses would be printed with the name of whichever tune they could be sung to and reproduced on a large scale to be pasted on lamp posts. Memorised by the population at large, these ditties would then be sung at work and in alehouses. Their down-to-earth observations show that the public were not unaware of the deficiencies of their new chief magistrates, and it's not too difficult to imagine entering the City of London in 1884 after the election of Michael Gibbs to hear the following being sung. It is worth noting, although it will doubtless become clear, that Gibbs's accession to the civic throne was by no means universally celebrated. That Gibbs was suspected of financial irregularity was an issue which raised its head later.

This Lord Mayor's day they haste away
Of every rank and station,
The poor and gay mark what I say,
Of all denominations;
I do declare we've got a Mayor,
We will soon find who's rum'un,
So here's a health to Gobble G—bbs,
The new Lord Mayor of London.

CHORUS.
Some people thought to keep me out,
Oh ! was not it a pity,
But here I am old Gobble G—bbs,
Lord Mayor of London city.
I went to great Westminster Hall,
And as I was returning,
Some roam'd about, and loud did shout,
Gog and Magog is in mourning,
But never mind, they soon will find,
So help my Peter Pompey,
As I'm a Mayor I'll make them stare,
As wild as any donkey.
I boldly stood and conquered Wood,
And flared away like flinders,
With a peck of coals inside my hat,
And my pockets full of cinders.
Some think for to blow their hide,
But they will be mistaken,
There'll be nothing else but sausage fry,
And a little eggs and bacon.

And when I sit as great Lord Mayor,
My words you may believe in,
Every one that is before me brought,
For going out a thieving,
Shall off to Newgate go,
Where such have long resorted,
And stand a chance to have a dance,
Or else to be transported.
Do you think there's any green in me,
You do make such a fuss then,
Oh ! won't I pull up all the randy
Dandy omnibus men,
Fine them to your hearts content,
And almost drive them mad then,
And so help my bob a month in quod,
I will give to every cabman.
The pretty girls who walk the streets,
With their sweet arms a kimbo,
Three times a week shall have a treat,
By popping into limbo.
All drunken swells I'll fleece full well,
And make them play fine capers,
And commit the lot who holloas
Hot smoking baked potatoes.
The City shall be all locked up,
Now take this as a warning,
From past eleven every night,
Till seven every morning,
The policemen all shall orders have,
To take all noisy creatures,

Dog's meat men and barbers clerks,

Snobs and chimney sweepers.

Although you see I am Lord Mayor

Of great big London city,

That I'm not made a Baronet,

I think is a great pity.

Magnay says tt's all my eye,

And Gibby's hopes are blighted,

Oh! won't I ask Sir Bobby Peel,

To try to get me Knighted.

Now while I sit as great Lord Mayor,

I'll make great alteration,

I will make the pig and parson swear,

Of every rank and station.

I will make 'em sing God save the Queen

And to conclude my ditty,

See here comes old Gobble G—bbs,

Lord Mayor of London city.

You will notice the tone of the ballad alters considerably on the 1815 election of Matthew Wood. Sung to the tune of 'The Roast Beef of Old England', this celebratory ode affects a note considerably more accepting.

COME listen awhile I'll not keep you long,

The City Lord Mayor is the theme of my song

Hark ! how his praises resound from the throng

Huzza for the Mayor of the City,

Huzza for the City Lord Mayor

His judgement in Office so well he display'd;

He studied his duties, not show or parade,
Then how could a better Election be made.
Then the present Lord Mayor of the City,
Huzza for the City Lord Mayor.—
His duties extend beyond limits of day,
And often at night thro the City he'll stray,
And Night-mares will frighten, I've heard people say
So will the Mayor of the City,
Huzza for the City Lord Mayor.
The time being come for the choice of Lord Mayor
The City Electors to Guildhall repair;
Determin'd were they, tho' a circumstance rare,
To re-elect Wood for the City,
Huzza for the City Lord Mayor.
Their efforts were crown'd with success in the end
By electing again the City's best f end,
And long may he live their rights to defend.
The present Lord Mayor of the City.
Huzza for the City Lord Mayor.
Impreserving the lives of three poor Irishmen,
His name will be echo'd again and again
Then what friend to justice can ever refrain,
From praising the Mayor of the City.
Huzza for the City Lord Mayor
To Butchers and Bakers, he next turns his eye,
Who have long fleec'd the poor they cannot deny
By charging a price which he proves is too high.
Thanks to the Mayor of the City,
Huzza for the City Lord Mayor,
His name will be handed by history's page;

His actions a model in ev'ry age,

And like him may all, who in future engage,

Deserve the best thanks of the City,

Huzza for the City Lord Mayor.

Then Alderman Wood must sure rule the roast,

Ofall the Lord Mayors that e'er grac'd the post;

Sonow to conclude I will give you a toast.

Here's a health to the Mayor of the City,

Muzza for the City Lord Mayor.

Unusually, Wood was re-elected in 1816, which may have been due to the many improvements he made within the City. Supporting proposals for a new London Bridge, he also openly took a stand against government oppression.

Not only do the broadside ballads provide a unique glimpse into the characters of London's Lord Mayors, they also give us an insight into the populace's opinion of the Lord Mayor's Show. In 1847, these celebratory verses appeared for John Kinnersley Hooper, whose mayoralty later became known for Chartist agitation:

Just listen to my ditty

All classes blythe and gay,

There's such doings in the City

Upon the Lord Mayor's day;

Driving, pushing, clinging,

The like you seldom saw,

Tens of thousands roving

To see the Lord Mayor's show.

Push along keep moving,

Gently, fast, and slow,
Old and young a roving
To see the Lord Mayor's day.
There's barbers, prigs, and sailors,
And merchants in a row,
Coalheavers, dustmen, tailors,
All at the Lord Mayor's show;
Ladies with Polka dresses,
So handy, gay, and fine,
Polka shifts and bustles,
And draggled tails behinds
Ladies mind your lockets,
Or gently off they goes,
Covey's mind your pockets,
I say get off my toes,
The Lord Mayor's show is coming;
A half a pint of gin?
One covey got a stunning
With a peeler's rolling pin.
There's Hooper in the carriage,
Hark how the bells do ring!
It beats a royal marriage,
He looks just like a king.
They tell me that his trade is
When he resides at home,
Dealing with the ladies
In linen rags and bones.
When the hob nails are counted,
Off goes the Lord Mayor's show,
To Guildhall handsome mounted

All classes in a row;
A dinner is provided
For them at the Guildhall,
When their bellies satisfied is,
Why then comes on the ball.
There is herrings, sprats, and muscles,
Fat turkeys, trouts, and eels,
There's Albert and Jack Russell,
Rothschild and Bobby Peel;
There's Stanley and Duke Nosey,
And the Prince of Wales so young,
They invited Vick so cosey,
But she said she couldn't come.
There's old King Gog and Magog,
And Whittington's tom cat,
When some can eat no longer
They will poke it in their hats;
Rothschild eat three pounds of bacon,
Prince Albert eat a duck,
Bob Peel and old Duke Nosay
Eat a large sheep's head and pluck.
When some can eat no longer,
They will tumble on the floor,
And the leavings the next morning,
Will be given to the poor;
And they before they get it
Must be recommended well,
And thousands will be lucky
If they only get a smell.
Said a doctor to a lady,

As thep went along cheapside,
I pray don't be offended marm,
Your garter is untied;
She caught him round the middle.
And him in the gutter rolled.
She broke his nose, and beat him
With a stunning barber's poll.
So push along keep moving,
And mind which way you go,
From every part they are roving,
For to see the Lord Mayor's show.

While these verses show that Lord Mayor's Day was still a widely celebrated event in the mid-nineteenth century, there was no doubt that it was less of a spectacle than in days gone by. In *Dickens's Dictionary of London* (1879), Charles Dickens Jr suggests that the general want of entertainment in general is the reason the show is well-attended. He writes,

The dull monotony, which is one of the saddest features of the life of the hard-working lower orders of London, is relieved by so little in the way of pageant or show, that it is no wonder that the most insignificant mercies are received with disproportionate gratitude. It is necessary to bear this well in mind in endeavouring to account for the popularity of the procession which blocks some of the principal City streets annually on 9 November. One redeeming point may be noticed. There are always plenty of bands and some military display; and there is so little to enliven the usual dinginess of a London November day, that the streaming flags and banners give unwonted life and colour to the dingy scene. It may, after all, be doubted whether he is not the wisest Lord Mayor who relies on the personal attractions of the *personnel* of the City for his show.

Citing 'beery knights in armour, circus elephants and shivery ladies from the back rows of the ballet', Dickens goes on to say that

whatever qualities may be requisite to secure civic honours, the organisation of shows finds no place amongst them. The course of the procession in the City proper, and the inconvenience to which men of business are put during its progress, depends upon the ward of which the Lord Mayor is alderman. In any case, Fleet-Street and the Strand are sure to have all the benefits and all the disagreeables of the show. A single experience will show that it is undesirable to take any trouble to see it twice. The best point of view is from the window of a friend who occupies rooms along the line of route, more especially if he have liberal ideas on the subject of lunch. The kerb-stone can in no way be recommended. The 9th of November is pickpockets' carnival, and one of the very worst mobs in London is that which closes up behind the final escort and follows the procession with howls and horseplay. If more shows were provided for the people – who, after all, may be supposed to require amusement as well as their betters – the Lord Mayor's annual 'march through Coventry' would probably better organised.

Dickens was not the only writer to put forward a less than flattering portrayal of the City's favourite show. Prolific diarist Samuel Pepys witnessed several shows of the 1660s which provided him with varying degrees of entertainment.

On 29 October 1660, the year of the Restoration, Pepys writes,

I up early, it being my Lord Mayor's day (Sir Richard Browne), and neglecting my office, I went to the Wardrobe, where I met my Lady Sandwich and all the children; and after drinking of some strange and incomparably good claret of Mr Remball's, he and Mr Townsend did take us, and set the young lords at one Mr Nevill's a draper in Paul's Churchyard; and my lady and my Lady Pickering and I to one Mr. Isaacson's a linendraper at the 'key' in Cheapside where there was a company of fine ladies, and we were very civilly treated, and had a very good place to see the pageants, which were many and I believe good for such things, but in themselves but poor and absurd.

On Lord Mayor's Day 1663, Pepys gives a further account of the mayoral celebrations when he describes the dinner given at Guildhall after the official ceremonies of the day:

Anon comes the Lord Mayor, who went up to the lords, and then to the other tables, to bid welcome; and so all to dinner. I sat near Proby, Baron, and Creed, at the merchant strangers' table, where tend good dishes to a messe, with plenty of wine of all sorts, of which I drank none; but it was very unpleasin that we had no napkins not change of trenchers, and drunk out of earthen pitchers and wooden dishes ... I expected musique, but there was noone, but only trumpets and drums, which displeased me. The dinner, it seems, is made by the mayor and two sheriffs for the time being, the Lord Mayor paying one half.

Whatever opinions exist about the Lord Mayor's Show, it is

nonetheless remarkable to think that after eight hundred years the show continues to be held and to entertain to this very day. Rich in cultural significance, and the culmination of months of planning and hard work, it is at the very least, as even the acerbic Dickens concedes, 'perhaps a thing to see once'.

8

JUSTICE IN THE CITY
1600–1750

Of all the characters to grace the City's civic throne, the eighteenth century's John Wilkes, Member of Parliament, journalist and sometime outlaw, was by far the most colourful. Variously described as a voracious wit, heady libertine and shameless self-promoter, by the time he ascended to the seat of London Lord Mayor in 1775 he had achieved such a formidable political reputation that even the King of England, George III, was said to have declared to his ministers that he 'would have nothing more to do with that devil Wilkes'. But in an age of heavy censorship it was Wilkes's irascible writings which fuelled a frenzy of public debate, and it was this, as opposed to his political career, that originally made his name. From the very start, Wilkes was linked to the burgeoning cause of liberty of speech and it was his own controversial publication which was to provide the primary platform for these views.

The *North Briton* was first launched on an unsuspecting public in the June of 1762. Highly contentious, its founding issue was notable for its ferocious attack on the Scottish nation, but it was its twelfth offering which led its reckless editor into a highly publicised duel with the highly strung Lord Talbot, whose horsemanship at the coronation he had seemingly insulted.

'I found Lord Talbot in an agony of passion,' Wilkes later wrote.

He said that I had injured, that I had insulted him, that he was not used to being injured or insulted; what did I mean? Did I or did I not write the North Briton? He would know; he insisted on a direct answer – here were his pistols, I replied that he would soon use them, that I desired to know by what right his lordship catechized me about a paper which did not bear my name ... His Lordship insisted on finishing the affair immediately. I told him that I should soon be ready, that I did not mean to quit him, but would absolutely first settle some important business. After the waiter had brought pen, ink and paper, I proposed that the door of the room might be locked, and not opened until our business was decided. Lord Talbot, on this proposition, became quite outrageous, declared that this was mere butchery, and that I was a wretch who sought his life ...

According to Wilkes, Lord Talbot heatedly insisted, 'You are a murderer, you want to kill me; but I am sure that I shall kill you; I know I shall, by God. If you fight, if you kill me, I hope you will be hanged ... I know you will.'

There followed a well-documented rendezvous on Bagshot Heath, of which Wilkes remembered the following:

We then left the inn and walked to the garden at some distance from the house. It was near seven and the moon shone very bright. We stood about eight yards distant, and agreed not to turn round before we fired but to continue facing each other. Harris gave the word. Both our fires were in very exact time, but neither took effect. I walked up immediately to Lord Talbot and told him that I now avowed the paper. His Lordship paid me the highest encomiums on my courage, and said he would declare everywhere that I was the noblest fellow God had ever made.

What Lord Talbot made of this account, taken from Wilkes's memoires, we will sadly never know, but what we can be sure of is that its effect did not harm Wilkes in the least. A fierce advocate of free speech, he in fact started to become recognised as a champion of liberty – opposing figures of authority who, in the class-constricted confines of eighteenth-century England, had previously remained beyond reproach. For this he grew in popularity both with the general public and also with the upper classes. From this point onwards he sought to promote his cause among the leading figures of the day, seemingly wasting no opportunity to improve his situation. Spirited, daring and often reckless, it must have seemed to eighteenth-century Londoners there was never a figure more destined to shine.

The first English-born monarch of the Hanoverian dynasty, George III had taken up his throne in 1760 amid much rejoicing, but among London's leading citizens the celebrations did not last long. Instead of offering his subjects strong and clear leadership, it seemed as though much of his authority was wielded to the increasingly unpopular Earl of Bute, and it was Wilkes's very public opposition to the earl which earned him a place in the hearts of the general public. Once again, the *North Briton* became the chief platform for Wilkes to make his scurrilous attacks on Bute, which he did – at one time even alluding to an improper relationship between Bute and the Princess Dowager of Wales. It wasn't until the *North Briton* reached its forty-fifth issue, however, that Wilkes's forthright editorial style landed him in hot water. On 23 April 1763, a stunned public must have held its collective breath as it read what was to be later termed as Wilkes's libellous commentary on the inept rule of king and the 'despotic' influence of Lord Bute:

The Scots Magazine Monday April 4 1763

The King's Speech has always been considered by the legislature, and by the public at large, as the speech of the minister. It has regularly, at the beginning of every session of parliament, been referred by both the houses to the consideration of a committee, and has been generally canvassed with the utmost freedom, when the minister of the crown has been obnoxious to the nation. The ministers of this free country, conscious of the undoubted privileges of so spirited a people, and with the terrors of parliament before their eyes, have even been cautious, no less, with regard to the matter, than to the expressions of speeches, which they have advised the sovereign to make from the throne at the opening of each session. They well know, that an honest house of parliament, true to their truth, could not fail to detect the fallacious arts, or to remonstrate against the daring acts of violence, committed by any minister ...

This week has given the public the most abandoned instance of ministerial effrontery ever attempted to be imposed on mankind. The minister's speech of last Tuesday is not to be paralleled in the annals of this country. I am in doubt whether the imposition is greater on the sovereign or on the nation. Every friend of his country must lament, that a prince of so many great and amiable qualities, whom England truly reveres, can be brought to give the sanction of his sacred name to the most odious measures, and

33. From a prosperous and well-known family, this is the coat of arms of London Mayor William Hardel, a Magna Carta surety. (Courtesy of Rs-nourse, under Creative Commons 3.0)

34. Taken from the Chroniques de France et d'Angleterre, Book 2, this painting of the Peasants' Revolt depicts the rebel groups meeting outside London as they prepare to invade the City. (British Library)

35. Magnus the Martyr was once the first church to be encountered when approaching the City from the south side of London Bridge. In 1759 the bridge was widened and an archway formed under the tower so the east footway of the bridge could pass under it. Three Lord Mayors are buried here. (© Ben Hatfield)

Left: 36. The unfortunate Richard Gurney, Lord Mayor, knight and baronet, was committed to the Tower of London for supporting Charles I. (© Ben Hatfield)

Right: 37. Lord Kitchener inspected the City of London Volunteers in November 1915, congratulating the Lord Mayor on their fine appearance. Kitchener's statue is located on the south side of Horse Guards Parade. (© Ben Hatfield)

38. One of the many duties London's first mayor, Henry Fitz-Ailwin, undertook was to collect the ransom money for Richard I after the king was taken hostage returning from the Third Crusade. Richard's statue now stands outside the Houses of Parliament. (© Ben Hatfield)

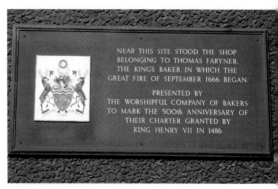

39. One of the most destructive events in the City's history, the Great Fire began in a bakery but soon made up to 10,000 citizens homeless. (© Ben Hatfield)

40. Old Billingsgate Market was designed by Sir Horace Jones and opened by the Lord Mayor in 1877. (© Ben Hatfield)

Left: 41. Thomas Gresham's statue stands outside the City's Royal Exchange. The original sixteenth-century building was described by Pepys as 'the eye of London'. (© Ben Hatfield)

Right: 42. The City Corporation initially provided the land for London's Royal Exchange. Here we can see Thomas Gresham's family emblem, the grasshopper, perched on the top. (© Ben Hatfield)

43. It was once the custom for the Lord Mayor and aldermen to meet at St Paul's Cross at 1 p.m. to hear the sermon on Good Friday. Political sermons were also preached here. (© Ben Hatfield)

55. This column, erected in 2000, marks the spot where the flames of the Great Fire of London were extinguished, thereby saving the historic building Temple Church. (© Ben Hatfield)

56. St Bartholomew the Less is the church of the Haberdashers' Company, to which 1631 Lord Mayor and Royalist Sir George Whitmore belonged. (© Ben Hatfield)

57. Samuel Pepys, Master of the Clothworkers' Company from 1677 to 1678.
(With kind permission of the Worshipful Company of Clothworkers)

58. This watercolour of Ironmongers' Hall was painted by Edward Haywood in 1796. (With kind permission from the Worshipful Company of Ironmongers)

59. 'A Friendly Dialogue Between a Liveryman and a Freeman of the City of London.' (With kind permission of the Worshipful Company of Clothworkers)

A Friendly

DIALOGUE

BETWEEN

A LIVERY-MAN

AND

A FREEMAN

OF THE

City of LONDON.

CONCERNING

The late Proceedings at *Guild-Hall*, in the Election of Sheriffs, and other Officers, for the Year ensuing.

By a true and most sincere Well-wisher to the Peace, Plenty, and Prosperity of this most Antient and Renowned Corporation, and to all the Members and Inhabitants thereof.
BEATI PACIFICI.

London Printed, and are to be Sold by *Richard Baldwin* near the *Oxford-Arms* in *Warwick-Lane*. 1695.

Left: 60. The Vintners' emblem. (With kind permission of the Worshipful Company of Vintners)

Below: 61. The opulent dining hall at Vintners' Hall, by Darren Woolway. (With kind permission of the Worshipful Company of Vintners)

62. The third Royal Exchange was opened by Queen Victoria in 1844. (With kind permission from the Worshipful Company of Mercers)

63. It was the second charter of 1394 which gave the Mercers a common seal. The Mercer Maiden is now the Mercers' emblem. (With kind permission from the Worshipful Company of Mercers)

64. Richard Whittington became master of the Mercers three times, in 1395, 1401 and 1408. (With kind permission from the Worshipful Company of Mercers)

65. Sir Thomas Gresham bequeathed money to the Corporation of London and the Mercers' Company for the foundation, in 1597, of Gresham College. (With kind permission from the Worshipful Company of Mercers)

66. Sir Christopher Wren's memorial to the Great Fire of London was completed in 1677 in 'perpetual remembrance of this dreadful visitation'. The east side of the pillar is inscribed with the names of the mayors in office while the pillar was erected – from Sir Richard Ford Knight in 1671 to Sir Thomas Davies in 1677. (Author's colletion)

67. Described by Sir John Betjeman as 'very municipal, very splendid', St Lawrence Jewry, located next to Guildhall, is the official church of the Corporation of London. (Author's collection)

68. The statue of St Thomas à Becket in St Paul's churchyard once played a key role in the mayoral processions of the Corporation of London. (© Ben Hatfield)

69. In 1914, 1,600 city workers were sworn in by Lord Mayor Sir W. Vansittart Bowater in the dry moat of the Tower. Known as the Stockbrokers Battalion, the men also referred to themselves as the ditchers because they had taken their oath in Tower Ditch. (© Ben Hatfield)

to the most unjustifiable, public declarations, from a throne ever renowned for truth, honour and unsullied virtue.

Lord Ligonier is now no longer at the head of the army but Lord Bute in effect is: I mean, that every preferment given by the crown will be found still to be obtained by his enormous influence, and to be bestowed only on the creations of the Scottish faction. The nation is still in the same deplorable state while he governs, and can make the tools of his power pursue the same odious measures ... A despotic minister will always endeavour to dazzle his prince with high-flown ideas of the prerogative and honour of the crown, which the minister will make a parade of firmly maintaining. I wish as much as any man in the kingdom to see the honour of the crown maintained in a manner truly becoming Royalty. I lament to see it sunk even to prostitution ... Is it possible such an indignity can have happened, such a sacrifice of the honour of the crown of England, as that a minister should already have kissed his Majesty's hand on being appointed to the most insolent and ungrateful court in the world, without a previous assurance of that reciprocal nomination which the meanest court in Europe would insist upon, before the proceeding to an act otherwise so derogatory to her honour?

But Wilkes had not finished yet. Saving his most damning words until the closing paragraphs of his piece, he went on to say,

The Stuart line has ever been intoxicated with the slavish doctrines of the absolute, independent, unlimited power of the crown. Some of that line were so weakly advised, as to endeavour to reduce them into practice: but the English nation was too spirited to suffer the least incroachment on the ancient liberties of this kingdom. The

King of England is only the first magistrate of this country but it is invested by law with the whole executive power. He is, however, responsible to his people for the due executions of the royal functions in the choice of ministers etc. equally with the meanest of his subjects in his particular duty. The personal character of our present amiable sovereign makes us easy and happy that so great a power is lodged in such hands ... but the favourite has given too just cause for him to escape the general odium. The prerogative of the crown is, to exert the constitutional powers instructed to it, in a way, not of blind favour and partiality, but of wisdom and judgment. This is the spirit of our constitution. The people too have their prerogative; and I hope the words of DRYDEN will be engraven on our hearts. Freedom is the English Subjects prerogative.

While the public gasped in awe and horror at Wilkes's latest attack, the authorities acted quickly, consulting both attorney Mr Charles Yorke and solicitor general Sir Fletcher Norton, who issued the damning verdict that the paper was 'an infamous and seditious libel; tending to inflame the minds, and alienate the affections of the people from his majesty, and excite to traitorous insurrections against the government'.

Prosecution, it seemed, was inevitable; and after detaining the printers and all those who had been involved in the production of this perfidious issue, on 29 April 1763 the ministry finally caught up with Wilkes, who confounded the king's messengers by refusing to accompany them. Such spirited resistance was ultimately to no avail. The officers simply returned the next day to seize Wilkes's papers while Wilkes himself was sent to the Tower.

Wilkes's supporters now got to work, and when the case was discussed in Parliament amid scenes of vocal chaos it was decided, by Chief Justice Lord Camden, that Wilkes's arrest was unlawful because he was a member of the House, and Wilkes was duly discharged. The nation's newspapers lapped up the latest instalment of the *Wilkes v Crown* saga, which, like the publication of No. 45, was widely reported. The same paper later added,

> Having been industriously represented as a proceeding wholly new and unusual, it may not be improper to acquaint the public, that upon Mr Wilkes's being brought by Habeas corpus yesterday before the judges of the court of common pleas, they were unanimously of opinion that the warrant for his commitment was in every respect, in point of form, agreeable to former precedents, and warranted by legal determinations; but Mr Wilkes, being a member of parliament, the judges were of opinion, he was entitled to privilege, and thereupon discharged him from his confinement.

Though Wilkes was now free, he was still pursued – this time by the attorney general who pursued him for libel. Undiminished and undeterred, Wilkes refused to cower. Now that he was unable to solicit a printer for the *North Briton*, he established a printing press himself, ignored all correspondence from the attorney general and committed himself to drawing as much attention to his cause as was humanly possible. The quarrel, wrote Woodcock in his comprehensive text on London's Lord Mayors, *Lives of Illustrious Lord Mayors and Aldermen of London*, had now become a national one, and if his adversaries employed the whole force of the government to silence his opposition, Wilkes was no less diligent in enlisting upon his side every kind of force to aid his design of inflicting as much mischief as possible, in a battle which reached fever pitch on 23 November. On this day it was decided that, contrary to the earlier ruling, the privileges of Parliament did not cover libel. This unexpected reversal of the decision granted by the Common Pleas caused such indignation that even Wilkes's political adversary Pitt felt compelled to leave his sickbed to protest Wilkes's cause. But it wasn't only leading figures in the political world who felt bound to make their outrage known.

As Woodcock explains, in London, the ferment was of a dangerous character:

> The sheriffs, pursuant to the vote of the House of Commons, attempted to burn the North Briton at the Royal Exchange; but the mob rose, attacked the hangman, from whose hands they rescued the paper and the sheriffs, assailed on all sides, were only too glad to escape with their lives. This daring outrage provoked still further the anger of Government; the most effectual measures were resorted to for suppressing any further signs of public feeling in the wrong direction, and the House of Commons resolved that the rioters were 'perpetrators of the public peace, dangerous to the liberties of the country, and obstructers of the public justice.'

Wilkes, however, refused to be outdone, launching a counter-attack on the under-Secretary of State, whom he charged with unlawfully confiscating his papers. The ensuing trial took place on 6 December 1763 and played out in Wilkes's favour – not only were general warrants declared to be illegal, but the proceedings against Wilkes found to be unlawful. Wilkes was compensated in the fullest way possible, being awarding £1,000 in damages in addition to payment of his legal costs.

While the jury had found financially in his favour, the episode still cost Wilkes dearly. Early the next year it was decided in the

House of Commons that John Wilkes, Esq., was indeed guilty of writing and publishing the paper entitled the *North Briton*, No. 45, and for this he was expelled from the house.

Wilkes might have lost his seat, but his political ambition was far from diminished and from his new base in France he plotted his return. It took Wilkes nearly seven long years before he was to once again make his mark upon the City of his birth, but in the February of 1768 he returned to London. In the elections of 1768, to the uncontained surprise of all involved, he put himself forward to represent his hometown. Losing by only the smallest of margins served merely to push Wilkes's ambition further still, and, remaining resolutely undeterred, only a few days passed before he put himself forward as a candidate for the Middlesex election – a decision which resulted in little short of mayhem – though from the outset, says Woodcock, his support from the public was clear:

> On the morning of the election, while the irresolution from the court, and the negligence of the prime minister, caused a neglect of all precautions, the populace took possession of all the turnpikes and avenues leading to the hustings, by break of day; and would suffer no man to pass who did not wear in his hat a blue cockade with 'Wilkes and No. 45' on a written paper. Riots took place in the streets, and the carriage of Sir William Proctor, the opposing candidate, was demolished.

This being a time when elections were not limited to a single day, the results were still uncertain at nightfall, though an element of the public made it clear what they wished the results to be. At the thought of the beloved leader of liberty returning to their midst, the Wilkes-supporting populace of London remonstrated in the streets with abandon. While a number of minor incidents occurred in the West End in the early hours of the evening, both Lord Bute and Lord Egmont's houses were later attacked by the mob, who, unable to force their way indoors, left after breaking windows. Even London's Lord Mayor himself, a pronounced anti-Wilkite, did not find himself safe from the fury of the mob. As the violence escalated, the rioters carelessly but purposefully made their way across London to break the windows of the mayoral residence of Mansion House. The Trained Bands, called into action on the say-so of the Lord Mayor, could not quell the violence. Even when Wilkes joined his votes in with Cooke so that they came in together and the ministerial candidate was defeated, the unrest, according to Woodcock, only continued to grow.

At the time it must have seemed impossible for Wilkes to win. Yet without money, time or property to aid him, he beat his opponents, Beauchamp-Proctor and Cooke, by a majority of 485 and 465 respectively. Though the poll was incredibly small by today's standards – just two thousand votes – there was no hint of any irregularity, though many observers found the news of his success difficult to believe: 'It is really an extraordinary event to see an outlaw and exile, of bad personal character, not worth a farthing … immediately carrying it for the principal country,' noted Benjamin Franklin, one of America's founding fathers, while other leading figures mirrored his disbelief. 'No person living, after Wilkes had been defeated in London, would have thought it possible for him to have carried his election for the county of Middlesex,' Lord Camden wrote.

Wilkes had indeed got lucky. While many of his opponents put his success down to the influence of the mob, in reality, when

Wilkes put himself forward for the Middlesex election he was connecting with a population very much dissatisfied with an overly intrusive London rule. The City's loss was their gain.

But while Wilkes had won his seat for Middlesex fair and square, the battle between the ministry and the nation's favourite radical was far from over. Surrendering himself to the authorities, he was promptly sentenced to an imprisonment of twenty-two months along with a £1,000 fine. On Thursday 28 April 1768, from the Court of the King's Bench, Wilkes made the following speech in which he stated he was the victim of ministerial vengeance. The following account, in relation to the republication of the *North Briton* No. 45, appeared in the *Derby Mercury* the next day:

As to the re-publication of the Number of the *North Briton* I cannot see that there is the smallest degree of guilt. I have often read, and examined with Care that famous paper. I know that it is in every part founded on the strongest evidence of facts. I find it full of duty and respect to the person of the king, although it arraigns in the severest manner, the conduct of his majesty's then ministers, and brings very heavy Charges home to them. I am persuaded they were well-grounded, because every one of those Ministers has since been removed. No one instance of falsehood has yet been pointed out in that pretended libel; nor was the word false in the information before the court. I am therefore perfectly easy under every Imputation respecting.

Upon Wilkes's imprisonment his supporters once again rose up from across the country in gestures of goodwill, vying with each other in their expressions of attachment. Says Woodcock:

Upwards of £20,000 were subscribed to form a fund for the composition of his debt and his future maintenance. Tradesmen offered gifts of their choicest ware, and ladies contributed their ornaments to deck the living shrine of liberty. To quote the language of a contemporary writer, 'Until the time of his first election for Middlesex, in March, 1768, through the whole of the year 1769, and even far in 1772 (a long reign for a people's favourite), he was the sole unparalleled political idol of the people, who lavished upon him all in their power it was to bestow, as if to prove, that in England it was possible for an individual to be great and important.' Through them alone a subscription was opened for the payment of his debts and £20,000 was said to have been raised for the purpose, and the discharging his fine. The Society for the support of the Bill or Rights presented him with £300. Gifts of plate, of wine, of household goods were daily heaped upon him. An unknown patriot conveyed to him, in a handsomely embroidered purse, five hundred guineas. An honest chandler enriched him with a box, containing of candles, the magic number of dozens, (45). High and low contended with each other who should most serve and celebrate him. Devices and emblems of all descriptions ornamented the trinkets conveyed to his prison; the most usual was the cap of liberty, placed over his crest: upon others was a bird with expanded wings, hovering over a cage beneath: a motto – 'I love liberty.' Every wall bore his name, and every window his portrait. In china, in bronze, or in marble he stood upon the chimney-pieces of half the houses in the metropolis; he swung upon the sign-post of every village, of every great road throughout the country.

Meanwhile, quick to turn the events of the election into an opportunity for popular entertainment, the ballad writers got to work:

Wilkes & Liberty forever
YOU hearty Britons pray attend,
We hope no o ts ſhall uſurvive,
While we maintain brave forty five.
O rare Wilkes for ever, O rare liberty.
When Mr. W-s did firſt contrive,
To write the number forty five,
It touch'd ſome people to the gall,
But Wilkes defiance bid to all.
Another thing appear'ſt quite ſtrange,
This pamphlet burnt all the Change,
But one a friend we'll not dispute,
He in the fire chuck'd a boot.
The Printer then immediately,
Was ordered to the pillory,
Butthere ſome friends did him ſurround
Colleccted for him many a pound.
Then Mr. Wilkes he did advance,
And took a journey into France,
But by his friends was ſentfor o'er,
To v x them as he did before.
The city we muſt not degrade,
We know their votes depend on trade,
But yet a joke we are free to paſs,
They ſay the mare's become an aſs.
The country then immediately,
Promoted Wilkes to high degree,
And of him they did make no ſcoff,
Like the pyeman now he'll take them off
        (from the National Library of Scotland)

Also appearing at this time was the resoundingly popular 'The
London Petition', sung to the tune of 'The Pilgrim'.

> YOU friends to Britifh freedom,
> Thefe lines I've pell'd pray
> heed'em,
> I wifh you did not need them,
> To urge to Liberty;
> Sine Walkes in prifon lying,
> And minifters are trying,
> To fet us all a crying,
> For the lofs of liberty.
> Each Middlefex elect on,
> Tho' follow'd by rejection,
> Will prove a ftrong affection.
> To Wilkes and liberty;
> Tho' poor wi s is rejected,
> And L—ll is protected,
> He never will be refpected,
> By friends to liberty.
> The London petition,
> Set forch a fad condition,
> Of honeft reputation,
> Of ftabs to liberty;
> It tells you of murders pardon'd;
> By minifters grows hardned,
> Who does not care a fair thing,
> For Englifh liberty.
> May great George give attention,
> To all that it does mention,

of every bafe intention,

To wrong our liberty;

That we might all have reafon,

To join in every feafon,

Sure it is no treafon,

To fing George and liberty.

May forrow ne'er for fake him,

But grips and cholick rack him;

And may the devil take him,

Who wrongs our liberty;

But may each freedom lover,

With happinefs run over,

And may we ftill difcover,

The foes to liberty.

Because of his stalwart opposition to the ruling classes Wilkes forged many alliances throughout his career, and though he was reckless and inclined to mischief there were many in the City who were sympathetic to his cause. When an attempt was made to arrest Wilkes for publishing parliamentary speeches, it was Lord Mayor Brass Crosby, along with Alderman Oliver, who came to his aid, ultimately enduring imprisonment in the Tower for supporting Wilkes's rights. Crosby's justly indignant explanation has subsequently echoed down the ages: 'No power on earth shall seize any citizen of London without me or another alderman.'

In 1774, Wilkes achieved the City's ultimate prize, being crowned Lord Mayor – in a typically extravagant ceremony – and was soon after elected again to Parliament for Middlesex, where he served for sixteen years.

Wilkes, as would be expected, thoroughly enjoyed his new role as London Lord Mayor, not least because of its inherently sociable nature. During his supremacy as the City's chief magistrate, Mansion House was said to have resounded with the sounds of balls and elaborate dinners. However, there was also a great deal of work to be done, and it was now that Wilkes's proclamations about liberty were issued with more force than usual, as we can see by the letters between the Right Hon. the Earl of Hertford, Lord Chamberlain of the King's Household, and the Right Hon. John Wilkes, Lord Mayor of London, printed on 14 May 1775:

April 11, 1775

My Lord,

The king has directed me to give notice that for the future his Majesty will not receive on the throne any address, remonstrance and petition, but from the body corporate of the city.

I therefore acquaint your Lordship with it as chief Magistrate of the City, and have the honour to be, My Lord, your Lordship's most obedient humble servant.

May 2, 1775

My Lord, It is impossible for me to express or conceal the extreme astonishment and grief I felt at the notice your Lordship's letter gave me as Chief Magistrate of the city [that for the future his Majesty will not receive on the throne any address, remonstrance and petition but from the body corporate of the City].

I entreat your Lordship to lay me with all humiliation at the king's feet, and, as I have now the honour to be Chief Magistrate, in my name to supplicate his Majesty's justice and goodness in behalf of the Livery of London, that he would be graciously pleased to revoke and order, highly injurious to their rights and privileges, which in this instance have been constantly respected and carefully preserved by all Royal Predecessors.

Going on to say that the livery of London had proved themselves to be 'zealous friends of liberty', Wilkes then reminds George of the ancient rights of the livery and questions the legitimacy of his actions.

> Your Lordship, I am sure will now no longer suffer a doubt to remain in your mind as to the legality of common halls, or of their extensive powers and therefore I presume to lay claim on behalf of the Livery of London to the ancient privileges of presenting to the king on the throne any address, petition or remonstrance. In this manner have the addresses of the Livery constantly been received both by his present Majesty and all his Royal predecessors, the kings of England. On the most exact research I do not find a single instance to the contrary ... Other rights and privileges of the city have been invaded by despotic Monarchs, by several of the accursed race of the Stuarts, but this in no period of our history. It has not even been brought into question till the present inauspicious era.

Part of Wilkes's letter has, even for Wilkes, an unusually bold tone: 'It cannot escape your Lordship's recollection that at all times, when the privileges of the capital were attacked, very fateful consequences ensued.'

Not only was Wilkes, as London's Lord Mayor, prepared to defend the rights of his own electorate, but he also played a crucial role in the run-up to the war with America, becoming increasingly vocal and active in supporting the colonists' cause:

On 22 August 1775 heralds proclaimed from the steps of the Royal Exchange that his royal majesty would on the next day make a proclamation. Knowing what was coming Lord Mayor Wilkes forbade the attendance of any City official except the town crier and, in defiance of custom, would not lend horses to the heralds. As expected George III proclaimed the colonists to be 'open and avowed rebels.' He demanded full attention and information about all persons who shall be found carrying on correspondence with, or in any manner or degree aiding or abetting the persons now in open arms and rebellion against our government.

John Wilkes: The Scandalous Father of Civil Liberty by
Arthur Cash

At this point it was now difficult in the extreme for anyone to even mention support for Americans, but Wilkes decided he would try it out: 'Wilkes tested the waters in a meeting with the Common Council on 29 September 1775 and read them a letter from John Hancock, president of American Congress. He urged the City of London, which he called the "patron of liberty" to work for peace but the livery was too afraid to reply, though they did send the letter to the newspapers.' Thus, we see in the *Stamford Mercury* on 5 October 1775 the following report:

Mr Wilkes then came forward and acquainted the Livery, 'that he had received a letter from the Continental Congress; that it was addressed through him to the Livery of London and was signed John Hancock. Moved, that the letter be read.'

Passed in the affirmative. Mr Wilkes read it.

'My Lord, Permit the Delegates of the People of the twelve ancient Colonies to pay your Lordship and the very respectable body of which you are head, the just tribute of gratitude and thanks, for the virtuous and unsoliticited resentment you have shewn to the violated rights of a free people. The City of London, my Lord, having in all ages approved itself the patron of Liberty and the support of just Government against lawless tyranny and oppression, cannot fail to make us deeply sensible of the powerful aid our cause must receive from such advocates. A cause, my Lord, worthy the support of the first City in the World, as it involves the fate of a great Continent and threatens to shake the foundations of a flourishing, and until lately, a happy empire.

North America, my Lord, wishes most ardently for a lasting connection with Great Britain on terms of just and equal liberty; less than generous minds will not offer, not brave and free ones be willing to receive.

A cruel war has at length been opened against us, and whilst we prepare to defend ourselves like the descendents of Britons, we still hope, that the mediation of wise and good citizens will at length prevail over despotism and restore harmony and peace, on permanent principles, to an oppressed and divided empire. We have the honour to be, my Lord, with great esteem, Your Lordship's Faithful friends and fellow subjects.

By order of Congress. Philadelphia July 8 1775.

Wilkes was unimpressed by the lack of support for the colonists and, in keeping with his usual style, did not hesitate to make his feelings known. His support for the principles of liberty, did, however, win him a huge following in America, where he came to be seen as the figurehead for all those who found themselves marginalised. Colonial newspapers all but buzzed with information about Wilkes's continual exploits on their behalf and two places in America – Wilkes-Barre in Pennsylvania and Wilkesboro in North Carolina – even took their name from the infamous author of No. 45. At one point, the citizens of Virginia and Maryland resolved to send Wilkes forty-five hogsheads of tobacco while forty-five women in Massachusetts joined to spin American linen to protest British politics. America, it seemed, had not forgotten Wilkes, and the phrase 'Wilkes and Liberty' was to be heard as much in the colonies as it was at home. Boston trader John Hancock named a ship *The Liberty* while others invited him to live in America. Most, however, thought they would be best served by his support from within the English nation.

Meanwhile, Wilkes refused to dampen his outspoken nature, and when the City livery met to elect Sawbridge as his mayoral successor Wilkes bluntly criticised the war as 'bloody, expensive and a threat to liberty'. In his stepping-down speech he further attacked ministerial plans to establish what he called 'despotism in New England and Popery in Canada', but public opinion in the City was changing fast; after Wilkes's failure to secure election in 1776 to the widely coveted and hugely lucrative post of City Chamberlain, the setback was widely attributed to his tireless support of the colonial cause.

At a time when London was great, the City was blessed with an abundance of spirited Lord Mayors, of whom William Beckford was another. Twice serving the office of chief magistrate, once in 1762 and again in 1769, it appears that with his duties in the House of Commons, being an officer of militia, provincial magistrate and alderman of London, he had spread his not inconsiderable talents rather thinly. In the City election of 1761, the accusation was made that he had not duly attended his duty as an alderman, and at a meeting of the livery for the nomination of representatives, Mr Beckford attended that he might justify himself:

Gentlemen of the livery and fellow citizens, I thought it my duty to attend here this day, both in justice to you, and to your faithful, humble servant. I had been informed, and my present experience convinces me I was truly informed that a very unfavourable opinion had gone forth against me, amongst my late worthy constituents permit me to say, gentlemen, with the boldness becoming an honest man, that I have not deserved it. It has been my chief pride to be a representative of the first city in the world and I shall relinquish such an honour with concern and mortification, but I will not flatter you in order to obtain a continuance of it. It is my duty to speak out and act as I ever have done with openness and integrity. My abilities may not be equal to those of many other gentlemen who you may choose to represent you; but I defy you to find anyone who will serve you with more zeal and attention than I have done.

Memoires of William Beckford of Fonthill, by William Beckford

A rousing burst of applause filled the air in response to this spirited defence, and he was declared Lord Mayor on St Michael's Day 1762, promising to discharge his duties to the best of his abilities and with dignity and weight.

Such was the charming vigour of this popular man that in 1770 he was elected for a second term on the City's civic throne. Citing his advanced years, he stoutly declined to accept the honour but later relented, penning his acceptance to the existing Lord Mayor Samuel Turner, Esq. with the following words:

My Lord Mayor,

I cannot resist the importunate request of my fellow citizens; their desires have overcome resolutions that I once thought were fixed and determined. The feeble efforts of a worn-out man to serve them can never answer their sanguine expectations. I will do my best, and will sacrifice ease and retirement – the chief comforts of old age – to their wishes.

I will accept of the office of Lord Mayor, I shall hope for the assistance of your Lordship and my brethren of the Court of Aldermen; the advantage and good effects of their advice were experienced on many occasions during my late mayoralty by your Lordships' most obedient and faithful humble servant. William Beckford.

While Beckford's official accession celebrations were said to surpass all others, the generous side of his nature did not allow him to forget the City's poor says Woodcock:

On the day on which he was sworn into office he ordered to be distributed to the parish of St Anne, Soho, to every poor man a leg of mutton, a half-peck loaf, three pounds of potatoes and half-a-crown in money; to every poor woman six pounds of beef, one quartern and one threepenny loaf and one shilling and sixpence in money, and to every indigent family one guinea.

Beckford certainly celebrated in style, but his larger-than-life status was not to last. He expired during his mayoralty and was succeeded by Barlow Trecothick.

If Beckford was known as much for his generosity as anything else, then Robert Waithman (1823) played a laudable role in enhancing civic and religious freedom; an obelisk erected opposite his house in Farringdon is a reminder of how much he had done.

In terms of permanently shaping the experiences of the citizens of London, though, for the last words we must return to Wilkes, the rakish Lord Mayor whose name, said that great orator

Gladstone, 'whether we choose it or not, must be enrolled among the great champions of English freedom'.

The *Bucks Herald* on Saturday 5 November proved this point by publishing an editorial many years after Wilkes's death in 1797. Of the often flamboyant member for Aylesbury, the paper wrote,

George the Third had been taught by his mother and by Lord Bolingbroke that he should be a king in fact as well as in name. He was told to espouse no party but to govern like the common father of his people. The tragedy was that he never wholly learned his lesson, for by striving to govern 'without party' he made the Cabinet a mere instrument of the Royal will and Parliament dependant on the king's purse. It was this system of favouritism and corruption, this system of harnessing the sovereign parliament to the chariot of royal ambition that aroused the anger of Edmund Burke and raised a state of ferment in the nation. In the ensuing conflict the people might indeed have triumphed over their rules, but democracy in 1765 stood for little beyond the mob. Men had died for Hampden; but it would be fantastic to die for Mr Wilkes.

Nevertheless the folly of the king opened up a career for this Mr Wilkes and thus gave the first impetus to the movement for popular rights. Nor were the nation's grievances insignificant. Corruption was practised everywhere, and parliamentary seats were advertised in the newspapers. In one letter to Lord North the king admits that the last general election cost near £50,000 to the Crown and in another letter George says: 'If the Duke of Northumberland requires some gold pills for the election it would be wrong not to give him some assistance.' But bribery was not the only cause of the national ferment and the Government's persecution of Wilkes gave additional force to the cry that justice was perverted, Parliament a subject for ridicule and the country in greater disorder than at any other time ... Before his death in 1797 Wilkes had fought a great fight against arbitrary power in his own land, and had initiated many of the reforms that ultimately were embodied in the famous Reform Bills of the next century. The inspiration of his example, it has been truly said, passed across the Atlantic and having helped to precipitate the War of Independence, returned as an even fiercer spirit to provoke the cataclysm of the French Revolution.

It remains to discover what sort of man he was, the paper continued, although it was undoubtedly true he had a fascinating manner. He 'could talk away his face in half an hour' and 'could beat the handsomest fellow in England in contest for a lady's favours if he had a fair start'. Of one of the greatest agitators of the eighteenth century, Gibbon, the great historian, generously concluded, 'I scarcely ever met with a better companion. He has inexhaustible spirits, infinite wit and humour and a great deal of knowledge.'

9

REFORM AND RIOT
1750–1900

In the early days of April 1856, Lord Mayor Sir David Salomans was to be found in the council chamber at Guildhall poring over a hastily assembled report from his sheriffs, Mr Alderman Kennedy and Mr Alderman Rose. After deliberating over its contents for many minutes, Salomans then entered into a long conversational debate with members of the court. Unable to reach a decision, the meeting was adjourned until the following week. The dilemma was not easy to solve. Involving an unsavoury incident at the notorious prison of Newgate, it was an unfortunate occurrence which struck terror and fear into all who heard it recounted.

Today, looking at the highly polished exterior of London's most famous criminal court – the Old Bailey – it is difficult to imagine that once, in its place, stood the most widely feared and notorious prison in the country, reserved for what were seen as the most hardened of criminals. In reality, many of the prisoners who were forced to endure the cramped and unsanitary conditions were guilty of nothing more than theft or counterfeit, but this didn't prevent the convicts exciting the general condemnation of the populace as a whole, as did the prison itself (in the early eighteenth century the very smell of it was said to sour the streets of London).

It is perhaps unsurprising to realise the horror elicited by any mention of Newgate, particularly in the days before prison reform. However, nineteenth-century City dwellers had ample reason to fear the squalid jail, for it was partly its notorious gallows, set in a side street, where many of London's prisoners met their inglorious end. It was these gallows, too, which were the scene of the aforementioned event which had prompted Alderman Sidney to remark to the Court of Aldermen just that Tuesday morning, 'I see from several of this morning's journals there is a great feeling in the public mind respecting it and certainly never in my life have I read a more horrible one than the one which describes the execution of yesterday.'

Newspapers up and down the country reported widely on the affair, which must have been the most distressing case Salomans had to deliberate on during his time in office, with the description in the *Huddersfield Chronicle* being particularly exacting. Describing the events of Saturday 5 April 1856 as 'one of those dreadful spectacles, happily now of rare occurrence', the *Chronicle* went on to detail the incident at the public execution of William Bousfield, which took place on Monday morning in front of the gaol of Newgate. Bousfield had been convicted of the horrific attack and seemingly motiveless murder of his wife (there were also three indictments against him for murdering his three children). Immediately after the crime was committed he turned himself in to the Bow Street police, was convicted, sentenced and incarcerated in Newgate, where, on the night before his execution was scheduled to take place, he attempted to end his own life by throwing himself into the lit fireplace in his cell.

Suffering from burns around his face and becoming overcome with listlessness, by the time Bousfield's execution was to take place the convicted man was unable to walk from his cell and had to be carried outside by prison officials.

After the customary signal from the sheriff, the execution party processed to the scaffold at Debtors' Door under the expectant gaze of around four thousand onlookers. It was noted that Calcraft, the executioner, was emitting a strong sense of anxiety as the party approached, though he could hardly have guessed at the horrors to follow: 'Scarcely two seconds had elapsed before Bousfield exhibited convulsive strength and power to the astonishment of all who had seen his apparent utter prostration for the previous hours,' the *Chronicle* reported.

> The sounds of the falling drop had scarcely passed away when there was a shriek from the crowd of 'he is up again' and, to the horror of every one, it was found that the prisoner, by a powerful muscular effort, had drawn himself up completely to the next level of the drop. His shoulders and arms were raised upwards, his legs being thrown in various directions to obtain a footing, in which he soon succeeded, by placing his right foot on the right edge of the scaffold, and by an extraordinary effort succeeding in placing his left foot close to it.

Apparently, the terrified executioner at this point ran from the scene, though with Bousfield's struggles becoming evermore fretful the sheriffs and in particular Mr Alderman Rose became so distressed that they entreated Calcraft to return. His extraordinary behaviour was later explained by the paper, which ended its report as follows: 'To account in some manner for the extraordinary conduct of Calcraft it appears that on Sunday he had received an anonymous letter advising him to go to the Horse Guards and get a helmet to wear on the occasion as the Kent Street roughs were determined to shoot him to put an end to any more executions.'

Even in a city well used to the barbaric scenes of public executions, the idea of an executioner departing the scene before his work was done aroused indignation and horror, and Salomans was now obliged to attend to the matter in unison with the gaol committee.

As chief justice for the City, it is perhaps inevitable that London's Lord Mayors are sometimes seen as legitimate targets for wronged individuals who are seeking public redress. Such was the case for the unfortunate new mayor Sir John Knill, whose inaugural festivities in November 1909 were unceremoniously disrupted by persons wishing to draw attention to their increasingly well-managed Suffragette cause. On Wednesday 10 November, the *Dundee Evening Telegraph* reported the shocking event:

The Lord Mayor's banquet in the Guildhall, London, last evening was interrupted – spoiled, as far as many of those present were concerned – by one of the most daring outrages of which the women at present suffering from collective hysteria have thus far been guilty.

A Suffragette incident was reported to have occurred during the reception. A woman in the evening toilet presented herself and is said to have attempted to gain admission on re-presenting that she had lost her ticket. While an attempt was being made to establish her identity and claim to admission, Mr Churchill arrived. The intruder made a dash for the Right. Hon gentleman, but was held back and had to content herself with shouting out some opprobrious epithets, and haranguing Mr Churchill for his ill-treatment of women. She was at once ejected.

The Lord Mayor rose to propose the toast to 'His Majesty the King'. He had not spoken a dozen words when – crash! A missile of some sort came through one of the stained glass windows – the window above the Wellington Statue, a few feet from the gallery in which were the Maids of Honour. A large hole was made in the top of the beautiful stained-glass picture, and cries of 'votes for women' could be heard from the outside.

It is difficult to describe the effect on the men and women in the Guildhall, the *Telegraph* continued:

Excited conversation completely drowned the voice of the Lord Mayor.

Mrs Asquith, who sat at the right of the Lord Mayor looked very frightened and angry. Her husband who must by now be so used to this kind of outrage as to expect it everywhere, had an expression like that of the smile on a figure of carved marble. The Maids of Honour were evidently in a condition of extreme alarm.

The lord mayor in an admirably steady voice, went on with his remarks. The toast to the king was drunk, and then a toast to the Queen and the rest of the Royal Family.

The two women were taken to Moor Lane Police Station.

In a case which widely caught the public's imagination, on Thursday 11 November the *Yorkshire Post and Leeds Intelligencer* adorned its editorial on the sentencing of the two women with the headline 'The suffragette outrage at the Guildhall' before going on to give the following account:

> The two suffragettes who were concerned in the Guildhall incident on Tuesday night at the Lord Mayor's banquet came before Alderman Johnston yesterday. Their names were Amelia Brown who was described as of 'no occupation' and Alice Paul, student, and both gave 4, Clement's Inn – the head quarters of the Women's Social and Political Union – as their address. They were charged with wilfully breaking a stained glass window and with being found on enclosed premises for an unlawful purpose. On Brown was found a bottle of milk, and on Paul at stomache-pump, which it is believed, they intended to present to the Prime Minister as an illustration of the forcible-feeding methods.

> The Alderman: What have you to say to the charge?
> Miss Brown: I did it as a political protest against our political laws.
> The Alderman: What have you to say, Paul?
> Miss Paul: I have broken no moral law.
> The Alderman: I cannot listen to this. What have you to say to the charge of breaking the window?
> Miss Paul: It was to justify our motive.
> Miss Brown; I do not see how you can convict me when I am not recognised by the law as being alive.

> The alderman said he could not see how these hysterical women could expect to promote the advancement of their cause by such conduct as damaging historic buildings in this way. Each defendant would be fined £5 and £2.10s costs, or one month's hard labour. They were both removed to the cells.

This was neither the first nor the last dealing London's Lord Mayors would have with the Suffragettes. On 11 May 1909, Mr Asquith and Mr Winston Churchill were guests of the Lord Mayor for a luncheon to celebrate the newly created Port of London Authority at Mansion House when they were accosted by suffragettes demanding to give them the vote. This, it transpired, was a mere precursor to the main event, which was the launching of rockets outside the Houses of Parliament later that same day.

The Suffragette movement had started in 1866, but it wasn't until 1905 that it became increasingly focused on direct action as a way to achieve results, some of which were tried in the Old Bailey. Emily Wilding Davison was prosecuted for damage to property and arson for placing a box of matches and other dangerous substances in a Post Office letter box on 9 January 1912, while on 14 May 1912 Emmeline Pankhurst was imprisoned for nine months for unlawfully and maliciously damaging property. The following year, under the same charge, she was sentenced to three years' penal servitude.

Perhaps the most famous trial to take place in the Old Bailey was the case of William Penn and fellow Quaker William Meade who, in 1670, were both arrested in Gracechurch Street, London, for the act of preaching. It wasn't the first time Penn had been arrested; in the September of 1667 the future founder of the province of Pennsylvania had been detained at a meeting of Quaker Friends, an assembly which was in direct contravention of the Conventicle Act of 1664, which made it illegal for groups of more than five people to worship together (with the exception of Church of England services). The Act stated that

if any person of the age of Sixteene yeares or upwards being a Subject of this Realme at any time after the first day of July which shall be in the yeare of our Lord One thousand six hundred sixty and fower shall be present at any Assembly Conventicle or Meeting under colour or pretence of any Exercise of Religion in other manner then is allowed by the Liturgy or practise of the Church of England in any place within the kingdome of England Dominion of Wales or Towne of Berwicke upon Tweede, at which Conventicle Meeting or Assembly there shall be five persons or more assembled together over and above those of the same Household, then it shall and may be lawfull to and for any two Justices of the Peace of the County Limit Division or Liberty wherein the offence aforesaid shall be committed, or for the Cheife Magistrate of the place where such offence aforesaid shall be committed (if it be within a Corporation where there are not two Justices of the Peace) And they are hereby required and enjoyned upon proofe to them or him respectively made of such offence either by confession of the party or Oath of Witnesses, or notorious Evidence of the Fact (which Oath the said Justices of the Peace and Cheife Magistrate respectively are hereby impowered and required to administer) to make a Record of every such offence.

Penn and Meade were duly put on trial, and when Penn demanded to see a written copy of the indictment against him his request was denied. He subsequently pleaded 'not guilty', effectively calling into question the validity of the charge against him. The day after Penn had questioned the legitimacy of the proceedings, both he and Meade were fined forty marks for the offence of not removing their distinctive hats in court. Citing rights afforded to citizens in the Magna Carta, the pair appealed but their remonstrances were ignored. On being accused by the Lord Mayor of disobeying not only martial power but civil also, Penn responded,

It is a great mistake; we did not make the tumult, but they that interrupted us: The jury cannot be so ignorant, as to think, that we met there, with a design to disturb the civil peace, since (1st) we were by force of arms kept out of our lawful house, and met as near it in the street as their soldiers would give us leave; and (2dly) because it was no new thing (nor with the circumstances expressed in the indictment), but what was usual and customary with us: it is very well known that we are a peaceable people, and cannot offer violence to any man.

The court's recorder then, unusually, put it to the jury that they should find Penn and Meade guilty, to which Penn objected:

It is intolerable that my jury should he thus menaced: Is this according to the fundamental laws? Are not they my proper judges by the Great Charter of England? What hope is there of ever having justice done, when juries are threatened, and their verdicts rejected? I am concerned to speak, and grieved to see such arbitrary proceedings. Did not the lieutenant of the Tower render one of them worse than a felon? And do you not plainly seem to condemn such for factious fellows, who answer not your ends? Unhappy are those juries, who are threatened to be fined, and starved, and ruined, if they give not in Verdicts contrary to their consciences.

Four of the jurors declined to act as the recorder had suggested, and instead of being found guilty of an 'unlawful assembly' the pair were instead found guilty of the much lesser offence of 'speaking in the street'.

The magistrate, incensed at the jurors' rebuff, demanded they be 'locked up without meat, drink, fire and tobacco'.

Eventually released on a writ of habeas corpus (a summons with the force of a court order), the jurors then sued the Lord Mayor and City Recorder in a successful case which made legal history when it was concluded that 'judges may try to open the eyes of the jurors but not to lead them by the nose':

Instead, of accepting their verdict as good in law, and for the true decision of the matter, according to the Great Charter (that constitutes them proper judges, and which bears them out with many other good laws, in what they agreed to, as a verdict, the court did most illegally and tyrannically fine and imprison them, as in the trial was expressed. And that notwithstanding the late just resentment of the House of Commons, in judge Keeling's Case, where they resolved, 'That the precedent and practice of fining, and imprisoning of juries, for their verdicts, were illegal.' And here we must needs observe two things.

1st. That the fundamental laws of England cannot be more slighted, and contradicted in any thing (next Englishmens being quiet destroyed) than in not suffering them to have that equal medium, or just nay of trial, that the same law has provided, which is by a jury.

2d. That the late proceeding of the court, at the Old Bailey, is an evident demonstration, that juries are now but mere formality, and that the partial charge of the Bench must be the verdict of the jury; for if ever a rape were attempted on the consciences of any jury, it was there. And indeed the ignorance of jurors of their authority by law, is the only reason of their unhappy cringing to the court, and being scared into an Anti-Conscience Verdict, by their lawless threats.

Lord Mayor Starling, however, refused to be deterred and the following year arrested Penn again for preaching without taking an oath.

Apprenticeship matters also provided a great deal of business in the City courts, largely because, in a city which leaned heavily on its trades and crafts, the apprentice system was a key part of the employment structure. Even before the City's first records for apprentices exist, it is safe to assume that the apprentice system was common – if only in the tradition of trades passing from father to son. The medieval City, however, tightly regulated the relationship between master and apprentice – a decision that kept its courts busy in the extreme. Today a rare letter survives from John Evans to his attorney in the Lord Mayor's Court. Evans was suing his master, Richard White, in 1695.

Sir, I would desier you to cleare me from my Master for I am a frade that he will kill me if that I stay with him any longer he has bete me so much that I am not able to stay with him he did bete me and made me all of a gore blood and stompt upon me and drag'd me upon downe so much that my mother thought that he had kild me that I am a frade to stay and a grate many times he dus a buse me he stompt upon my beley and bete me after a gros maner and now my mother is dead I am afrade that he will kill me now I have no body to stand my frind now he will not give what he promost me now when my mother was dead he would not give me my cloths to go to the berin I was faute to buy cloths my self and he did lock me up and made me give him forty shillings before he would let me go oute of the roome. I am you servant to command, John Evanes.

London Metropolitan Archives ref. CLA/024/08/056

On the morning of 2 June 1780, St George's Fields was the focal point for the gathering of a large crowd who were to march to Parliament with a petition to repeal the Catholic Relief Act of two years earlier. The primary aim of the bill was relatively innocuous – it had been designed to swell the ranks of the army with English Catholics, which at that point was at war with America. However, a pervasive uneasiness remained, to the point that Lord George Gordon, who led the Scottish campaign, decided to march to the Commons with a petition of around 44,000 signatures calling for repeal, an act which resulted in more than six days of disorder across London. Catholic churches were targeted, along with such City institutions as the Bank of England and Newgate prison. But certain high-profile individuals also found themselves under attack. Say Ian Haywood and John Seed in *The Gordon Riots: Politics, Culture and Insurrection in Late Eighteenth-Century Britain*:

> In the first phase there was a series of attacks on Catholic chapels and private houses in various parts of London, especially around Moorfields, an area adjoining the City of London that contained many Irish workers. The most high-profile target was a rich silk merchant named Malo. Having been refused assistance by Bracklet Kennett, London's Lord Mayor, Malo watched his house and its contents suffer the same fate as all the Catholic chapels in the area; even his beloved canaries were immolated as 'Popish birds'.

Other individuals also found themselves at the centre of the fray. Says Haywood:

> Other targets included prominent political figures suspected of Catholic sympathies, including Sir George Savile, who sponsored

the Catholic Relief Act, and Lord Mansfield, the Lord Chief Justice.

The burning of Savile's house in Leicester Fields (present-day Leicester Square) was so intense that it illuminated the night sky, an anticipation of the larger conflagration to come.

In the recriminations that followed, many questions were asked: why had the City of London not done more to halt the protest? Why had ordinary citizens been forced to side with the mob or become a target themselves? Says Haywood: 'One consequence of the "great supineness …", in the king's words, was that many Londoners could only appease the mob by wearing blue cockades and either shouting "No popery" or chalking the same phrase on their front doors.' All in all, 285 citizens died and, says Haywood, during the riots, 'a total of more than 450 people had been arrested, and of these 160 went forward for trial at the Old Bailey Southwark, or Guildford. Eighty-five were found not guilty, but twelve were imprisoned and another was whipped, whilst sixty-two were sentenced to death, though in the end, only twenty-five were hanged.'

The *Scots Magazine*, on Saturday 1 July 1780, ran the following article making public the details of the trial:

The Recorder gave his charge to the grand jury in the court of session at the Guildhall, which was greatly crowded on Monday, June 26 – He said he should not think he had acquitted himself in the discharge of his duty, if he did not endeavour to throw out some hunts whereby the gentlemen might understand the nature of the extraordinary business that would come before them. He then entered into a discrimination of the offences recently committed and gave a description of the crimes. The grand jury (he said) should distinguish between misdemeanors and felonies. Those who directed their attention to any particular chapel, were guilty of misdemeanour or felony, according to the part they acted: and those who combined for a general destruction, were guilty of high treason against the State. The learned Serjeant reprobated the proceedings of the lawless rabble in terms of great indignation. He compared them to the havock which a conqueror makes in an enemy's country; and said, the devastations lately made were astonishing, and terrible in their effects. After touching on the late dreadful scenes with some energy, he desired the jury would blot them from their memories when they cam upon their duty, and decide without the smallest prejudice; they were to receive and consider evidence with caution, and particularly to remember the confusion of the times, which was such as would render it highly incumbent in their testimony. On the one hand, the grand jury were to be the guardians of the liberty of the subject, and to prevent improper motives having an influence to overturn the principles of fair and impartial justice taking place towards every man charged as a public offender. It was there province also to bring criminals of so singular a degree to the bar of Justice, that they may be dealt with according to their deserts. They were to act with firmness and impartiability and regardless of threats and without favour or affection. Having said much more on the subject the Recorder concluded with thanking them for coming forward with alacrity at this particular period to perform a very disagreeable and troublesome office, not altogether free from the most serious danger.

In addition to the Lord Mayor acting as chief justicar for its numerous courts, another privilege the City of London enjoys is the right to its own military, which in the very earliest times

– before standing armies or even the police were thought of – consisted of what were known as the Trained Bands. Relied on to keep law and order, these trained bands, under the jurisdiction of London's Lord Mayor, were ordinary men who fulfilled a statutory requirement to defend their City in times of crisis. The Militia Act of 1558 resulted in a bona fide militia being put in place across the country, but historian Ian Beckett dates the creation of these militia groups to the much earlier date of between the seventh and ninth centuries. Stating that the militia, the oldest of all auxiliary, had their beginnings in the 'military obligations imposed on the freemen in the Anglo-Saxon kingdoms such as Kent, Murcia and Wessex', Beckett explains that this expectation for action in times of emergency was later to be made law under the Statute of Westminster 1285. In *A History of the British Standing Army* by Clifford Walton, Walton also points out that

at least as early as 1512 it had been requisite to pass an Act ordering every male over seven and under sixty to be practised in the bow at the Public butts continually; and in the Instructions for Musters and Arms issued by order of the Privy Council in 1623 that the Non-Commissioned Officers of the Trained Bands (or Militia) were to exercise their several files with the musquet 'upon Sundays after evening prayer and upon Holidays (as it hath been formerly used for the Bow)', and that the Officers were to exercise the whole parade 'once in a month or six weeks'.

The rules, says Walton, were as follows:

Each person in the County whose estate was equivalent to £500 a-year (or a personal estate in money and goods of the value of

£6,000, exclusive of house-furniture) was liable to furnish 'a horse, horseman, and arms'. Each person having an estate of the value of £50 a-year (or personal estate of £600 value exclusive of stock upon the soil) was bound to find a foot soldier and arms. Persons holding estate of intermediate value were to pay a proportionate quote towards finding one horse soldier for every aggregate of such estates amounting to the fixed standard; and in like manner, the lesser holders were conjointly to maintain foot-soldiers, the liability of some being limited to as little as one-tenth of a soldier.

Those who found the men were to furnish them with a specified quantity of ammunition, and were also to find pay for them at the daily rates of two shillings for a Horse-solider and one shilling for an infantry soldier; but there was no prohibition against serving in person.

The muster-days were not to exceed fourteen in the year; and no man could be compelled to serve out of the kingdom in any case, and not even out of his own County, except in the case of invasion or civil war.

According to legislation in the time of Henry IV, ordained clergy were exempt from the demands of this early form of military service, but for all other eligible men Walton explains that the consequences of not serving could be severe:

> The disciplinary provisions empowered Lords-Lieutenant to punish ordinary delinquencies by fines not exceeding five shillings, or by imprisonment not exceeding twenty days: but for desert the penalty was a fine of twenty pounds or three months' imprisonment, and for failing to appear at the appointed time of muster one pound or five days' imprisonment.

Appointed to their positions by the Lord Mayor and aldermen, the City's Trained Bands used the Artillery Garden in Bishopsgate as their training ground and were expected to defend the capital from both foreign invasion and from local rebellion, though in reality London's Lord Mayors used the Trained Bands for a variety of different purposes. On 31 January 1612, for instance, we see Sir James Pemberton being asked to allow the City's Trained Bands 'in the shows and magnificences prepared for the marriage of the Princess Elizabeth, the king's eldest daughter'. This was a request for which Pemberton was required to 'appoint 350 of the best shot of those bands to be ready by 13 February, for which they should be at no charge, but should have the provision of powder and match delivered to them'.

A commonly held view of the Trained Bands – that they were ill prepared and ill equipped – is given credence by John Corbett in the *Historical Relation of the Military Government of Gloucester* of 1645, where he appraises their experience as follows: 'The trained bands accounted ⁄the maine support of the ralme and bulwarke against unexpected invasions were effeminate in their courage and uncapable of discipline, because the whole course of their life was alienated from warlike employment.'

In letters from the Lords of the Council to London's Lord Mayor we can see this view is also echoed, increasingly anxiously, by Charles I, who in 1616 writes to London's chief magistrate to say that he has been informed that the City was 'altogether unprovided with arms, and could not furnish the trained numbers without borrowing one of another, and that there was scarcely sufficient match and powder in the whole City for one day's training'.

In January 1627 we see that Lord Mayor Sir Cuthbert Aket received a letter from the Lords of the Council, strongly advising him to ensure the Trained Bands were kept in a state of readiness. The king, it transpires, had heard that the bands were generally ill provided and badly furnished – that not only were the defects great in those who showed their horses and arms, but that many had actually been forced to borrow horses and arms, and many more had gone without. Wary of what he termed 'hostile and dangerous' times, the king further advised the Lord Mayor that the horse companies within his lieutenancy were to come before the king with their captains and officers on Hounslow Heath by nine o clock in the morning of 21 April next. The Lord Mayor was further advised to take care that the 'several bands were supplied with full numbers, and that the men, arms and horses were fit for service'. As part of these demands, the king also stated that the troops were to be 'trained and exercised frequently together, and that the men to be directed two or three times a week at their own dwellings, to rise their houses armed, and thus accustom themselves to the use of their weapons'. It is unlikely that anyone would have dared to disobey this command, particularly since the king made a further pointed threat: 'If any man should appear at the general muster with a borrowed horse or arms, or in other unfitting manner, His Majesty would proceed against him as a contempner of his commands and a betrayer of his honour and the safety of his kingdom. If any persons made default the Lord Mayor should send them in safe custody before the Council.'

Many monarchs relied on the Trained Bands, but Charles I was particularly anxious they should be kept in a state of readiness. In a letter dated last of May 1628, from the Lords of the Council to the Lord Mayor, the nervous monarch's feelings were clear,

The present state of Christendom was such as to require all things to be in readiness for defence, and because the times requiring more than ordinary care, they the more earnestly recommended the mustering and training both of horse and foot within the City, the defects of which had induced the king to determine to take a personal inspection of many of them, but which he had forgone on account of the cost it would have entailed.

Yet again, on 30 April 1635, the Lords of the Council implored the Lord Mayor to ensure the Trained Bands were ready for combat, this time due to the threat

upon information from abroad of the great preparations both by sea and land of the neighbouring Princes and States – requiring him to cause an exact view and muster to be taken of the arms and trained forces of the City, and to see that their arms were complete, and all the soldiers and officers able to perform their duties: that they were well affected in religion and took the oath of allegiance; that the trained bands were ready to assemble at an hour's warning and that all able men untrained between 16 and 60 were enrolled. The Lord Mayor should also endeavour to increase the Trained Bands and see them completely furnished and exercised, and require the best sort of men to provide themselves with arms for their own use. He should likewise take order that as many of the untrained men as possible might be furnished and exercised and reduced into bands; that the arms of recusants which had been sequestered should be repaired and kept fit for use at the cost of the owners; and that no recusants should be exempt from showing at every muster the arms chargeable upon them, but that the persons to wear their arms should be chosen by his Deputy Lieutenants, at the charge of the said recusants; and that after every muster the arms should be delivered back and kept in sequestration as before; that the several proportions of ammunition should be put in magazine for use on all occasions; that a Provost Marshal should be appointed for the apprehending and punishment of vagabonds and idle persons not in any lawful vocation; and that an exact account of the state of the forces should be sent to the Council by the 10th June next.

It is likely Charles came to regret his decision to keep the City's armed bands in a perpetual state of readiness – for it was this large and well-prepared force which fought against him during the troublesome days of the Civil War.

Undeniably, not all of the threats against law and order in the City of London would have required such a forceful response. Had you been wandering the streets of the walled City in the late sixteenth century you would doubtless have heard the distinctive sound of the Royal Exchange's bell, which rang both at midday and 6 p.m. to summon its merchants to the trading floor. Built between Cornhill and Threadneedle Street between 1566 and 1570, the first building was described by Pepys as 'The Eye of London' and was graced by Elizabeth I; however, it wasn't long before it came to attract a less welcome sort of person, as outlined by Walter Thornbury in his book *The Royal Exchange in Old and New London: Volume 1*, where he explains that 'the new Exchange, like the nave of St Paul's, soon became a resort for idlers'. On Sundays and holidays, Thornbury adds, 'great numbers of boys, children and young rogues meet there and shout holloa so that honest citizens cannot quietly walk there for their recreation and the parishoners of St Bartholomew's could not hear the sermon'.

Citing the inquest book for 1590, Thornbury finds many legal cases against the groups of citizens who gathered at the Royal

Exchange, including the prosecution of women who are tried for selling apples and oranges at the Exchange gate in Cornhill. These women are also to be found 'amusing themselves in cursing and swearing to the great annoyance and grief of the inhabitants and passersby'. In 1592, Thornbury further finds that the merchants are becoming increasingly bothered by a strange and pungent aroma that is finding its way onto the Flemish-style trading floor. This turns out to be the smell of broiling herrings, sprats and bacon, for which a tavern keeper, operating from vaults underneath the Exchange, is duly fined. By 1622 there are protests about the dog sellers and rat catchers who have made the South Gate of the Royal Exchange their place of business, but Thornbury also describes a more unusual grievance:

> It was also seriously complained of that bear-wards, Shakespeare's noisy neighbours in Southwark, before special bull or bear baitings, used to parade before the Exchange, generally in business hours and there make proclamation of their entertainments which caused tumult and drew together mobs. It was usual, on these occasions to have a monkey riding on a bear's back and several discordant minstrels fiddling to give additional publicity to the coming festival.

From the Bawdy House Riots of 1668 to the Spitalfields Riots of 1769, London's Lord Mayors have also become accustomed to dealing with the outbreak of violent disorders. However, in 1517 Sir John Rest found himself dealing with an unusually violent situation in what is now referred to in the City's annals as Evil May Day. Historically a time of celebrating the goddess Flora, we rely on that great chronicler Stow to inform us of the intricacies of the May Day rites at a time when 'every man, except impediment, would, in May Day in the morning, walke into the sweete meddowes and greene woods, there to rejoice their spirits with the beauty and savour of sweet flowers, and with an harmony of birds, praysing God in their kind'.

But the celebrations were not limited to rural areas. Stow continues:

> I find also, that in the month of May, the citizens of London (of all estates) lightly in every parish, or sometimes two or three parishes joining together had their severall Mayings and did fetch in May-poles, with divers war-like shows, with good archers, morice dauncers, and other devices for pastime, all the day long, and towards the evening, they had stage plays and bonefires in the streets'.

In 1517 chronicler Edward Hall, then a young student of twenty years, explained the anxiety that arose as the tension between 'citizens and aliens' grew. 'The multitude of straungers was so greate about London, that the pore Englishe artificers coude skace get any living. And worst of all, the straungers were so proude, that they disdained, mocked, and oppressed the Englishmen, whiche was the beginning of the grudge.'

Ill feeling finally manifested itself on May Day, when rioters ran through the streets of London with clubs, stones and bricks, assaulting French, Italian and Venetian merchants and setting fire to their homes. The rioters acted with such ferocity that the London Watch was completely helpless to stem the violence; but, says W. Woodcock, the City authorities were determined to bring the perpetrators to justice:

But the Mayor was on the watch, and at once captured and sent to the Tower and other places of confinement three hundred of their number including women and lads not above thirteen or fourteen years old. They were tried in the Guildhall on the 4th and on the 7th a John Lincoln and twelve others were brought forth for execution – a sentence that was later annulled as Hall describes in detail on Thursday May 22 at Westminster Hall in front of the king and that the mayor and aldermen were there in their best livery by nine-o-clock. Then the king commanded that all the prisoners should be brought forth. Then came in the poor younglings, and the old false knaves, bound in ropes, all along, one after another, in their shirts, and every one a halter about his neck, to the number of four hundred men and eleven women. And when all were come before the king's presence, the Cardinal rose, laid to the Mayor and Commonalty their negligence and to the prisoners he declared they had deserved death for their offence. Then all the prisoners together cried, 'Mercy, gracious Lord, mercy!' Then the lords all together besought his Grace of mercy, at whose request the king pardoned them all.

Across the centuries London's Lord Mayors may have presided over the hearings of some terrible calamites, but they have also experienced tragedy themselves. During the sessions of May 1750, Gaol fever (an epidemic typhus) had taken hold in Newgate prison and its environs, and it was in a highly infected courtroom that the trial of Captain Clark for the murder of Captain Turner took place in front of a large crowd of onlookers. It was remarked that the Lord Chief Justice and the recorder, who sat on the Lord Mayor's right hand, caught the infection while the rest of the bench, on the left, escaped – a fact attributed to the draught that carried the infected air in that direction. Simply entering the court that day caused the death of Sir Samuel Pennant, Lord Mayor, along with several members of the Bar.

If London's Lord Mayors were not above falling prey to the diseases of the time, then neither were they beyond the reproach of the general public. On Tuesday 19 January 1897, the *Hull Daily Mail* reported,

> The Lord Mayor of London has received, on the back of a visiting card of a person living at Redhill, the following intimation:
>
> 'My Lord Mayor, you are a fool and a consummate idiot to refuse Mr Hyndman a hearing on Saturday. I will shoot you dead the first opportunity. This is not an idle threat.'
>
> The communication is thought to be a hoax but the police are investigating the matter.

10

LORD MAYORS AT WAR
1900–1945

When asked of his greatest achievement in office, Charles Johnston, Lord Mayor of London from 1914 to 1915, didn't hesitate in his response. Speaking of the pride he felt in having fathered the distinctly successful volunteer force that was the National Guard of the City of London, he spoke in glowing terms of the volunteers' achievements, before concluding, 'I rejoice to have taken the leading part in its inception and incorporation.'

Johnston had every reason to feel proud. What had started merely as a speculative concept during the course of conversation soon grew to become the most valuable asset in the City of London's home defence, not only providing precious resources in terms of manpower on the home front but also freeing up eligible men to go and fight abroad. No man from the volunteer force ever served on the front line, but their efforts were no less appreciated for that. Hour after hour, day after day, as the conflict turned into weeks, months and years, the volunteers of the National Guard of the City of London came together to watch over the City and its citizens. Digging trenches, helping with air-raid duties and even guarding prisoners of war, men in their hundreds answered the City's call to arms. When Lord Mayor Thomas Vansittart Bowater had addressed Londoners on the outset of war, he had said,

> Keep your heads. There is no need for panic. Try and go on in the ordinary way. It is however necessary to exercise economy for the good of the community; and above and beyond all to render such assistance as lies in your power to those poorer than yourselves. All who can should offer their services to the nation in whatever capacity is open and acceptable.

When Johnston formed the group, he created the perfect vehicle to harness that good intent. Promising that the Corporation of London would offer its full support to the movement, he swiftly prepared for its conception, naming his new outfit the National Guard. Not everyone was in favour of this title, thus when the Guard became affiliated with the Central Volunteer Association its official title was changed to become the City of London National Guard Volunteers, which took on the grey-green uniform of the existing volunteer training corps. On 6 December 1914 the formation of the City's National Guard was announced in the press, and the public was quick to respond. Just ten days later, on 26 December, Guildhall opened its doors to the first ever meeting of the City of London National Guard Volunteers, at which Johnston became chairman. In attempting to estimate how many volunteers they could realistically expect to attract, the City's chief officers had settled on a figure of around a thousand men, though in reality the number was hundreds more. But while attracting manpower proved to be a straightforward task, shaping the volunteers who were of variable ages and experience required a certain amount of planning – and it was in this that Johnston did his utmost to provide the unit with his support.

Accompanying his protégés on route marches, attending their manoeuvres, trench-digging and parades, Johnston also found the time to attend to the bureaucratic business of the Grand Committees, and on the rare occasion he wasn't immersed in this work he used his position of Lord Mayor to heighten the profile of the Guard. The king's review in the grounds of Buckingham Palace, the Church Parade at St Paul's Cathedral in June 1915 and the inspection of the regiment by Lord Kitchener in November 1915 were all his idea, and were valuable ones at that. Not only did they promote the Guard, legitimising it in the eyes of the nation, but they also provided a sense of validation and honour for the volunteers themselves. Describing Kitchener's inspection, *The Daily Mirror*, on 4 November 1915, wrote,

Over 3000 men were inspected by the secretary for war. It was difficult to believe that many of these volunteers were over sixty years of age. A few men were there who were over seventy and one 'Tommy' was seventy-two. When Lord Kitchener arrived he looked quickly along the ranks of men in front of him with evident pleasure. After his inspection Lord Kitchener congratulated the officers on the smart appearance of the men and said: 'You have done good work.'

The famous Secretary of State for War, Field-Marshall Lord Kitchener, was also glowing in his praise for the Lord Mayor: 'I have pleasure in congratulating you, my Lord Mayor, on the fine appearance presented by the National Guard. The work they have taken up so well, I have no doubt they will continue to perform.'

Yet the scheme itself wasn't without its problems. Although at the outset there had been no shortage of eager hands ready and willing to volunteer, in reality the sheer amount of time that was called for meant that, initially, the drop-out rate was also high. Quite often the recruits were men with households to support and they could scarce afford the time away from their own responsibilities. In addition, in its preliminary stages the scheme by today's standards would doubtless be considered rather ad hoc – not only were members expected to pay a subscription but also to provide their own uniforms and even their own arms. Happily, a later call for donations furnished Johnston's men with all the bayonets and rifles they could possibly need.

When Johnston created the City's National Guard, it wasn't the first time a London Lord Mayor had taken responsibility for raising a volunteer force. In 1803, as war raged with France, six cavalry troops reporting to the Lord Mayor joined with London troops. Though similar, Johnston's effort was on a much larger scale, and his recruits took on a number of diverse roles. On 30 March 1915 the *Manchester Evening News* reported that a large number of German prisoners of war were to be interned in the Crystal Palace and that their custodians were to be members of the City of London National Guard.

Although it had been just a matter of weeks after the outbreak of war that the ominous German airships, the Zeppelins, dropped their deadly loads on Antwerp, Belgium, it wasn't until 1915 that the bombs reached British soil, with the first attack on London taking place on 31 May. While seven people were killed that day, it was the suddenness and the sheer drama of these air attacks which played on the public's imagination. For the very first time, Londoners were forced to defend themselves against a wholly new and perilous type of assault – but the City's protectors were ready. The first air-raid attack on London resulted in the Volunteer Guard carrying out air-raid duties at St Bartholomew's Hospital, where procedures were swiftly worked out as to how to best help those who were wounded should the need for evacuation arise. Large halls were set aside for drills and familiarising the Guard with the hospital and how it was laid out. The volunteers learned the difficult task of how to evacuate by stretcher, and the different ways of carrying those unable to walk. To further complicate matters, since the hospital was in darkness, the volunteers were only able to work by torchlight.

Duties started every night at 7 p.m., and if volunteers were given the 'all clear' before midnight then they were allowed to go home, or in the case that they lived too far away they were given a hospital mattress for the night.

Simple but strikingly effective, it was an idea which received great attention across the country. On 9 February 1916, the *Yorkshire Evening Post* explained:

Each night a special detachment of nearly 100 members of the City of London National Guard Volunteers is on duty at one big hospital, where a scheme has been evolved to meet the possibility of air raids. Under the mattresses of all the beds a sheet of strong canvas with a large hem at each side is placed. By the simple expedient of slipping a pole through each of these sheets, the bed, mattress, clothes, and patient are removed in one moment. Three men are required for the operation, two at the head and one at the foot. The volunteers are taught to remove the invalids with despatch and to carry them to certain places of safety.

From guarding prisoners of war to safeguarding the sick and infirm, no ideas were left unexplored when it came to the National Guard. The suggestion from Mr Manning Foster to establish the Guard's own magazine resulted in Sir Charles Johnston being approached. The idea was heartily agreed, approved by the Grand Committee, and the *National Guard Magazine* put out its first issue in March 1915, featuring Sir Charles on the cover. Every Corps received a free copy of the magazine, which from then on became subscription-based. Demand increased quickly as the magazine was not just taken by volunteers and their families but by officers, ladies and men of other regiments – regular and volunteer. Copies of the magazine also found their way into clubs and hotels, and with readers in Canada, New Zealand, Australia, France, Egypt and India, news of London's remarkable volunteer force found its way far across the globe.

In addition to raising awareness of the volunteers' efforts, the magazine was also successful in fundraising for a number of causes. The Wounded Allies Relief Committee received £300 and money was also raised for Surrey War Charities. More than £3,000 was donated to military hospitals, while the National Guard Bands and the Empire Union Club also received funds.

A further manner in which the magazine helped others was by the creation of a fund which provided cigarettes to troops returning from the front, also granting loans and providing gifts of money if needed. Both of these schemes helped to increase morale and were much in demand. The demand for cigarettes, for example, was so great that additional appeals had to be made in order to send enough to the many thousands of returning troops, while soldiers' families benefitted from the loans, which were often used for transport fares. It was to the eternal credit of the magazine and its staff that they never failed to go out of their way to provide assistance to those who asked.

The devotion he had shown to the volunteers throughout the year of his mayoralty led Charles Johnston to be known as the father of the National Guard, and after his year in office it could have been no surprise that he continued to work as hard as he could for the benefit of the Guard. But how would the volunteers fare under his successor?

Sir Charles Wakefield, London's wartime Lord Mayor from 1915 to 1916, was by all accounts a popular bet: 'A better choice for a war year it would be difficult to make,' concluded *The Daily Mirror* of 29 September 1915, describing Wakefield as: 'a sturdy, vigorous-looking man in the early fifties with well-cut features and an iron-grey moustache'. Certainly, this outgoing character knew how to capture the support of the public, offering £500 to the first man who brought down a Zeppelin on British soil. He was also savvy enough, even in times of supreme adversity, to realise the value of a positive approach. In his first address as Lord Mayor, in Cordwainers' Hall on 9 November, he stoutly declared, 'We shall win through, but it will require further patience, courage and sacrifice. If peace based on righteousness, truth, honour and liberty should come to Europe this year, then it will indeed be a memorable year.'

As is generally the case in wartime, the importance of keeping morale high cannot be underestimated, and part of this is to keep 'business as usual'. Thus, in the midst of conflict, the Lord Mayor's Show of 1915 took place as was customary, but in that particular year two hundred members of the City of London Volunteers proudly took their places in what was essentially a much-needed recruitment show. Parading captured guns and German prisoners of war, the procession was timed to coincide with no less than ten recruiting meetings as it made its way through the streets of the City. But compared to the multi-hued flamboyancy of previous shows, Charles Wakefield's inaugural celebrations were of a distinctly monotone nature. Said *The Grantham Journal* on Saturday 13 November 1915:

> It was Khaki, Khaki, all the way. That, in a sentence, describes the Lord Mayor's Show of 1915. Here, trundling along the London streets through a deluge of rain, was one of our own familiar motor buses, converted for war purposes, its gaudy colours shrouded in a coating of drab grey paint, full inside and out with leather-coated, sheepskin-covered soldiers, looking just as they look when they are being moved up to the communication trenches. There was an aeroplane, though not a German one, and there were four of the field guns captured at Loos to serve as a further reminder of what our Army is doing on the other side of the Channel. Nor were the defences of London forgotten. Guns of the anti-aircraft corps, mounted on motorcars figured in the procession, and behind them came a search light, also mounted on a motor, in testimony of what Sir Perry Scott is doing to protect us from further Zeppelin raids.

Not only did the Lord Mayor's Show become a vehicle for recruitment that year – it also served as a grand farewell. Many of the troops who turned out on parade that day, impeccably attired in their heavy woollen uniforms, marched straight through the cheering crowds and immediately on to war.

It was in 1916, under the mayorship of Sir Charles Wakefield, that the Guard, in recognition of its enormous achievements, ceased to exist as a separate entity and joined the City of London Volunteer Regiment as battalions 4, 5 and 6. In a solemn ceremony, the volunteers now had to swear their allegiance to King George V and promise to defend him against 'all of his enemies and opposers'.

Its incorporation into the regiment meant the volunteers and their new regiment now attended a review, with around 1,600 marching through Horse Guards Parade to rousing melodies from the band and the cheers of a jubilant crowd. *The National Guard in the Great War* by A. E. Manning Foster gives a detailed account of a 'perfect day with a cloudless sky'.

It was twenty minutes past five, when, in the distance, a little cavalcade with the Union Jack flying, could be seen advancing rapidly through the regiments. Lord French rode at the head. No time was wasted. He rode round the regiments to make his inspection, and in ten minutes was back at the saluting base.

Lord French gathered around him the officers commanding the various regiments, and, addressing them from horseback, said he had been commanded by the king to tell them how very sorry he was that he was unable to take the review himself. He would have been delighted, and was most anxious to do so, but they knew what a number of engagements he had and how difficult it was to arrange these things. His Majesty desired him, however, to tell them how highly he appreciated their devoted loyalty and energy, and everything they had done.

His Majesty's Government — he thought he might certainly speak on their behalf — and the War Office also greatly appreciated their services.

'An idea seems to have got abroad — I don't know how they get abroad in war time but they do — -that you were not wanted. There was never such an idea. I want you to get that idea out of your mind. You are all regarded as a most valuable force and one which can be turned to the best account.

It has given me deep pleasure to come here to see such a fine body of men and to congratulate you all most heartily upon a splendid turn-out at so short a notice. It is miraculous to me that you should have been got together in such numbers in such a short time and in such a soldierly manner. It must be a surprise to any soldier who is looking on.'

It was the adaptability of the men of the National Guard and their willingness to do any sort of work that was the hallmark of their success. At the Wounded Allies Fair at the Caledonian Market in June 1916, they policed the market, acting as gatekeepers, money changers, collectors, auctioneers and general handymen – word soon going round that if anyone was in difficulty they should send for the National Guard.

The year 1916 also saw a number of new official duties for the Guard – mostly station work (the meeting and ferrying round of soldiers who had returned home 'on leave' and were to be accompanied across the capital or to 'rest houses'). Medical work was also new, and in this the Guard worked closely with the Australian, New Zealand and Canadian forces. The Guard also now acted as lookouts at vulnerable points and were responsible for guarding German prisoners. But it was to remain their work in looking after soldiers returning from the front for which they were most remembered in 1916.

'God will bless you for looking after men returning from the front. It will remain a fragrant memory for all time, and when the war is over you will have the consciousness of knowing that in the days of darkness and difficulty you responded to the call and did your best here, as our brave boys in khaki have done their best in other spheres,' said Wakefield in 1916, speaking these poignant words at the Guildhall.

As any effective organisation has to, the National Guard continued to evolve throughout the war years, responding to new legislation and new twists in the fast-moving theatre of war. One of the most important matters to affect its members was the Volunteer Act, passed on 22 December 1916 and becoming law in 1917. Giving effect to agreements on the part of members of volunteer corps to attend drills or undergo training or perform military duty, this Act also had the effect of officially legitimising the corps, thereby making them liable to comply with the official terms. From this point onwards the volunteers could not take absence without leave and could also be taken into military custody and tried. As section three states, 'A Volunteer who has entered into any such agreement shall, during the continuance of the agreement, while engaged in any drill exercise or training, or while performing any military duty, be subject to military law as a soldier, and the Army Act shall apply accordingly.' This Act sat alongside the Volunteer Act of 1863, which had never been repealed.

It wasn't long after the corps had been formed that the Lord Mayor's chaplain, Reverend Becker, vicar of St Botolph's, Aldergate Street, was appointed chaplain of the Guard while Reverend Rosedale, chaplain to the Worshipful Company of Horners and the Worshipful Company of Coachmakers, became his assistant.

By 1917 it was generally considered that the threat of Zeppelin attacks was significantly reduced; it was the German heavy aircraft Gotha bombers, not the Zeppelin menace, which caused the devastation London experienced during the two unexpected daylight raids of 13 June and 17 July – a time when it was reported that the casualties flowed into London's hospitals on 'all manner of transport from a coster's barrow to a Red Cross ambulance'.

Although the attacks took everyone by surprise, the response was immediate and overwhelming. King George himself visited the London hospitals just two hours after the bombs had hit to offer comfort to those injured in the attack. The bombs had fallen so near the hospital and yet as if by a miracle the building itself escaped a direct hit.

The work of the volunteers was valuable in the extreme, as we can see from the letter written by Lord Sandhurst, chairman of the governors of St Barts, in which he pays heartfelt praise to the City's volunteers:

> I desire on behalf of the governors of the hospital to assure you how deeply sensible we are of our indebtedness for services rendered in undertaking definite duties in the military wing. It is, I can assure you, no exaggeration to say that if it had not been for the assistance we received from voluntary helpers, it would have been extremely difficult to have carried on the work as efficiently as the reputation of St Bart's demands. The work thus done has, you can be assured, been most truly appreciated by the ward sisters, whom you have done so much to assist.

Lord Sandhurst then presented the ambulance section with a new ambulance.

The role that the City's Lord Mayors had to play in the war effort was not confined to the Volunteer National Guard. On 29 August 1914, Lord Mayor Sir W. Vansittart Bowater travelled to the Tower to swear in the 1,600 City Workers who had joined what became known as the Stockbrokers Battalion. Earlier that day they had been inspected in Temple Gardens and marched to the Tower of London's dry moat, where they were sworn in. Throughout their service they referred to themselves as the Ditchers, because they had been sworn in Tower Ditch. Throughout the First World War the Tower also acted as a military depot where arms and munitions could be safely stored. It was also a place where spies were executed – on 6 November 1914 a firing squad of grenadier guards executed German officer Carl Hans Lody, who before his dawn execution wrote a letter addressed to the commanding officer of the 3rd Battalion Guards saying that the guards and sentries had never neglected their duties towards him and 'have shown always the utmost courtesy and consideration towards me'.

While London's Lord Mayors played a crucial role in recruiting volunteers, they were also responsible for swelling the ranks of the regular forces – a task carried out to good effect. On Tuesday 1 February 1916, the *Daily Mirror* reported on 'London's Fine Response to the Lord Mayor's Appeal' as follows:

The Lord Mayor's three weeks recruiting rally of the men of the City of London ended yesterday, and it has been a great success, Sir Charles Wakefield told *The Daily Mirror*. For over three weeks there has been steady flow of City recruits, including not a few well-known merchant princes, to the Mansion House, where the Lord Mayor placed every room except his own bedroom at the disposal of the special recruiting staff. Many hundreds have been attested under the Derby group system, and very considerable numbers have enlisted directly. A feature of the great rally, and one very greatly appreciated busy City men, was the speed with which recruits were dealt with. A perfect system had been organised by Chaplain Rees, the chief recruiting officer, and the medical officers, with the result that the average time it has taken for a man to become a fully fledged soldier of the king at the Mansion House has not exceeded twenty minutes. The record, however, stands at much less than this—only nine minutes! 'I am extremely pleased with the results attained. They have exceeded all my expectations. Hundreds of men of the historic old City have answered appeal, and have been particularly delighted and gratified to see such a large percentage of the younger men coming forward.'

Another time when the City of London involved itself in the creation of a volunteer force was during the Boer War. In 1899, as England reeled from the heavy defeats suffered during the first phase of the Boer War, Senior Army Officer Lord Garnet Wolseley began negotiations with the City's chief magistrate to establish a force of volunteers to be sent to support troops in South Africa. Supported financially by the wealthy livery companies, City officials – including the Lord Mayor, sheriffs and five aldermen – officiated over the swearing-in ceremony of the new recruits the City Imperial Volunteers, on the very first day of the following year. Having been granted the honour of the Freedom of the City on 12 January, the troops left for Africa the very next day, returning to the City on 29 October 1900 to be officially welcomed back by the Corporation of London. It was, as Lord Mayor Alfred Newton had explained in an editorial to the *London Evening Standard* earlier that year, a complex, time-consuming but ultimately satisfying endeavour:

The City Volunteers
To the Editor of the *Standard*
Monday 5 Feb 1900

Sir-From the moment when the Commander in Chief did me the honour of placing in my hands, as Chief Magistrate of the City of London, the organisation of a regiment of thoroughly qualified Volunteers for service in South Africa, I have been profoundly impressed with the responsibility of the trust and the importance of every promise made on behalf of the Corporation and City of London being fulfilled in its integrity.

The original promise was 1000 Metropolitan Volunteers, all recommended by their Commanding Officers, all between 20 and 35 years, all bachelors, and that at least 250 should be mounted. That was on the 20 December, and now, on 3 February, the City of London, with the approval of the military authorities, has completely equipped and despatched to the seat of war upwards of 1550 selected volunteers of whom 500 men and 17 officers are already in Capetown, all approved by the General Officer commanding Infantry, having their saddlery with them, and their horses ready at the Cape. Four small Maxim guns, with 200,000 rounds of ammunition, have also been shipped. A highly-trained battery of Field Artillery, mainly provided by the Honourable Artillery Company through the zealous co-operation of the Earl of Denbigh, composed of 140 men and officers, left the Royal Albert Dock to-day by the Steamship Montfort. This section takes with it four twelve and a-half pounder quick-firing guns and ample ammunition, together with their full complement of 110 horses purchased here, as they must be of a stouter type than the Cape horses. The City has also, which was not originally intended, provided the entire camp and tent equipment for the whole force when it leaves Capetown, and, at the request of the authorities, to do a good deal in the direction of land transport without interfering with the responsibility of the Headquarters Staff in South Africa in respect of maintenance of the corps.

Explaining the success of the Corps in such a short space of time, he adds,

As soon as Lord Wolseley accepted my offer, made on behalf of the Corporation and City, I was in the position of an autocrat in the business and the power of the purse was promptly placed at my disposal – in the first instance by the Corporation with its grant of £25,000, by the City Livery Companies, the large Shipowners, Bankers, Merchants, the Honourable Artillery Company, its members, and the citizens generally. The Metropolitan Volunteer Commanding Officers vied with each other as to who could send the most men, do the most work, and be the most useful. The result is, that with the exception of a few State officers from the Regular Arm, the officers of the City Imperial Volunteers are gentlemen engaged in civil pursuits but who have spent years efficiently performing their duties ...

Several City firms have furnished contingents of their expert employees, whose services at the Guildhall in the preparation and distribution of 'kits' have been of great assistance. The payment of accounts is now progressing, and at the first opportunity an audited statement of receipts and expenditure will be presented.

In Conclusion, I would state that the whole force has gone to the front with no burning desire for glory, but with a determination to do its duty, and with an intense loyalty and devotion to their beloved Soverign. I am, Sir, your obedient servant. Alfred, J. Newton, Lord Mayor, Mansion House E.C., February 3.

As we can see, the support of London's Lord Mayors during wartime was crucial to the City's success – and this was also true of their fundraising efforts. During the Second World War, Sir William Coxton's Lord Mayor Red Cross and St John Fund raised considerable sums with its Penny-A-Week scheme, with new firms registering at the rate of about forty a day. Coxton ensured maximum publicity for his scheme, asking the nation's employers to see that their workers knew about the scheme and its vital importance. To the workers he said that everyone in a job could afford 1*d* a week. As did many Lord Mayors who presided over the City in times of crisis, Coxton knew the value of boosting morale, particularly to the country's allies. On Saturday 21 September 1940, he made the following bold broadcast to New York: 'London has steeled herself for resistance and for victory; nothing can daunt her resolution.'

CONCLUSION

On 29 September 2015, on the ancient feast of Michaelmas, the liverymen of London City gather together to vote for the two candidates to be put forward for the post of London's Lord Mayor. Voting in the Guildhall's Common Hall, it is ultimately the Court of Aldermen who will assign the weighty responsibility of London Lord Mayor, taking office at the Silent Ceremony.

Taking place on the Friday before the second Saturday in November (the day before the very public splendour of the Lord Mayor's Show) the almost wordless Silent Ceremony is carried out behind closed doors. Described by the Worshipful Company of Marketors as 'the most whimsical and anachronistic' of the City's traditions. The ceremony is witnessed by the City officers, aldermen, the livery company masters and the city's liverymen.

The Lord Mayor's Show, (the grand procession in which the new Lord Mayor proceeds to the Strand's Royal Courts of Justice to swear allegiance to the Sovereign before the Justices of the High Court), remains, more than 800 years after it first began, one of the highlights of the City's calendar. So how is it that the traditional pomp and heraldry of the Lord Mayor's office continues to thrive in the modern world? After all, while the post of Lord Mayor dates back to the twelfth century, many of the other City offices have equally lengthy histories. The City's Swordbearer, for instance, first esquire of the Lord Mayor's household, can trace his position back to 1419, while the City Remembrancer, whose duty it is to ensure that the privilege and traditions of the City are at all times adhered to, first appeared in official records during Elizabethan times. Surprisingly, there are many similarities. As leader of the Corporation of the City of London, the Lord Mayor still serves as the key spokesperson for the local authority and, while he may no longer be expected to raise a king's ransom or to risk his own liberty to secure the rights of the City, he is still required to act on behalf of both the businesses and residents in the City. His presence still gives weight to ceremonial occasions, such as the 2013 appearance at Baroness Thatcher's Funeral, when the Lord Mayor carried the Sword of Mourning ahead of the Queen and Prince Phillip into St Paul's Cathedral.

While the relationship between City and Crown is today largely ceremonial, past differences have led to turbulence and bitter confrontation as London's Lord Mayors found themselves pitted against the tyrannical deeds of greedy monarchs, losing their liberty and even their lives to protect the City and its rights. It is fair to say, too, that the civic throne has been graced in its time by a number of more frivolous personalities, among them George Bolles, Lord Mayor in 1617, who surrounded himself with such finery and ceremony that James I was reported to have remarked that he had thought there was no King in England beside himself.

But behind the gilded coach, lavish entertainments and elaborate ceremonial costumes, it is worth remembering that for much of the City's history the post of Lord Mayor was, intriguingly, the very highest position a commoner could expect to reach – a fact of which many of London's chief magistrates were acutely aware. In 1839, Sir Chapman Marshall spoke at a public dinner for Metropolitan Charity Schools explaining that he had come to London in 1803 without a shilling and without a friend, adding: 'you witness in me what may be done by the earnest application of honest industry; and I trust that my example may induce others to aspire by the same means to the distinguished situation which I have now have the honour to fill.'

This sentiment was echoed by Sir John Pirie, who at his inaugural dinner in 1842 admitted: 'I little thought forty years ago, when I came to London a poor lad from the banks of the Tweed, that I should ever arrive at so great a distinction.'

Whatever their beginnings and no matter how challenging their time in office, the mark that London's Lord Mayors have made upon their city can never be fully erased. While it is true that the conduits of the City no longer flow with wine as they did in the days of Henry VIII and that much of the medieval city perished in the great fire, there is much, as we have seen, that remains. Ultimately, though, perhaps the most meaningful way we can recognise the contribution that London's mayors have made to the City is not through the statues and structures that remain, but through the eyes of the citizens who lived through each mayoralty and were personally affected by their acts. The feelings that London's populace had for its chief magistrates is perhaps best summed up in these touching verses found in the National Library of Scotland, dedicated to the memory of the Right Honourable William Beckford, twice Lord Mayor of London (1762 and 1769)

> Come mourn with me ye sons of freedom
> And pray listen to my song,
> We've lost a pillar of the city,

For alas! great Beckford's gone;
Know grim death that king of terrors,
When his dart he does display,
King's and princes to him's but trifles,
They like great Beckford must obey.

How his name will shine in story
When your children does it read
How he strove for Freedom's glory,
But alas! it was decreed,
That he with us must be no longer,
But to heaven above must go,
For our rights not could plead stronger
Than great Beckford you all do know,

He was the man on all occasions,
The Livery they well do know,
With Remonstrance or Petitions
When desir'd did boldy go,
The frowns of young men he'd despise,
Their jeering language he did defy,
Nor could they stop the man we priz'd,
Who was resolv'd to make reply.

O how the poor are all-lamenting
Because their benefactor's dead,
Some hundred was each day depending
On him for their daily bread
But now he's gone to be rewarded,
For his goodness to great and small,

Few like him will be recorded,
Who from his word did never fall.

So don't rejoice ye foes to freedom
Because a lover of it's gone.
Death is sure pray all remember,
You must follow ere't be long,
But some there is now left behind him,
Will support what he's begun
May they like Beckford shine in glory,
And die like him, Britannia's son.

Appendix 1

LIST OF LORD MAYORS

Henry	H	FITZ-AILWIN	1189	Draper	Died in office
Roger	R	FITZALAN	1212	Mercer	
Serlo	S	LE MERCER	1215	Mercer	
William	W	HARDELL	1215	Draper	
James	J	ALDERMAN	1216	Not Known	
Salomon	S	DE BASING	1217	Not Known	
Serlo	S	LE MERCER	1218	Mercer	
Richard	R	RENGER	1222	Not Known	
Roger	R	LE DUKE	1227	Not Known	
Andrew	A	BUCKEREL	1231	Grocer	Died in office
Richard		RENGER	1238	Not Known	Died in office
William	W	JOYNIER	1239	Not Known	
Gerard	G	BAT	1240	Not Known	
Reginald	R	DE BUNGHEYE	1240	Not Known	
Ralph	R	ASHWY	1241	Mercer	
Michael	M	TOVY	1244	Not Known	
John	J	GISORS	1246	Grocer	
Peter	P	FITZALAN	1246	Not Known	
Michael	M	TOVY	1247	Not Known	
Roger	R	FITZROGER	1249	Not Known	
John	J	NORMAN [1]	1250	Not Known	
Adam	A	DE BASING	1251	Mercer	
John	J	TULESAN	1252	Draper	
Nicholas	N	BAT	1253	Not Known	Resigned
Ralph	R	HARDEL	1254	Draper	Deposed
William	W	FITZRICHARD	1258	Draper	Royal Nominee
John		GISORS	1258	Grocer	
William	W	FITZRICHARD	1259	Draper	Royal Nominee
Thomas	T	FITZTHOMAS	1261	Not Known	Deposed

John	J	WALERAND	1265		Warden appointed by the Crown
Hugh	H	FITZOTHO	1265		Warden appointed by the Crown
John	J	DE LA LINDE	1265		Warden appointed by the Crown
William	W	FITZRICHARD	1266	Draper	Royal Nominee
Alan	A	LA ZUCHE	1267	Grocer	Warden appointed by the Crown
Thomas	T	DE IPPEGRAVE	1268		Warden appointed by the Crown
Stephen	S	DE EDDEWORTH	1268		Warden appointed by the Crown
Hugh	H	FITZOTHO	1269		Warden appointed by the Crown
John	J	ADRIEN	1270	Draper	
Walter	W	HERVEY	1271	Not Known	Deposed
Henry	H	LE WALEYS	1273	Not Known	
Gregory	G	DE ROKESLEY	1274	Goldsmith	
Henry		LE WALEYS	1281	Not Known	
Gregory	G	DE ROKESLEY	1284	Goldsmith	
Ralph	R	DE SANDWICH	1285		Warden appointed by the Crown
John	J	LE BRETON	1289		Warden appointed by the Crown
Ralph	R	DE SANDWICH	1289		Warden appointed by the Crown
John	J	LE BRETON	1293		Warden appointed by the Crown
Henry		LE WALEYS	1298	Not Known	
Elias	E	RUSSELL	1299	Draper	
John	J	LE BLUND	1301	Draper	
Nicholas	N	DE FARNDONE	1308	Goldsmith	
Thomas	T	ROMEYN	1309	Grocer	
Richer	R	DE REFHAM	1310	Mercer	Deposed
John	J	DE GISORS	1311	Grocer	
Nicholas		DE FARNDONE	1313	Goldsmith	
John		DE GISORS	1314	Grocer	
Stephen	S	DE ABYNDON	1315	Draper	
John	J	DE WENGRAVE	1316	Not Known	Royal Nominee
Hamo	H	DE CHIGWELL	1319	Fishmonger	
Nicholas		DE FARNDONE	1320	Goldsmith	
Robert	R	DE KENDALE	1321		Warden appointed by the Crown
Hamo	H	DE CHIGWELL	1321	Fishmonger	
Nicholas		DE FARNDONE	1323	Goldsmith	
Hamo		DE CHIGWELL	1323	Fishmonger	
Richard	R	DE BETOYNE	1326	Grocer	
Hamo		DE CHIGWELL	1327	Fishmonger	
John	J	DE GRANTHAM	1328	Grocer	

Simon	S	SWANLOND	1329	Draper	
John	J	DE PULTENEY	1330	Draper	
John	J	DE PRESTONE	1332	Draper	
John	J	DE PULTENEY	1333	Draper	
Reginald	R	DE CONDUIT	1334	Vintner	
John	J	DE PULTENEY	1336	Draper	
Henry	H	DARCI	1337	Draper	
Andrew	A	AUBREY	1339	Grocer	
John	J	DE OXENFORD	1341	Vintner	Died in office
Simon	S	FRAUNCIS	1342	Mercer	
John	J	HAMOND	1343	Grocer	
Richard	R	LE LACER	1345	Mercer	
Geoffrey	G	DE WICHINGHAM	1346	Mercer	
Thomas	T	LEGGY	1347	Skinner	
John	J	LOVEKYN	1348	Fishmonger	
Walter	W	TURKE	1349	Fishmonger	
Richard	R	DE KISLINGBURY	1350	Draper	
Andrew		AUBREY	1351	Grocer	
Adam	A	FRAUNCEYS	1352	Mercer	
Thomas		LEGGY	1354	Skinner	
Simon		FRAUNCIS	1355	Mercer	
Henry	H	PICARD	1356	Vintner	
John	J	DE STODEYE	1357	Vintner	
John		LOVEKYN	1358	Fishmonger	
Simon	S	DOLSELEY	1359	Grocer	
John	J	WROTH	1360	Fishmonger	
John	J	PECCHE	1361	Fishmonger	
Stephen	S	CAVENDISSHE	1362	Draper	
John	J	NOTT	1363	Grocer	
Adam	A	DE BURY	1364	Skinner	Impeached
John		LOVEKYN	1366	Fishmonger	
James	J	ANDREU	1367	Draper	
Simon	S	DE MORDONE	1368	Fishmonger	
John	J	DE CHICHESTER	1369	Goldsmith	
John	J	BERNES	1370	Mercer	
John	J	PYEL	1372	Mercer	
Adam		DE BURY	1373	Skinner	
William	W	WALWORTH	1374	Fishmonger	
John	J	WARDE [1]	1375	Grocer	
Adam	A	STABLE	1376	Mercer	
Nicholas	N	BREMBRE	1377	Grocer	
John	J	PHILIPOT	1378	Grocer	
John	J	HADLE	1379	Grocer	
William		WALWORTH	1380	Fishmonger	
John	J	DE NORTHAMPTON	1381		Draper
Nicholas	N	BREMBRE	1383	Grocer	
Nicholas	N	EXTON	1386	Fishmonger	

Nicholas	N	TWYFORD	1388	Goldsmith	
William	W	VENOUR	1389	Grocer	
Adam	A	BAMME	1390	Goldsmith	
John	J	HEENDE	1391	Draper	Deposed and Imprisoned
Edward		DALYNGRIGGE	1392		Warden appointed by the Crown
Baldwin		RADYNGTON	1392		Warden appointed by the Crown
William	W	STAUNDON	1392	Grocer	
John		HADLE	1393	Grocer	
John	J	FRESSHE	1394	Mercer	
William	W	MORE	1395	Vintner	
Adam		BAMME	1396	Goldsmith	Died in office
Richard	R	WHITTINGTON	1397	Mercer	May-Oct 1397
Richard		WHITTINGTON	1397	Mercer	
Drew	D	BARENTYN	1398	Goldsmith	
Thomas	T	KNOLLES	1399	Grocer	
John	J	FRAUNCEYS	1400	Goldsmith	
John	J	SHADWORTH	1401	Mercer	
John	J	WALCOTE	1402	Draper	
William	W	ASKHAM	1403	Fishmonger	
John		HEENDE	1404	Draper	
John	J	WODECOK	1405	Mercer	
Richard		WHITTINGTON	1406	Mercer	
William		STAUNDON	1407	Grocer	
Drugo		BARENTYN	1408	Goldsmith	
Richard	R	MERLAWE	1409	Ironmonger	
Thomas		KNOLLES	1410	Grocer	
Robert	R	CHICHELE	1411	Grocer	
William	W	WALDERNE	1412	Mercer	
William	W	CROWMERE	1413	Draper	
Thomas	T	FAUCONER	1414	Mercer	
Nicholas	N	WOTTON	1415	Draper	
Henry	H	BARTON	1416	Skinner	
Richard		MERLAWE	1417	Ironmonger	
William	W	SEVENOKE	1418	Grocer	
Richard		WHITTINGTON	1419	Mercer	
William	W	CAUNTBRIGGE	1420	Grocer	
Robert		CHICHELE	1421	Grocer	
William		WALDERNE	1422	Mercer	
William		CROWMERE	1423	Draper	
John	J	MICHELL	1424	Fishmonger	
John	J	COVENTRE	1425	Mercer	
John	J	REYNWELL	1426	Fishmonger	
John	J	GEDNEY	1427	Draper	
Henry		BARTON	1428	Skinner	
William	W	ESTFELD	1429	Mercer	
Nicholas		WOTTON	1430	Draper	

John	J	WELLES	1431	Grocer
John	J	PERNEYS	1432	Fishmonger
John	J	BROKLE	1433	Draper
Robert	R	OTELE	1434	Grocer
Henry	H	FROWYK	1435	Mercer
John		MICHELL	1436	Fishmonger
William		ESTFELD	1437	Mercer
Stephen	S	BROUN	1438	Grocer
Robert	R	LARGE	1439	Mercer
John	J	PADDESLE	1440	Goldsmith
Robert	R	CLOPTON	1441	Draper
John	J	HATHERLE	1442	Ironmonger
Thomas	T	CATWORTH	1443	Grocer
Henry		FROWYK	1444	Mercer
Simon	S	EYRE	1445	Draper
John	J	OLNEY	1446	Mercer
John	J	GEDNEY	1447	Draper
Stephen		BROUN	1448	Grocer
Thomas	T	CHALTON	1449	Mercer
Nicholas	N	WYFOLD	1450	Grocer
William	W	GREGORY	1451	Skinner
Geoffrey	G	FELDYNGE	1452	Mercer
John	J	NORMAN [2]	1453	Draper
Stephen	S	FORSTER	1454	Fishmonger
William	W	MAROWE	1455	Grocer
Thomas	T	CANYNGES	1456	Grocer
Geoffrey	G	BOLEYN	1457	Mercer
Thomas	T	SCOTT	1458	Draper
William	W	HULYN	1459	Fishmonger
Richard	R	LEE	1460	Grocer
Hugh	H	WICHE	1461	Mercer
Thomas	T	COOKE	1462	Draper
Matthew	M	PHILIP	1463	Goldsmith
Ralph	R	JOSSELYN	1464	Draper
Ralph	R	VERNEY	1465	Mercer
John	J	YONGE	1466	Grocer
Thomas	T	OULEGRAVE	1467	Skinner
William	W	TAILLOUR	1468	Grocer
Richard		LEE	1469	Grocer
John	J	STOCKTON	1470	Mercer
William	W	EDWARD	1471	Grocer
William	W	HAMPTON	1472	Fishmonger
John	J	TATE [1]	1473	Mercer
Robert	R	DROPE	1474	Draper
Robert	R	BASSETT	1475	Salter
Ralph		JOSSELYN	1476	Draper
Humphrey	H	HAYFORD	1477	Goldsmith

Richard	R	GARDYNER	1478	Mercer	
Bartholomew	B	JAMES	1479	Draper	
John	J	BROWNE	1480	Mercer	
William	W	HARYOT	1481	Draper	
Edmund	E	SHAA	1482	Goldsmith	
Robert	R	BILLESDON	1483	Haberdasher	
Thomas	T	HILL	1484	Grocer	Died in office (the plague)
William	W	STOKKER	1485	Draper	Died in office (the plague)
John	J	WARDE [2]	1485	Grocer	Sept-Oct 1485
Hugh	H	BRYCE	1485	Goldsmith	
Henry	H	COLET	1486	Mercer	
William	W	HORNE	1487	Salter	
Robert	R	TATE	1488	Mercer	
William	W	WHITE	1489	Draper	
John	J	MATHEWE	1490	Mercer	
Hugh	H	CLOPTON	1491	Mercer	
William	W	MARTIN	1492	Skinner	
Ralp	R	ASTRY	1493	Fishmonger	
Richard	R	CHAWRY	1494	Salter	
Henry		COLET	1495	Mercer	
John	J	TATE [2]	1496	Mercer	
William	W	PURCHASE	1497	Mercer	
John	J	PERCYVALE	1498	Merchant Taylor	
Nicholas	N	AILWYN	1499	Mercer	
William	W	REMYNGTON	1500	Fishmonger	
John	J	SHAA	1501	Goldsmith	
Bartholomew	B	REDE	1502	Goldsmith	
William	W	CAPEL	1503	Draper	
John	J	WYNGER	1504	Grocer	
Thomas	T	KNESEWORTH	1505	Fishmonger	
Richard	R	HADDON	1506	Mercer	
William	W	BROWNE [1]	1507	Mercer	Died in office
Lawrence	L	AYLMER	1508	Draper	Mar-Oct 1508
Stephen	S	JENYNS	1508	Merchant Taylor	
Thomas	T	BRADBURY	1509	Mercer	Died in office
William		CAPEL	1510	Draper	Jan-Oct 1510
Henry	H	KEBYLL	1510	Grocer	
Roger	R	ACHLELEY	1511	Draper	
William	W	COPYNGER	1512	Fishmonger	Died in office
Richard		HADDON	1513	Mercer	Feb-Oct 1513
William	W	BROWNE [2]	1513	Mercer	Died in office
John		TATE [2]	1514	Mercer	May-Oct 1514
George	G	MONOUX	1514	Draper	
William	W	BOTELER	1515	Grocer	
John	J	REST	1516	Grocer	
Thomas	T	EXMEWE	1517	Goldsmith	
Thomas	T	MIRFYN	1518	Skinner	

James	J	YARFORD	1519	Mercer
John	J	BRUGGE	1520	Draper
John	J	MILBORNE	1521	Draper
John	J	MUNDY	1522	Goldsmith
Thomas	T	BALDRY	1523	Mercer
William	W	BAYLEY	1524	Draper
John	J	ALEYN	1525	Mercer
Thomas	T	SEMER	1526	Mercer
James	J	SPENCER	1527	Vintner
John	J	RUDSTONE	1528	Draper
Ralph	R	DODMER	1529	Mercer
Thomas	T	PARGETER	1530	Salter
Nicholas	N	LAMBARDE	1531	Grocer
Stephen	S	PECOCKE	1532	Haberdasher
Christopher	C	ASCUE	1533	Draper
John	J	CHAMPNEYS	1534	Skinner
John		ALEYN	1535	Mercer
Ralph	R	WARREN	1536	Mercer
Richard	R	GRESHAM	1537	Mercer
William	W	FORMAN	1538	Haberdasher
William	W	HOLLYES	1539	Mercer
William	W	ROCHE	1540	Draper
Michael	M	DORMER	1541	Mercer
John	J	COTES	1542	Salter
William	W	BOWYER	1543	Draper	Died in office
Ralph		WARREN	1544	Mercer	April-Oct 1544
William	W	LAXTON	1544	Grocer
Martin	M	BOWES	1545	Goldsmith
Henry	H	HUBERTHORN	1546	Merchant Taylor
John	J	GRESHAM	1547	Mercer
Henry	H	AMCOTTS	1548	Fishmonger
Rowland	R	HILL	1549	Mercer
Andrew	A	JUDDE	1550	Skinner
Richard	R	DOBBIS	1551	Skinner
George	G	BARNE [1]	1552	Haberdasher
Thomas	T	WHYTE	1553	Merchant Taylor
John	J	LYON	1554	Grocer
William	W	GARRARDE	1555	Haberdasher
Thomas	T	OFFLEY	1556	Merchant Taylor
Thomas	T	CURTES	1557	Fishmonger	Imprisoned
Thomas	T	LEIGH	1558	Mercer
William	W	HEWET	1559	Clothworker
William	W	CHESTER	1560	Draper
William	W	HARPER	1561	Merchant Taylor
Thomas	T	LODGE	1562	Grocer
John	J	WHYTE	1563	Grocer
Richard	R	MALORYE	1564	Mercer

Richard	R	CHAMPYON	1565	Draper	
Christopher	C	DRAPER	1566	Ironmonger	
Roger	R	MARTYN	1567	Mercer	
Thomas	T	ROWE	1568	Merchant Taylor	
Alexander	A	AVENON	1569	Ironmonger	
Rowland	R	HEYWARD	1570	Clothworker	
William	W	ALLEN	1571	Mercer	
Lionel	L	DUCKETT	1572	Mercer	
John	J	RYVERS	1573	Grocer	
James	J	HAWES	1574	Clothworker	
Ambrose	A	NICHOLAS	1575	Salter	
John	J	LANGLEY	1576	Goldsmith	
Thomas	T	RAMSAY	1577	Grocer	
Richard	R	PYPE	1578	Draper	
Nicholas	N	WOODROFFE	1579	Haberdasher	
John	J	BRANCHE	1580	Draper	
James	J	HARVYE	1581	Ironmonger	
Thomas	T	BLANKE	1582	Haberdasher	
Edward	E	OSBORNE	1583	Clothworker	
Thomas	T	PULLYSON	1584	Draper	
Wolstan	W	DIXIE	1585	Skinner	
George	G	BARNE [2]	1586	Haberdasher	
George	G	BONDE	1587	Haberdasher	
Martin	M	CALTHORP	1588	Draper	Died in office
Richard	R	MARTIN	1589	Goldsmith	May-Oct 1588
John	J	HARTE	1589	Grocer	
John	J	ALLOT	1590	Fishmonger	Died in office
Rowland	R	HEYWARD	1591	Clothworker	Sep-Oct 1591
William	W	WEBBE	1591	Salter	
William	W	ROWE	1592	Ironmonger	Died in office (plague)
Cuthbert	C	BUCKELL	1593	Vintner	Died in office (plague)
Richard		MARTIN	1594	Goldsmith	July-Oct 1594
John	J	SPENCER	1594	Clothworker	
Stephen	S	SLANYE	1595	Skinner	
Thomas	T	SKINNER [1]	1596	Clothworker	Died in office
Henry	H	BILLINGSLEY	1596	Haberdasher	Dec-Oct 1597
Richard	R	SALTONSTALL	1597	Skinner	
Stephen	S	SOAME	1598	Grocer	
Nicholas	N	MOSLEY	1599	Clothworker	
William	W	RYDER	1600	Haberdasher	
John	J	GARRARDE	1601	Haberdasher	
Robert	R	LEE	1602	Merchant Taylor	
Thomas	T	BENNETT	1603	Mercer	
Thomas	T	LOWE	1604	Haberdasher	
Leonard	L	HALLIDAY	1605	Merchant Taylor	
John	J	WATTS	1606	Clothworker	
Henry	H	ROWE	1607	Mercer	

Humphrey	H	WELD	1608	Grocer	
Thomas	T	CAMBELL	1609	Ironmonger	
William	W	CRAVEN	1610	Merchant Taylor	
James	J	PEMBERTON	1611	Goldsmith	
John	J	SWYNNERTON	1612	Merchant Taylor	
Thomas	T	MIDDLETON	1613	Grocer	
Thomas	T	HAYES	1614	Draper	
John	J	JOLLES	1615	Draper	
John	J	LEMAN	1616	Fishmonger	
George	G	BOLLES	1617	Grocer	
Sebastian	S	HARVEY	1618	Ironmonger	
William	W	COKAYNE	1619	Skinner	
Frances	F	JONES	1620	Haberdasher	
Edward	E	BARKHAM	1621	Draper	
Peter	P	PROBIE	1622	Grocer	
Martin	M	LUMLEY	1623	Draper	
John	J	GORE	1624	Merchant Taylor	
Allan	A	COTTON	1625	Draper	
Cuthbert	C	HACKET	1626	Draper	
Hugh	H	HAMMERSLEY	1627	Haberdasher	
Richard	R	DEANE	1628	Skinner	
James	J	CAMBELL	1629	Ironmonger	
Robert	R	DUCYE	1630	Merchant Taylor	
George	G	WHITMORE	1631	Haberdasher	
Nicholas	N	RAINTON	1632	Haberdasher	
Ralph	R	FREEMAN	1633	Clothworker	Died in office
Thomas	T	MOULSON	1634	Grocer	Mar-Oct 1634
Robert	R	PARKHURST	1634	Clothworker	
Christopher	C	CLITHEROW	1635	Ironmonger	
Edward	E	BROMFIELD	1636	Fishmonger	
Richard	R	VENN	1637	Haberdasher	
Morris	M	ABBOT	1638	Draper	
Henry	H	GARRAWAY	1639	Draper	
Edmund	E	WRIGHT	1640	Grocer	
Richard	R	GURNEY	1641	Clothworker	
Isaac	I	PENINGTON	1642	Fishmonger	
John	J	WOLLASTON	1643	Goldsmith	
Thomas	T	ATKYN	1644	Mercer	
Thomas	T	ADAMS	1645	Draper	
John	J	GAYER	1646	Fishmonger	
John	J	WARNER	1647	Grocer	Died in office
Abraham	A	REYNARDSON	1648	Merchant Taylor	Dismissed by Parliament
Thomas	T	ANDREWES	1649	Leatherseller	April-Oct 1649
Thomas	T	FOOT	1649	Grocer	
Thomas		ANDREWES	1650	Leatherseller	
John	J	KENDRICKE	1651	Grocer	
John	J	FOWKE	1652	Haberdasher	

Thomas	T	VYNER	1653	Goldsmith	
Christopher	C	PACK	1654	Draper	
John	J	DETHICK	1655	Mercer	
Robert	R	TICHBORNE	1656	Skinner	
Richard	R	CHIVERTON	1657	Skinner	
John	J	IRETON	1658	Clothworker	
Thomas	T	ALLEYN	1659	Grocer	
Richard	R	BROWNE	1660	Merchant Taylor	
John	J	FREDERICK	1661	Grocer	
John	J	ROBINSON	1662	Clothworker	
Anthony	A	BATEMAN	1663	Skinner	
John	J	LAWRENCE	1664	Haberdasher	
Thomas	T	BLUDWORTH	1665	Vintner	
William	W	BOLTON	1666	Merchant Taylor	
William	W	PEAKE	1667	Clothworker	
William	W	TURNER	1668	Merchant Taylor	
Samuel	S	STARLING	1669	Draper	
Richard	R	FORD	1670	Mercer	
George	G	WATERMAN	1671	Skinner	
Robert	R	HANSON	1672	Grocer	
William	W	HOOKER	1673	Grocer	
Robert	R	VYNER	1674	Goldsmith	
Joseph	J	SHELDON	1675	Draper	
Thomas	T	DAVIES	1676	Draper	
Francis	F	CHAPLIN	1677	Clothworker	
James	J	EDWARDS	1678	Grocer	
Robert	R	CLAYTON	1679	Draper	
Patience	P	WARD	1680	Merchant Taylor	
John	J	MOORE [1]	1681	Grocer	
William	W	PRICHARD	1682	Merchant Taylor	
Henry	H	TULSE	1683	Grocer	
James	J	SMYTH	1684	Draper	Nominated by king
Robert	R	GEFFERY	1685	Ironmonger	Nominated by king
John	J	PEAKE	1686	Mercer	Nominated by king
John	J	SHORTER	1687	Goldsmith	Nominated by king and died in office
John	J	EYLES [1]	1688	Haberdasher	Nominated by king
John	J	CHAPMAN	1688	Mercer	Died in office
Thomas	T	PILKINGTON	1689	Skinner	Mar-Oct 1689
Thomas	T	PILKINGTON	1689	Skinner	
Thomas	T	STAMPE	1691	Draper	
John	J	FLEET	1692	Grocer	
William	W	ASHURST	1693	Merchant Taylor	
Thomas	T	LANE	1694	Clothworker	
John	J	HOUBLON	1695	Grocer	
Edward	E	CLARKE	1696	Merchant Taylor	
Humphrey	H	EDWIN	1697	Skinner	
Francis	F	CHILD [1]	1698	Goldsmith	

Richard	R	LEVETT	1699	Haberdasher	
Thomas	T	ABNEY	1700	Fishmonger	
William	W	GORE	1701	Mercer	
Samuel	S	DASHWOOD	1702	Vintner	
John	J	PARSONS	1703	Fishmonger	
Owen	C	BUCKINGHAM	1704	Salter	
Thomas	T	RAWLINSON [1]	1705	Vintner	
Robert	R	BEDINGFELD	1706	Merchant Taylor	
William	W	WITHERS	1707	Fishmonger	
Charles	C	DUNCOMBE	1708	Goldsmith	
Samuel	S	GARRARD	1709	Grocer	
Gilbert	G	HEATHCOTE	1710	Vintner	
Robert	R	BEACHCROFT	1711	Clothworker	
Richard	R	HOARE [1]	1712	Goldsmith	
Samuel	S	STANIER	1713	Draper	
William	W	HUMFREYS	1714	Ironmonger	
Charles	C	PEERS	1715	Salter	
James	J	BATEMAN	1716	Fishmonger	
William	W	LEWEN	1717	Haberdasher	
John	J	WARD	1718	Merchant Taylor	
George	G	THOROLD	1719	Ironmonger	
John	J	FRYER	1720	Fishmonger	
William	W	STEWART	1721	Goldsmith	
Gerard	G	CONYERS	1722	Salter	
Peter	P	DELME	1723	Fishmonger	
George	G	MERTTINS	1724	Skinner	
Francis	F	FORBES	1725	Haberdasher	
John	J	EYLES [2]	1726	Haberdasher	
Edward	E	BECHER	1727	Draper	
Robert	R	BAYLIS	1728	Grocer	
Robert	R	BROCAS	1729	Grocer	
Humphrey	H	PARSONS	1730	Grocer	
Francis	F	CHILD [2]	1731	Goldsmith	
John	J	BARBER	1732	Goldsmith	
William	W	BILLERS	1733	Haberdasher	
Edward	E	BELLAMY	1734	Fishmonger	
John	J	WILLIAMS	1735	Mercer	
John	J	THOMPSON	1736	Vintner	
John	J	BARNARD	1737	Grocer	
Micajah	M	PERRY	1738	Haberdasher	
John	J	SALTER	1739	Merchant Taylor	
Humphrey		PARSONS	1740	Grocer	Died in office
Daniel	D	LAMBERT	1741	Vintner	Mar-Oct 1741
Robert	R	GODSCHALL	1741	Ironmonger	Died in office
George	G	HEATHCOTE	1742	Salter	June-Oct 1742
Robert	R	WILLIMOTT	1742	Cooper	The first Lord Mayor not to belong to one of the great 12 livery companies

Robert	R	WESTLEY	1743	Merchant Taylor	
Henry	H	MARSHALL	1744	Draper	
Richard	R	HOARE [2]	1745	Goldsmith	
William	W	BENN	1746	Fletcher	
Robert	R	LADBROKE	1747	Grocer	
William	W	CALVERT	1748	Brewer	
Samuel	S	PENNANT	1749	Ironmonger	Died in office
John	J	BLACHFORD	1750	Goldsmith	May-Oct 1750
Francis	F	COCKAYNE	1750	Vintner	
Thomas	T	WINTERBOTTOM	1751	Clothworker	Died in office
Robert	R	ALSOP	1752	Ironmonger	June-Nov 1752
Crisp	C	GASCOYNE	1752	Brewer	The first Lord Mayor to inhabit the mayoral residence, Mansion House
Edward	E	IRONSIDE	1753	Goldsmith	Died in office
Thomas	T	RAWLINSON [2]	1753	Grocer	
Stephen	ST	JANSSEN	1754	Stationer	
Slingsby	S	BETHELL	1755	Fishmonger	
Marshe	M	DICKINSON	1756	Grocer	
Charles	C	ASGILL	1757	Skinner	
Richard	R	GLYN	1758	Salter	
Thomas	T	CHITTY	1759	Salter	
Mathew	M	BLAKISTON	1760	Grocer	
Samuel	S	FLUDYER	1761	Clothworker	
William	W	BECKFORD	1762	Ironmonger	
William	W	BRIDGEN	1763	Cutler	
William	W	STEPHENSON	1764	Grocer	
George	G	NELSON	1765	Grocer	
Robert	R	KITE	1766	Skinner	
Thomas	T	HARLEY	1767	Goldsmith	
Samuel	S	TURNER	1768	Clothworker	
William		BECKFORD	1769	Ironmonger	Died in office
Barlow	B	TRECOTHICK	1770	Clothworker	June-Nov 1770
Brass	B	CROSBY	1770	Goldsmith	
William	W	NASH	1771	Salter	
James	J	TOWNSEND	1772	Mercer	
Frederick	F	BULL	1773	Salter	
John	J	WILKES	1774	Joiner	
John	J	SAWBRIDGE	1775	Framework Knitter	
Thomas	T	HALLIFAX	1776	Goldsmith	
James	J	ESDAILE	1777	Cooper	
Samuel	S	PLUMBE	1778	Goldsmith	
Brackley	B	KENNETT	1779	Vintner	
Watkin	W	LEWES	1780	Joiner	
William	W	PLOMER	1781	Tyler	
Nathaniel	N	NEWNHAM	1782	Mercer	
Robert	R	PECKHAM	1783	Wheelwright	
Richard	R	CLARK	1784	Joiner	

Thomas	T	WRIGHT	1785	Stationer
Thomas	T	SAINSBURY	1786	Bowyer
John	J	BURNELL	1787	Glover
William	W	GILL	1788	Stationer
William	W	PICKETT	1789	Goldsmith
John	J	BOYDELL	1790	Stationer
John	J	HOPKINS	1791	Grocer
James	J	SANDERSON	1792	Draper
Paul	P	LE MESURIER	1793	Goldsmith
Thomas	T	SKINNER [2]	1794	Haberdasher
William	W	CURTIS	1795	Draper
Brook	B	WATSON	1796	Musician
John	JW	ANDERSON	1797	Glover
Richard	R	CARR GLYN	1798	Salter
Harvey	HC	COMBE	1799	Brewer
William	W	STAINES	1800	Carpenter
John	J	EAMER	1801	Salter
Charles	C	PRICE	1802	Ironmonger
John	J	PERRING	1803	Clothworker
Peter	P	PERCHARD	1804	Goldsmith
James	J	SHAW	1805	Scrivener
William	W	LEIGHTON	1806	Fishmonger
John	J	ANSLEY	1807	Merchant Taylor
Charles	C	FLOWER	1808	Framework Knitter
Thomas	T	SMITH	1809	Leatherseller
Joshua	JJ	SMITH	1810	Ironmonger
Claudius	CS	HUNTER	1811	Merchant Taylor
George	G	SCHOLEY	1812	Distillers
William	W	DOMVILLE	1813	Stationer
Samuel	S	BIRCH	1814	Cook
Matthew	M	WOOD	1815	Fishmonger
Christopher	C	SMITH	1817	Draper
John	J	ATKINS	1818	Merchant Taylor
George	G	BRIDGES	1819	Wheelwright
John	JT	THORP	1820	Draper
Christopher	C	MAGNAY	1821	Merchant Taylor
William	W	HEYGATE	1822	Merchant Taylor
Robert	R	WAITHMAN	1823	Framework Knitter
John	J	GARRATT	1824	Goldsmith
William	W	VENABLES	1825	Stationer
Anthony	A	BROWN	1826	Fishmonger
Matthias	MP	LUCAS	1827	Vintner
William	W	THOMPSON	1828	Ironmonger
John	J	CROWDER	1829	Makers of Playing Cards
John	J	KEY	1830	Stationer
Peter	P	LAURIE	1832	Saddler
Charles	C	FAREBROTHER	1833	Vintner

Henry	H	WINCHESTER	1834	Cutler
William	WT	COPELAND	1835	Goldsmith
Thomas	T	KELLY	1836	Plaisterer
John	J	COWAN	1837	Wax Chandler
Samuel	S	WILSON	1838	Weaver
Chapman	C	MARSHALL	1839	Innholder
Thomas	T	JOHNSON	1840	Cooper
John	J	PIRIE	1841	Plaisterer
John	J	HUMPHREY	1842	Tallow Chandler
William	W	MAGNAY	1843	Stationer
Michael	M	GIBBS	1844	Fishmonger
John	J	JOHNSON	1845	Spectaclemaker
George	G	CARROLL	1846	Spectaclemaker
John	JK	HOOPER	1847	Vintner
James	J	DUKE	1848	Spectaclemaker
Thomas	T	FARNCOMB	1849	Tallow Chandler
John	J	MUSGROVE	1850	Clothworker
William	W	HUNTER	1851	Upholder
Thomas	T	CHALLIS	1852	Butcher
Thomas	T	SIDNEY	1853	Girdler
Francis.	FG	MOON	1854	Stationer
David	D	SALOMONS	1855	Cooper
Thomas	TQ	FINNIS	1856	Bowyer
Robert	RW	CARDEN	1857	Cutler
David	DW	WIRE	1858	Innholder
John	J	CARTER	1859	Clockmaker
William	W	CUBITT	1860	Fishmonger
William	WA	ROSE	1862	Spectaclemaker
William	W	LAWRENCE	1863	Carpenter
Warren	WS	HALE	1864	Tallow Chandler
Benjamin	BS	PHILLIPS	1865	Spectaclemaker
Thomas	T	GABRIEL	1866	Goldsmith
William	WF	ALLEN	1867	Stationer
James	JC	LAWRENCE	1868	Carpenter
Robert	R	BESLEY	1869	Loriner
Thomas	T	DAKIN	1870	Spectaclemaker
Sills	SJ	GIBBONS	1871	Salter
Sydney	SH	WATERLOW	1872	Stationer
Andrew	A	LUSK	1873	Spectaclemaker
David	DH	STONE	1874	Spectaclemaker
William	WJR	COTTON	1875	Haberdasher
Thomas	T	WHITE	1876	Vintner
Thomas	TS	OWDEN	1877	Innholder
Charles	C	WHETHAM	1878	Leatherseller
Francis	FW	TRUSCOTT	1879	Stationer
William	W	MCARTHUR	1880	Spectaclemaker
Whittacker	JW	ELLIS	1881	Merchant Taylor

Henry	HE	KNIGHT	1882	Spectaclemaker
Robert	RN	FOWLER	1883	Spectaclemaker .
George	GS	NOTTAGE	1884	Spectaclemaker
Robert		FOWLER	1885	Spectaclemaker .
John	J	STAPLES	1885	Leatherseller
Reginald	R	HANSON	1886	Merchant Taylor
Polydore	P	DE KEYSER	1887	Spectaclemaker
James	J	WHITEHEAD	1888	Fanmaker
Henry	HA	ISAACS	1889	Loriner
Joseph	J	SAVORY	1890	Goldsmith
David	D	EVANS	1891	Haberdasher
Stuart	S	KNILL	1892	Goldsmith
George	GR	TYLER	1893	Stationer
Joseph	J	RENALS	1894	Spectaclemaker
Walter	WH	WILKIN	1895	Broderer
George	G	FAUDEL-PHILLIPS	1896	Spectaclemaker
Horatio	HD	DAVIES	1897	Spectaclemaker .
John	JV	MOORE [2]	1898	Loriner
Alfred	AJ	NEWTON	1899	Fanmaker
Frank	F	GREEN	1900	Glazier
Joseph	JC	DIMSDALE	1901	Grocer
Marcus	M	SAMUEL	1902	Spectaclemaker
James	JT	RITCHIE	1903	Shipwright
John	J	POUND	1904	Leatherseller
Walter	WV	MORGAN	1905	Cutler
William	WP	TRELOAR	1906	Loriner
John	JC	BELL	1907	Haberdasher
George	GW	TRUSCOTT	1908	Stationer
John	J	KNILL	1909	Goldsmith
Vezey	TV	STRONG	1910	Stationer
Thomas	TB	CROSBY	1911	Turner
David	D	BURNETT	1912	Loriner
Vansittart	TV	BOWATER	1913	Girdler
Charles	C	JOHNSTON	1914	Innholder
Charles	CC	WAKEFIELD	1915	Haberdasher
William	WH	DUNN	1916	Wheelwright
Charles	CA	HANSON	1917	Pattenmaker .
Horace	H	MARSHALL	1918	Stationer
Edward	EE	COOPER	1919	Musician
James	J	ROLL	1920	Horner
John	JJ	BADDELEY	1921	Framework Knitter
Edward	EC	MOORE	1922	Fruiterer
Louis	LA	NEWTON	1923	Loriner
Alfred	AL	BOWER	1924	Vintner
William	WR	PRYKE	1925	Painter Stainer
George.	GR	BLADES	1926	Gardener .
Charles	CA	BATHO	1927	Pavior

Kynaston	JEK	STUDD	1928	Fruiterer
William	WA	WATERLOW	1929	Stationer
Phene	WP	NEAL	1930	Horner
Maurice	M	JENKS	1931	Haberdasher
Percy	PW	GREENAWAY	1932	Stationer
Charles	CH	COLLETT	1933	Glover
Stephen	SHM	KILLIK	1934	Fanmaker
Percy	P	VINCENT	1935	Gold & Silver Wiredrawer
George	GT	BROADBRIDGE	1936	Loriner
Harry	HEA	TWYFORD	1937	Framework Knitter
Frank	FH	BOWATER	1938	Girdler
William	WG	COXEN	1939	Cordwainer
George	GH	WILKINSON	1940	Stationer
John	JD	LAURIE	1941	Saddler
Samuel	SG	JOSEPH	1942	Cutler
Frank	FE	NEWSON-SMITH	1943	Turner
Frank	FS	ALEXANDER	1944	Shipwright
Charles	C	DAVIS	1945	Fanmaker
Bracewell	B	SMITH	1946	Spectaclemaker
Frederick	FM	WELLS	1947	Carman
George	G	AYLWEN	1948	Merchant Taylor
Frederick	F	ROWLAND	1949	Horner
Denys	DCF	LOWSON	1950	Grocer
Leslie	HL	BOYCE	1951	Loriner
Rupert	R	DE LA BÈRE	1952	Skinner
Noel.	NV	BOWATER	1953	Vintner
Seymour	HWS	HOWARD	1954	Gardener
Cuthbert	CL	ACKROYD	1955	Carpenter
Cullum	GJC	WELCH	1956	Haberdasher
Denis	DH	TRUSCOTT	1957	Stationer
Harold	SH	GILLETT	1958	Basketmaker
Edmund	EVM	STOCKDALE	1959	Carpenter
Bernard	B	WALEY COHEN	1960	Clothworker
Frederick	FA	HOARE	1961	Spectaclemaker
Ralph	RE	PERRING	1962	Tin Plate Worker
James	CJ	HARMAN	1963	Painter Stainer
James	J	MILLERS	1964	Coachmaker
Lionel	JLP	DENNY	1965	Vintner
Robert	RI	BELLINGER	1966	Broderer
Gilbert	GS	INGLEFIELD	1967	Haberdasher
Charles	AC	TRINDER	1968	Fletcher
Ian	I F	BOWATER	1969	Haberdasher
Peter	P	STUDD	1970	Merchant Taylor
Edward	HE	HOWARD	1971	Gardener
Alan	AR	MAIS	1972	Pavior
Hugh	HWS	WONTNER	1973	Feltmaker
Murray	HM	FOX	1974	Wheelwright

Lindsay	LR	RING	1975	Armourer
Robin	RP	GILLETT	1976	Master Mariner
Peter	PBR	VANNECK	1977	Gunmaker
Kenneth	KR	CORK	1978	Horner
Peter	PDH	GADSDEN	1979	Clothworker
Ronald	R	GARDNER-THORPE	1980	Painter Stainer
Christopher	C	LEAVER	1981	Carman
Anthony	A	JOLLIFFE	1982	Painter Stainer
Mary	AS	DONALDSON	1983	Gardener
Alan	A	TRAILL	1984	Cutler
Allan	WA	DAVIS	1985	Painter Stainer
David	DK	ROWE-HAM	1986	Wheelwright
Greville	GD	SPRATT	1987	Ironmonger
Christopher	C	COLLETT	1988	Glover
Hugh	HCP	BIDWELL	1989	Grocer
Alexander	AM	GRAHAM	1990	Mercer
Brian	BG	JENKINS	1991	Ch Accountant
Francis	F	MCWILLIAMS	1992	Loriner
Paul	PH	NEWALL	1993	Baker
Christopher	CR	WALFORD	1994	Makers of Playing Cards
John	LJ	CHALSTREY	1995	Apothecary
Roger	RW	CORK	1996	Bowyer
Richard	RE	NICHOLS	1997	Salter
Peter	P	LEVENE	1998	Carman
Clive	CH	MARTIN	1999	Stationer
David	DHS	HOWARD	2000	Gardener
Michael	JMY	OLIVER	2001	Ironmonger
Gavyn	GF	ARTHUR	2002	Gardener
Robert	RG	FINCH	2003	Solicitor
Michael	MB	SAVORY	2004	Poulter
David	DW	BREWER	2005	Merchant Taylor
John	J	STUTTARD	2006	Glazier
David	D	LEWIS	2007	Solicitor
Ian	I D	LUDER	2008	Cooper
Nick		ANSTEE	2009	Butcher
Michael		BEAR	2010	Pavior
David		WOOTTON	2011	Fletcher
Roger		GIFFORD	2012	Musician
Fiona		WOOLF	2013	Solicitor
Alan		YARROW	2014	Fishmonger

Appendix 2

LIST OF LONDON SHERIFFS

Sheriff	Year
Bokointe, John	1190
de Haverell, William	1190
Duket, Nicholas	1191
Nevelun, Peter	1191
le Duk, Roger	1192
fitz-Alan, Roger	1192
fitz-Alulf, William	1193
fitz-Isabel, William	1193
Alderman, Jukel	1194
Besaunt, Robert	1194
de Antioche, Godard	1195
fitz-Durand, Robert	1195
Blund, Robert	1196
Duket, Nicholas	1196
de Bel, Robert	1197
fitz-Alulf, Constantine	1197
Blunt, Richard	1198
fitz-Alulf, Ernulf	1198
Alderman, James	1199
de Deserto, Roger	1199
de Aldermanbury, Simon	1200
fitz-Alice, William	1200
Blund, Norman	1201
de Cayo, John	1201
Brun, Walter	1202
Chamberleyn, William	1202
Brond, Hamond	1203
de Haverell, Thomas	1203
de Winton, Richard	1204
fitz-Eliandi, John	1205
fitz-Gerard, Edmund	1205
le Mercer, Serlo	1206
of St. Alban's, Henry	1206
de Winton, Robert	1207
Hardel, William	1207
le Duc, Peter	1208
Nele, Thomas	1208
Blund, William	1209
Nevelun, Peter	1209
de Witebi, Adam	1210
Garland, John	1211
Elyland, Ralph	1212
juvenis, Constantine	1212
Bat, Peter	1213
fitz-Alice, Martin	1213
de Basing, Hugo	1214
de Basing, Salomon	1214
Nevelun, Andrew	1215
Blund, William	1216
Senturer, Benedict	1216
Bukerel, Thomas	1217
Elyland, Ralph	1217
le Spicer, Joce	1218
Lambart, Thomas	1221
Lambart, Thomas	1222
fitz-William, Martin	1225
Cocham, Henry	1227
de Woborne, John	1230
le Bufle, Walter	1231
de Edmonton, Henry	1232
of Coventry, Jordan	1236
de Coudres, John	1238
de Wylhale, John	1238
Viel Jnr, John	1241
Eswy, Radulph	1242

Blunt, Hugh	1243	de Basing, William	1308
de Arcubus, Ralph	1244	le Boteler, James	1308
of Bentley, Adam	1245	of St. Edmond, James	1309
le Feure, Humphrey	1250	de Palmer, Roger	1309
Picard, Richard	1253	de Blakeneye, Peter	1310
de Linton, Robert	1254	Cambridge, John	1310
de Oystergate, Stephen	1254	Corp, Simon	1310
de Walemunt, Henry	1254	de Welleford, Richard	1311
de Cateloigne, Robert	1257	Merwod, Simon	1311
Grapefige, William	1257	Lambyn, John	1312
de Mountpiler, Robert	1262	de Welleford, Richard	1312
de Suffolke, Osbert	1262	Lutkin, Adam	1312
de Ford, Thomas	1263	Burdeyn, Robert	1313
de Badencourt, Lucas	1266	de Gartone, Hugh	1313
de Bodele, John	1271	de Chigwell, Hamo	1314
Paris, Richard	1271	de Godchep, Hamo	1315
Cosyn, Peter	1273	Redynge, William	1315
Adrien Jnr, John	1277	le Palmer, Ralph	1316
le Mazeliner, William	1278	de Caustone, William	1316
de Basinge, Robert	1278	Furneis, William	1317
de la More, Ralph	1279	Priour, John	1317
Box, Thomas	1279	Dalling, John	1318
de Chigwell, Richard	1281	Poyntel, John	1318
le Blund, Walter	1282	de Prestone, John	1319
Goodcheape, Jordan	1283	Produn, William	1320
Box, Martin	1283	de Conduit, Reginald	1320
Cornhill, Stephen	1284	de Hakeneie, Richard	1321
Wade, John	1285	Elie, Richard	1322
Hauteyn, Walter	1286	de Grantham, John	1322
Cros, Thomas	1286	de Oxenford, John	1323
de Estanes, Thomas	1287	de Salisbury, Adam	1323
St. Edmond, Fulk	1289	Gille, Alan	1324
le Coteler, Solomon	1289	de Folesham, Benedict	1324
Romeyn, Thomas	1290	Mordon, Gilbert	1325
de Leyre, William	1290	Chaunteclere, Roger	1326
Box, Hamo	1291	de Rothyng, Richard	1326
Amersbury, Martin	1293	Darci, Henry	1327
Rokesley Jnr, Robert	1293	Fraunceys, Simon	1328
Box, Henry	1294	de Gisors, Henry	1329
de Hallingberi, Adam	1295	le Lacer, Richard	1329
of Suffolke, Thomas	1296	Harewolde, Thomas	1330
de Storteford, John	1297	de Mockyng, John	1331
de Storteford, William	1297	Husbond, John	1332
de Fyngrie, Henry	1299	Pike, Nicholas	1332
Champs, Richard	1300	Haunsard, William	1333
de Hauering, Lucas	1300	Hamond, John	1333
de Bosenho, Peter	1301	Turke, Walter	1334
le Callere, Robert	1301	de Bricklesworth, William	1336
de Bureford, John	1303	de Northall, John	1336
de Lincoln, John	1304	Neel, Walter	1337
de Paris, Roger	1304	Marberer, Hugh	1338
Thunderley, Reginald	1305	de Pountfrey, William	1338
de Conduit, Geoffrey	1306	de Thorneye, William	1339
Bolet, Simon	1306	Lucas, Adam	1340
Drury, Nigel	1307	Deumars, Bartholomew	1340

de Rokele, John	1341	Bryan, John	1418
de Kislingbury, Richard	1342	Botiler, John	1419
Lovekyn, John	1342	Welles, John	1420
Syward, John	1343	Boteler, John	1420
de Wychingham, Geoffrey	1344	Weston, William	1421
Hemenhall, Edmond	1345	Gosselyn, Richard	1421
de Gloucester, John	1345	Estfeld, William	1422
Clopton, William	1346	Wandesford, Thomas	1423
de Croydon, John	1346	Brokle, John	1425
de Basyngstoke, Richard	1347	Melreth, William	1425
Dolseley, Simon	1348	Arnold, Robert	1426
de Lenne, Ralph	1349	Higham, John	1426
Worcester, William	1350	Abbot, John	1428
Nott, John	1350	Dufthous, Thomas	1428
Stayndrop, Gilbert	1351	Russe, William	1429
Wroth, John	1351	Holland, Ralph	1429
Little, John	1353	Chertsey, Walter	1430
Smelt, Richard	1354	Hatherle, John	1431
Brandon, Thomas	1355	Olney, John	1432
Forster, Walter	1355	Lynge, John	1433
Cavendisshe, Stephen	1357	Eyre, Simon	1434
Buris, John	1358	Morstede, Thomas	1436
de Bernes, John	1358	Chapman, William	1437
de Benyngton, Simon	1359	Hales, William	1437
Denis, John	1360	Dyke, Hugh	1438
de Berneye, Walter	1360	Marshal, Robert	1439
de St. Albans, John	1362	Malpas, Philip	1439
Hiltoft, John	1363	Rich, Richard	1441
de Croydon, Richard	1363	Beaumond, Thomas	1442
de Mytford, John	1364	Nordon, Richard	1442
de Briklesworth, John	1365	Wiche, Hugh	1444
Irlond, Thomas	1365	Feldynge, Geoffrey	1445
of Lee, Thomas	1366	Boleyn, Geoffrey	1446
Warde, John	1366	Marowe, William	1448
Dikeman, William	1367	Hulyn, William	1449
Girdelere, Robert	1368	Dere, William	1450
Wimondham, Adam	1368	Middleton, John	1450
Holbech, Hugh	1369	Feelde, John	1451
Geyton, Robert	1370	Walderne, John	1453
Stable, Adam	1371	Cook, Thomas	1453
Hatfield, Robert	1371	Taillour, William	1454
Fyfhide, John	1373	Oulegrave, Thomas	1455
Wodehous, William	1374	Yonge, John	1455
Neuport, William	1375	Steward, John	1456
Vynent, Thomas	1390	Verney, Ralph	1456
Louthe, William	1404	Reyner, Thomas	1457
Speleman, Stephen	1404	Edward, William	1457
Barton, Henry	1405	Nedeham, Richard	1458
Duke, Thomas	1408	Plummer, John	1459
Reynwell, John	1411	Lambarde, John	1460
Micoll, John	1413	Lok, John	1461
Sutton, John	1413	Hampton, William	1462
Widyngton, Robert	1416	James, Bartholomew	1462
Coventre, John	1416	Muschampe, Thomas	1463
Read, Henry	1417	Stone, John	1464

Waver, Henry	1465	Dauntsey, William	1530
Bryce, Henry	1466	Altham, Edward	1531
Stalbrook, Thomas	1467	Gresham, Richard	1531
Smyth, Simon	1468	Pyncheon, Nicholas	1532
Haryot, William	1468	Martyn, John	1532
Aleyn, John	1471	Preest, John	1532
Shelley, John	1471	Reynolds, Richard	1532
Bryce, Hugh	1475	Kytson, Thomas	1533
Horne, William	1476	Leveson, Nicholas	1534
Stokker, John	1477	Lewen, Thomas	1537
Byfeld, Robert	1478	Gresham, John	1537
Hardyng, Robert	1478	Gybson, Nicholas	1538
Danyell, Thomas	1480	Wilkenson, William	1538
Chawry, Richard	1481	Huntlowe, Thomas	1539
White, William	1482	Fayrey, John	1539
Wood, Thomas	1491	Suckley, Henry	1541
Browne, William	1491	Hill, Rowland	1541
Fabyan, Robert	1493	Curtes, Thomas	1546
Wynger, John	1493	Ayliffe, John	1548
Ailwyn, Nicholas	1494	Yorke, John	1549
Warner, John	1494	Cowper, John	1551
Somer, Henry	1495	Maynard, John	1552
Kneseworth, Thomas	1495	Duckett, Lionel	1564
Haddon, Richard	1496	Hawes, James	1565
Rede, Bartholomew	1497	Nicholas, Ambrose	1566
Wyndout, Thomas	1497	Boxe, William	1570
Jenyns, Stephen	1498	Branche, John	1571
Bradbury, Thomas	1498	Pullyson, Thomas	1573
Bronde, Richard	1499	Harte, John	1579
Wilforth, James	1499	Allott, John	1580
Hawes, John	1500	Buckle, Cuthbert	1582
Stede, William	1500	Haydon, John	1582
Hede, Henry	1501	Billingsley, Henry	1584
Aylmer, Lawrence	1501	Ratclyffe, Anthony	1585
Watts, Robert	1503	Prannell, Henry	1585
Hawes, Christopher	1503	Elkyn, William	1586
Browne Jnr, William	1504	Howse, Robert	1586
Grove, Roger	1505	Skinner, Thomas	1587
Boteler, William	1507	Catcher, John	1587
Kirkby, John	1507	Offley, Hugh	1588
Exmue, Thomas	1508	Saltonstall, Richard	1588
Smyth, Richard	1508	Barnham, Benedict	1591
Doget, John	1509	Ryder, William	1591
Milborne, John	1510	Houghton, Peter	1593
Symonds, Ralph	1517	Style, Oliver	1604
Skevynton, John	1520	Jones, Francis	1610
Breton, John	1521	Jeye, Henry	1613
Pargeter, Thomas	1521	Lumley, Martin	1614
Champneys, John	1522	Gore, John	1615
Roche, William	1524	Gore, William	1615
Hollyes, William	1527	Cotton, Allan	1616
Long, John	1528	Hacket, Cuthbert	1616
Dormer, Michael	1529	Johnson, Robert	1617
Champyon, Walter	1529	Herne, Richard	1618
Choppyn, Richard	1530	Hammersley, Hugh	1618

Cambell, James	1619	Bethel, Slingsby	1680
Deane, Richard	1619	Shute, Samuel	1681
Allen, Edward	1620	North, Dudley	1682
Ducye, Robert	1620	Rich, Peter	1682
Handford, Humphrey	1622	Dashwood, Samuel	1683
Hodges, John	1622	Gostlyn, William	1684
Parkhurst, Robert	1624	Vandeput, Peter	1684
Poole, John	1625	Thorowgood, Benjamin	1685
Clitherow, Christopher	1625	Kinsey, Thomas	1685
Abdy, Anthony	1630	Rawlinson, Thomas	1686
Cambell, Robert	1630	Fowle, Thomas	1686
Cranmer, Samuel	1631	Parsons, John	1687
Pratt, Henry	1631	Firebrace, Basil	1687
Andrewes, Henry	1632	Edwin, Humphrey	1688
Gurney, Richard	1633	Thomson, Samuel	1688
Harrison, Gilbert	1633	Fleet, John	1688
Highlord, John	1634	Lethuillier, Christopher	1689
Cordell, John	1634	Houblon, John	1689
Soame, Thomas	1635	Ashhurst, William	1691
Gayer, John	1635	Hedges, William	1693
Abell, William	1636	Cole, William	1694
Garrard, Jacob	1636	Sweetapple, John	1694
Atkyn, Thomas	1637	Wills, Edward	1695
Rudge, Edward	1637	Buckingham, Owen	1695
Penington, Isaac	1638	Blewitt, Samuel	1696
Wollaston, John	1638	Woolfe, John	1696
Adams, Thomas	1639	Collett, James	1697
Warner, John	1639	Gracedieu, Bartholomew	1697
Towse, John	1640	Duncombe, Charles	1699
Reynardson, Abraham	1640	Jeffreys, Jeffrey	1699
Garrett, George	1641	Beachcroft, Robert	1700
Clarke, George	1641	Furnese, Henry	1700
Browne, Richard	1648	Bateman, James	1702
Ireton, John	1651	Woolfe, Joseph	1703
Riccard, Andrew	1651	Buckworth, John	1704
Bigg, Walter	1653	Humfreys, William	1704
Vyner, Robert	1666	Stanier, Samuel	1705
Sheldon, Joseph	1666	Benson, William	1706
Davies, Thomas	1667	Crowley, Ambrose	1706
Ward, Patience	1670	Peers, Charles	1707
Smyth, James	1672	Green, Benjamin	1707
Tulse, Henry	1673	Hopson, Charles	1708
Geffery, Robert	1673	Guy, Richard	1708
Herne, Nathaniel	1674	Dunk, Thomas	1709
Lethuillier, John	1674	Eyles, Francis	1710
Gold, Thomas	1675	Stewart, William	1711
Shorter, John	1675	Clarke, Samuel	1712
Peake, John	1676	Forbes, Francis	1713
Stampe, Thomas	1676	Sharpe, Joshua	1713
Rawsterne, William	1677	Breedon, Robert	1714
Beckford, Thomas	1677	Knipe, Randolph	1714
Chapman, John	1678	Cook, Charles	1716
Lewis, Simon	1679	Master, Harcourt	1717
Raymond, Jonathan	1679	Ambrose, Thomas	1718
Cornish, Henry	1680	Bull, John	1718

Tash, John	1719	Fenn, James	1787
Caswall, George	1720	Bloxam, Matthew	1787
Billers, William	1720	Baker, Thomas	1789
Feast, Felix	1723	Brander, Alexander	1792
Hopkins, Richard	1723	Tebbs, Benjamin	1792
Eyles, Joseph	1724	Hamerton, Charles	1793
Murden, Jeremiah	1725	Perchard, Peter	1793
Lock, John	1726	Burnett, Robert	1794
Ogborne, William	1726	Eamer, John	1794
Grosvenor, John	1727	Glode, Richard	1795
Lombe, Thomas	1727	Liptrap, John	1795
Fuller, John	1730	Mellish, Peter	1798
Shard, Isaac	1730	Champion, William	1798
Pindar, Thomas	1731	Blackall, John	1799
Russell, Samuel	1731	Flower, Charles	1799
Lambert, Daniel	1733	Rawlins, William	1801
Westley, Robert	1733	Cox, Robert Albion	1801
Rawling, Benjamin	1736	Alexander, James	1802
Rous, William	1736	Welch, Richard	1802
Russell, Thomas	1737	Scholey, George	1804
Brooke, James	1738	Domville, William	1804
Westbrooke, William	1738	Branscomb, James	1806
Smith, William	1741	Miles, Jonathan	1806
Eggleton, Charles	1742	Smith, Christopher	1807
Scott, Robert	1750	Phillips, Richard	1807
Alexander, William	1750	Heygate, William	1811
Torriano, John	1754	Blades, John	1812
Whitbread, Ive	1755	Hoy, Michael	1812
Master, Alexander	1758	Marsh, Thomas Coxhead	1813
Dandridge, James	1758	Leigh, Joseph	1814
Errington, George	1759	Reay, John	1814
Vaillant, Paul	1759	Bell, Thomas	1815
Hart, William	1760	Thorp, John Thomas	1815
Bankes, Henry	1762	Kirby, Robert	1816
Harris, Thomas	1764	Alderson, George	1817
Crosby, Brass	1764	Desanges, Francis	1817
Charlwood, Benjamin	1765	Gwynne, Lawrence	1818
Kennett, Brackley	1765	Roberts, Thomas	1818
Darling, Robert	1766	Parkins, Joseph Wilfred	1819
Esdaile, James	1766	Williams, James	1820
Baker, William	1770	Whittaker, George Byrom	1823
Martin, Joseph	1770	Laurie, Peter	1823
Bull, Frederick	1771	Kelly, Thomas	1825
Lewes, Watkin	1772	Farebrother, Charles	1826
Sayre, Stephen	1773	Winchester, Henry	1826
Lee, William	1773	Stable, Charles	1827
Hart, John	1774	Spottiswoode, Andrew	1827
Kitchin, Henry	1778	Wilde, Edward Archer	1828
Burnell, John	1778	Booth, Felix	1828
Crichton, William	1780	Copeland, William Taylor	1828
Nicholson, William	1781	Richardson, William Henry	1829
Cole, Benjamin	1782	Ward, Thomas	1829
Taylor, Robert	1782	Poland, William H	1830
Skinner, Thomas	1783	Marshall, Chapman	1830
Higgins, Charles	1786	Pirie, John	1831

Peek, Richard	1832	Burt, George	1878
Humphery, John	1832	Bayley, Edmund Kelly	1879
Illidge, John	1834	Woolloton, Charles	1879
Raphael, Alexander	1834	Waterlow, Herbert Jameson	1880
Salomons, David	1835	Ogg, William Anderson	1881
Johnson, John	1836	Savory, Joseph	1882
Duke, James	1836	Smith, Clarence	1883
Montefiore, Moses	1837	Cowan, Phineas	1883
Carroll, George	1837	Faudel-Phillips, George	1884
Evans, William	1839	Clarke, Thomas	1885
Wheelton, John	1839	Kirby, Alfred	1886
Farncomb, Thomas	1840	Higgs, William Alpheus	1887
Rogers, Alexander	1841	Davies, Horatio David	1887
Pilcher, Jeremiah	1842	Newton, Alfred James	1888
Moon, Francis Graham	1843	Harris, Walter Henry	1889
Sidney, Thomas	1844	Farmer, William	1890
Chaplin, William James	1845	Harris, Augustus Henry Glossop	1890
Laurie, John Laurie	1845	Foster, Harry Seymour	1891
Kennard, Robert William	1846	Hand, George	1894
Hill, Charles	1847	Cooper, John Robert	1895
Cubitt, William	1847	Rogers, Robert Hargreaves	1896
Goodheart, Jacob Emanuel	1848	Dewar, Thomas Robert	1897
Nicoll, Donald Nicoll	1849	Probyn, Clifford	1898
Hodgkinson, George Edmund	1850	Bevan, Alfred Henry	1899
Cotterell, Thomas	1851	Lawrence, Joseph	1900
Swift, Richard	1851	Brooks Marshall [Lord Marshall], Horace	1901
Croll, Alexander Angus	1852	Brooke-Hitching, Thomas Henry	1902
Wallis, George Appleton	1853	Reynolds, Alfred James	1903
Crosley, Charles Decimus	1854	Woodman, George Joseph	1904
Keats, Frederick	1856	Bowater, Thomas Vansittart	1905
Mechi, John Joseph	1856	Dunn, William Henry	1906
Allen, William Ferneley	1857	Wakefield, Charles Cheers	1907
Conder, Edward	1858	Baddeley, John James	1908
Lusk, Andrew	1860	Slazenger, Ralph	1909
Cockerell, George Joseph	1861	Roll, James	1909
Twentyman, William Holme	1861	Buckingham, Henry Cecil	1910
Jones, Hugh	1862	Briggs, George	1911
Cave, Thomas	1863	Painter, Frederic George	1913
Nissen, Hilary Nicholas	1863	Bower, Alfred Louis	1913
Figgins, James	1865	de Lafontaine, Henry Cart	1914
Lycett, Francis	1866	Shead, Samuel George	1915
Mcarthur, William	1867	Newton, Louis Arthur	1916
Hutton, Charles William Cookworth	1868	Haysom, George	1916
Vallentin, James	1869	Hepburn, Harry Frankland	1917
Jones, Robert	1870	Blades [Lord Ebbisham], George Rowland	1917
Paterson, John	1870	Fletcher, Banister Flight	1918
Truscott, Francis Wyatt	1871	Smith, William Robert	1918
Young, Richard	1871	Ashdown, Curtis George	1919
Bennett, John	1871	Eves, Charles	1919
Perkins, Frederick	1872	Knights, Henry Newton	1920
Johnson, John Henry	1873	Wishart, Sidney	1920
Shaw, James	1874	McKay, George Mills	1921
Breffit, Edgar	1875	Studd, John Edward Kynaston	1922
East, William Quatermaine	1876	Killik, Stephen Henry Molyneux	1922
Bevan, Thomas	1878	Dron, Thomas Middleton	1923

Sennett, Richard Christopher	1923	Gadsden, Peter Drury Haggerston	1970
Downer, Harold George	1924	Rayner, Neville	1971
Agar, Francis Agar	1925	Horlock, Henry Wimburn Sudell	1972
Shepherd, Harry Percy	1926	Hart, Cyril Anthony	1973
Vincent, Percy	1926	Olson, Andrew Hugh Fitzgerald	1974
Davenport, Henry Edward	1927	Hedderwick, Ronald Arthur Ralph	1975
Green, Frederick Daniel	1927	Cole, Alexander Colin	1976
Coxen, William George	1928	Brown, Bernard Joseph	1977
Bowater, Frank Henry	1929	Ballard, Kenneth Alfred	1978
Collins, Daniel George	1930	Hart, John Garrow Maclachan	1979
Wilkinson, George Henry	1931	Inglefield, David Gilbert Charles	1980
Threlford, William Lacon	1932	Eskenzi, Anthony Noel	1981
Joseph, Samuel George	1933	Two aldermanic sheriffs	1982
Pearse, John Slocombe	1934	Fitzgerald, Rodney Cyril Alban	1983
Waldron, William James	1935	Two aldermanic sheriffs	1984
McRea, Charles James Hugh	1936	Neary, Jack Edward	1985
Champness, William Henry	1937	Two aldermanic sheriffs	1986
Rowland, Frederick	1938	Saunders, Richard	1987
Lowson, Denys Colquhoun Flowerdew	1939	Block, Simon Anthony Allen	1988
Trentham, George Percy	1940	Edwards, Ronald Dere Keep	1989
Boot, Horace Louis	1940	Taylor, John	1990
de la Bère, Rupert	1941	Perring, John Raymond	1991
Hewett, Robert Roy Scott	1942	Moss, Anthony David	1992
Wood, Gervase Ernest	1943	Gotch, Jeremy Millard Butler	1993
Dickson, Charles Gordon	1946	Charkham, Jonathan Philip	1994
Hammett, Richard Christmas	1947	Ayers, Kenneth Edwin	1995
Richardson, Thomas Guy Fenton	1948	Knowles, Stanley Keith	1996
Wells, Stanley Walter	1949	Two aldermanic sheriffs	1997
Lovely, Percy Thomas	1950	Harris, Brian Nicholas	1998
Fox, Sidney Joseph	1952	Halliday, Pauline Ann	1999
Tremellen, Norman Cleverton	1953	Branson, Nigel Anthony Chimmo	2000
Prince, Leslie Barnett	1954	Mauleverer, David Robin	2001
Allen, William Gilbert	1955	Clarke, Martin Courtenay	2002
Walker, Samuel Richard	1957	Bond, Geoffrey Charles	2003
Cook, John Edward Evan	1958	Cobb, David	2004
Derry, Cyril	1959	Kearney, Kevin	2005
Kirk, Adam Kennedy	1960	Regan, Richard	2006
Rawson, Christopher Selwyn	1961	Two aldermanic sheriffs	2007
Greenaway, Alan Pearce	1962	Gillon, George	2008
Edgar, Gilbert Harold Samuel	1963	Cook, Peter	2009
Ley, Arthur Harris	1964	Sermon, Richard Sermon	2010
Sweett, Cyril	1965	Mead, Wendy	2011
Toye, Herbert Graham	1966	Pullman, Nigel Reginald	2012
Ring, Lindsay Roberts	1967	Waddingham, Adrian	2013
McNeil, Kenneth Gordon	1968	Adler, Fiona	2014
Beck, Richard Theodore	1969	Rigden, Christine	2015

BIBLIOGRAPHY

Alana, Magdelena. *The Great Fire of London of 1666*. The Rosen Publishing Group, 2003.

Appleford, Amy. *Learning to Die in London: 1380–1540*. University of Pennsylvania Press, 2015.

Ashley, Maurice. *Financial and Commercial Policy under the Protectorate*. Frank Cass, 1962.

Ashley, Maurice. *The English Civil War*. Sutton, 2001.

Bamme, Adam. Available online at http://www.historyofparliamentonline. org/volume/1386-1421/member/bamme-adam-1397 [Accessed 9 May 2015].

Bayman, Dr Anna Thomas. *Dekker and the Culture of Pamphleteering in Early Modern London*. Ashgate Publishing, 2014.

Barron, Caroline. *London in the Later Middle Ages: Government and People 1200-1500*. Oxford University Press, 2005.

Barron, Caroline. *Revolt in London: 11th to 15th June 1381*. Museum of London 1981

Bemiss, Samuel M. (ed.) *The Three Charters of the Virginia Company of London*. Williamsburg, Virginia: Virginia's 350th Anniversary Celebration Corp, 1957.

Bergeron, David Moore. *Textual Patronage in English Drama: 1570–1640*. Ashgate Publishing, 2006.

Brooke, Christopher and Gillian Keir. *London 800–1216: The Shaping of a City*. London, Secker &Warburg, 1975.

Browning, Charles H. *Magna Charta Barons 1915: Baronial Order of Runnymede*

Bucholz, O. and Joseph P. Ward. *London: A Social and Cultural History, 1550-1750*. Cambridge University Press, 2012.

Carpenter, John. *Liber Albus: The White Book*. London, Reed and Pardon Printers, Paternoster Row. Translated by Henry Thomas Riley MA.

Cash, Arthur. *John Wilkes: The Scandalous Father of Civil Liberty*. Yale University Press, 2007.

Caufield, James. *The High Court Justice: Comprising Memoirs of the Principal Persons Who Sat in Judgment on King Charles the First*. London, 1820.

Clode, Charles M. *London During the Great Rebellion*. Harrison and Sons, St Martin's Lane, 1892.

Craven, Wesley Frank. *Dissolution of the Virginia Company*. Oxford University Press, 1932.

Curl, James Stevens. *The City of London and the Plantation of Ulster*. BBC History Online. Available online at http://www.bbc.co.uk/history/war/plantation [Accessed 9 July 2015].

De Krey, Gary S. *London and the Restoration: 1659-1683*. Cambridge University Press, 2005.

Dobson, Richard Barrie. *The Peasants' Revolt of 1381*. Macmillan, 1983.

Dodsley, Robert and Phillip Dormer Stanhope, Earl of Chesterfield. *The Chronicle of the Kings of England from William the Norman to the Death of George 3rd*. London, 1821.

Drew, Katherine Fischer. *Magna Carta*. Greenwood Publishing Group, 2004.

Early English Laws. Available online at http://www.earlyenglishlaws.ac.uk/reference/essays/writs/ [Accessed 22 April 2015].

Firth, C. H. and R. S. Rait. 'May 1643: An Ordinance concerning the Trained Bands of the Cities of London and Westminster, and the County of Middlesex, for their better appearance and execution of their Duties, as often as they shall be called thereunto, by their Captains or other Officers.' in *Acts and Ordinances of the Interregnum: 1642-1660*. London, 1911. Pp. 137–8. Available online at http://www.british-history.ac.uk/no-series/acts-ordinances-interregnum/pp137-138 [Accessed 15 June 2015].

Fissel, Charles Mark. *English Warfare: 1511–1642*. Routledge, 2001.

Fitzgerald, Percy. *The Life and Times of John Wilkes, M. P., Lord Mayor of London and Chamberlain*. London, 1888.

Foster, A. E. Manning. *The National Guard in the Great War: 1914-1918*. Cope & Fenwick, 1920.

Fryde, E. B. *The Great Revolt of 1381*. Historical Association pamphlet, General Series 100. Corporation of London, 1981.

Gillespie, James and Anthony Goodman (eds). *Richard 2nd: The Art of Kingship*. Clarendon Press, 2003.

Gossett, Suzanne (ed.) *Thomas Middleton in Context*. Cambridge University Press, 2011.

Grizzard, Frank E. and D. Boyd Smith. *Jamestown Colony: A Political, Social and Cultural History*. ABC-Clio, 2007.

Henry I's charter: Corporation of London Records Office, Liber Horn, f.362v. Transcription in C. Brooke, G. Keir and S. Reynolds, 'Henry I's charter for the City of London," Journal of the Society of Archivists, vol.4 (1973), 575-76

Henry I coronation charter – Based on the translation in Albert Beebe White and Wallace Notestein, eds., Source Problems in English History, Harper and Brothers, New York,1915. With reference to Douglas and Greenway, eds., English Historical Documents 1042-1189, Eyre Methuen, London, 1982 and Richard Thomson, An Historical Essay on the Magna Charta of King John, John Major, London, 1829.

Hakluyt, Richard and Edmund Goldsmid (eds). *The Principall Navigations, Voyages, Traffiques and Discoveries of the English Nation: 1885-1890.*

Hariot, Thomas. *A Brief and True Report of the NewFoundLand of Virginia.* 1588.

Herbert, William. *The History of the Twelve Great Livery Companies of London*. London, 1834.

Hill, George. *An Historical Account of the Plantation in Ulster at the Commencement of the Seventeenth Century.* 1877.

Hone, William. *The Every-Day Book and Table Book*, Volume 2. Assignment for Thomas Tegg, 73 Cheapside.

Jupp, Peter C. and Clare Gittings. *Death in England: An Illustrated History.* Manchester University Press, 1999.

Kinney, Arthur F. (ed.) *A Companion to Renaissance Drama*. John Wiley & Sons, 2008.

Lancashire, Anne. *London Civic Theatre*. Cambridge University Press, 2002.

Lawrence, Hannah. *Historical Memoirs of the Queens of England: Society in England During the Middle Ages*. London, 1838.

Moote, Lloyd M. and Dorothy C. *In The Great Plague: The Story of London's Most Deadly Year.* The John Hopkins University Press, 2004.

Nichols, John Gough. *London Pageants*. J.B. Nichols and Son, 1831.

Nichols, John Bower and John Chessel Bucker. *A Brief Account of the Guildhall of the City of London*. London, 1819.

Noorthouck, John. 'Book 1, Ch. 11: Charles I' in *A New History of London Including Westminster and Southwark*. Pp. 154–74. London, 1773. Available online at http://www.british-history.ac.uk/no-series/new-history-london/pp154-174 [Accessed 30 August 2015].

Page, William (ed.) 'Whittington's College' in *A History of the County of London: Volume 1, London Within the Bars, Westminster and Southwark*.

Pp. 578–80. London, 1909. Available online at http://www.british-history. ac.uk/vch/london/vol1/pp578-580 [Accessed 17 May 2015].

Pepy's Diary. Available online at http://www.pepysdiary.com/ encyclopedia/1348/ [Accessed 14 March 2015].

Porter, Stephen. *London and the Civil War*. MacMillan, 1996.

Porter, Stephen. *The Great Fire of London*. The History Press, 2011.

Sheppard, Francis. *London: A History*. Oxford University Press, 2000.

Statute of Labourers, 1351. Available online at http://www.britannia.com/ history/docs/laborer2.html [Accessed 19 April 2015].

Stow, J. *A Survey of London*. Whittaker and Co., London, 1598.

Stow, J. *A Survey of London*. Reprinted from the text of 1603. Available online at http://www.british-history.ac.uk/no-series/survey-of-london-stow/1603 [Accessed 4 April 2015].

Strype, John. *A Survey of the Cities of London and Westminster: 1720*. Available online at http://www.hrionline.ac.uk/strype/ [Accessed 7 June 2015].

Sutcliffe, Anthony. *London: An Architectural History*. Yale University Press, 2006.

The Brut, or The Chronicles of England. Available online at https://archive. org/stream/brutorchronicles00brieuoft#page/6/mode/2up. [Accessed 3 April 2015].

The History of the King's Works, Vol. 1: The Middle Ages. London, 1963. HM Stationery Office, 1976.

The History of Parliament. 'Whittington, Richard'. Available online at http://www.historyofparliamentonline.org/volume/1386-1421/member/ whittington-richard-1423 [Accessed 12 July 2015].

The Irish Society, *A concise view of the origin, constitution and proceedings of the Honorable Society of the Governor and Assistants of London*. London, 1822.

The Three Charters of the Virginia Company of London with Seven Related Documents: 1606–1621. Virginia 350th Anniversary Celebration Corporation,

May 21, 2011. Ebook no. 36181. Available online at http://www.gutenberg. org/files/36181/36181-h/36181-h.htm [Accessed 19 April 2015].

Thomas, A. H. (ed.) 'Roll A 6: 1349–1350' in *Calendar of the Plea and Memoranda Rolls of the City of London: Volume 1, 1323–1364*. Pp. 224–40. Available online at http://www.british-history.ac.uk/ plea-memoranda-rolls/vol1/pp224-240 [Accessed 7 June 2015].

Thomas, Peter D. G. *John Wilkes: A Friend to Liberty*. Oxford University Press, 1996.